ALSO BY MICHAEL T. KAUFMAN

In Their Own Good Time
Rooftops and Alleys

MAD DREAMS,
SAVING GRACES

MAD DREAMS, SAVING GRACES

POLAND: A NATION IN CONSPIRACY

MICHAEL T. KAUFMAN

RANDOM HOUSE / NEW YORK

Library of Congress Cataloging-in-Publication Data

Kaufman, Michael T.
Mad dreams, saving graces.

Includes index.
1. Poland—History—1980–   . 2. Kaufman,
Michael T.   I. Title.
DK4442.K38 1989   943.8'05   88-43198
ISBN 0-394-55486-8

Manufactured in the United States of America
24689753
First Edition
BOOK DESIGN BY JOANNE METSCH

For Rebecca

Poland is a symbol—a symbol of all which the best of the human race have loved, and for which they have fought. Everywhere in Europe where there has been any fighting for freedom in this century, the Poles have taken part in it, on all battlefields, on all barricades. They have sometimes been mistaken in their views of the enterprises to which they lent their arms, but they believed they were fighting for the good of humanity, they regarded themselves as the bodyguard of freedom and they still look on anyone who fights for freedom as a brother.

Conversely, it may also be said that everywhere [in Europe] where there is any fighting for freedom, there is fighting for Poland. The future fate of Poland is wholly dependent on that of Europe; for if the idea of the right of the people to independence and the right of every nation to full political freedom continually gains ground in the world, then the hour is drawing near when the resurrection of Poland shall be something more than a hope.

——Georg Brandes,
a Danish literary and social critic,
writing in 1885

CONTENTS

1: Fadeout from Red   3

2: Into Conspiracy   12

3: Bearings   29

4: Legends   43

5: Impasse   63

6: Underground Civilization   79

7: The Party   101

8: The General   119

9: A Priest Is Missing   134

10: The Killers   150

11: The Ghosts of Jews   167

12: May Day, May Day, May Day   194

13: On the Farm   212

14: Reform, Oh Yes, Reform   231

15: The Last Chapter   252

Acknowledgments   269

MAD DREAMS, SAVING GRACES

ONE

FADEOUT FROM RED

VERY BRIEFLY, THE antecedent action: Some seventy years ago, three powerful empires suddenly collapsed in war and revolution. At the point where they converged lived the Poles. For the previous 123 years they had been the subjects of foreigners, their nation segmented and lying under the control of Germans, Russians, and Austro-Hungarians. Then with the armistice of 1918 a new European order was proclaimed. At its heart lay a revivified, reconstituted Poland. That Poland and that Europe lasted for only twenty years. They perished in rapid succession after Hitler's armies invaded Poland to begin the Second World War and when, two weeks later, Stalin's forces seized the country's eastern half. Poland disappeared again, swallowed in a pincer movement of the dominant totalitarian powers of our century. For the next six years, as Europe was devastated by war, Poland lay at the epicenter of agony, the major killing field. Then, with Nazi fascism vanquished, Europe was once more reorganized, this time bisected by the agreements of Yalta and Potsdam. Of those nations consigned to the Eastern, Soviet sphere, the largest, most populous, and most unwilling to go was Poland. Still, despite the

3

continuing frustrations and occasional furious Polish outbursts, the arrangement held for more than forty years.

Now, for the fourth time in this century, Europe may be facing another rearrangement as the Soviet Communist system weakens and molders. This time, however, the Poles are playing a significant role in the process. There was nothing they did or could have done either to bring about or avert the two world wars. They had no voice at Yalta or Potsdam. But they have to a great degree dismantled and weakened Communism. They have exposed the rot and the impotency of Soviet power to the point that new leaders in Moscow are being forced to follow Polish experiences with reform, however gingerly. Through the upheaval of Solidarity and the national conspiracy that followed the free union's suppression, Poles have forced governments on both sides of the European divide to weigh their yearnings in considering possible political configurations for the continent as a new century and a new millennium approach.

Obviously, the destabilization of Poland endangers the peace of the continent. And Poland, the Soviet Union's largest European ally, is volatile. Under a failing communism it is being pauperized. It is threatened with ecological disasters. There are some who even think it might soon become a behavioral sink, the kind of mismanaged hellhole in which laboratory rats start to eat or banish their young.

In a way—the same vague and casual way as I knew about the threat of the eroding ozone layer—I was aware of some of this before I was sent to cover Poland for *The New York Times* in 1984. But it was not until months after my arrival in Warsaw that I began to sense just how markedly the divisions of contemporary Europe were again fraying. Soviet power, Soviet hegemony, and the Soviet-centered ideology of Communism were all in accelerating retreat throughout the globe. The inefficiency of communist patterns of development had been exposed. Messianic Communism was being rejected everywhere. But the major crucible of

the world's governmental systems remained Europe and, not sur-
prisingly, there the greatest changes were being forged once more
in Poland, a bogey borderland along a civilizational fault line.

It has long been the conceit of Poles that they live at the belly-
button of universal history, serving as the protectors of Christen-
dom in those reaches where the authority of Rome begins to give
way to that of Byzantium. They have for a very long time seen
themselves as the suffering Christ of nations, enduring oppression
for the promise of general deliverance. Their young men who
fought in the Napoleonic Wars, in the American Revolution, in
the Crimea, went off crying "For your freedom and ours," and
assigned to themselves an importance that usually went unrec-
ognized. At times such romantic self-consciousness was exaggerated and overblown, but now the claims for international attention
made more sense. As the Solidarity movement first arose, waned,
and rose again, it seemed evident that of all the places where
Soviet-style totalitarian Communism had been imposed, it has
changed most radically and dramatically in Poland. The ideology
is teetering. Economic planning has been discredited. The party
is bankrupt. The army has taken over. Jazz and jeans have pre-
vailed over march tempos and blue serge suits. Farmers own their
own land. Everyone wants privatization. The pope is a Pole.
Reagan was more popular than Jaruzelski, the Voice of America
more credible than Warsaw radio.

I came to Poland after the furor of Solidarity's rise and the
shock of its fall. In the three and a half years I spent in Warsaw
there were few surging and turbulent crowds. There were, in fact,
very few newsworthy events. Several amnesties were proclaimed
and a popular priest was killed by secret policemen. The pope
made his third visit and every few months the government promised yet more economic reforms, which never fully took root. Yet,
it was precisely while I was there that in gradual daily shifts,
consciousness was changing profoundly, even critically. I often
felt as if I was living through a period like the Reformation. Martin
Luther had nailed his challenging theses to the door, and day by

day the world was being viewed differently by more and more people. At work and in homes ordinary language was changing as men and women reassessed their own private possibilities and the possibilities of social change. People were speaking where they had whispered. Some were shouting. Adolescents and old people joined the ranks of those who lost their fear of prison. Old dogma was collapsing. Old slogans became embarrassing. Hardly anyone believed history was a science anymore, not even those whom the party charged with national pathfinding.

For a journalist it was both very exciting and very frustrating. As the throngs of striking workers that had commanded the attention of the world press vanished, the story also had shifted from the streets. Along with much of Polish society, it had gone underground. The changes that were taking place were profound but they were subtle, more elusive and harder to communicate than the rhythmic cries of the hundreds of thousands who had once chanted *"Sol-i-dar-ność"* in open squares. In an age of television, the sight of Lech Wałęsa addressing workers and challenging the dictatorship of the proletariat was very clear and powerful. But then came martial law and such images on Western television gave way to other crowd scenes in other places: Iran, the Philippines, Korea. Meanwhile in Poland, the action had withdrawn beyond camera range to basements, where emboldened high school pupils printed their own newspapers, or to police stations, where frustrated detectives gave up chasing after such students because there were just too many of them. The "story" was taking place in factories, where angry people worked more and more slowly, cursing their bosses louder and more often. Or at dinner tables, where parents told their children that emigration offered them their only chance for a normal life. It was fascinating to observe, like watching the incremental advance of adolescence, or the slow retreat of a plague.

During all of my stay in Poland, the government and party figures spurned appeals for national dialogue and refused to talk to those leaders who had emerged as the free trade union grew.

6

Indeed, they chased them and arrested them and kept them in jail for long periods. But then they let them out and sometimes left them alone. Nonetheless, a bizarre, ritualized form of dialogue was, in fact, taking place. The government was not talking to the opposition, but both the government and the opposition were talking to the same Polish nation, seeking to discredit each other, competing for tolerance, faith, and support.

As more uncensored books emerged from underground presses, the editors of the official presses permitted greater disclosure in their own publications. I tried to record the slowly ebbing tide of Orwellian newspeak, and I sought to explain how a government that had ignored public opinion as its Marxist duty was suddenly taking soundings and experimenting with "bourgeois" forms of public persuasion. Nothing like this had ever taken place under Soviet-style Communism. Often it seemed that political developments were unfolding as theatrical rituals. For example, the amnesties of political prisoners appeared to have been institutionalized as a rudimentary form of the social contract. First, a weak government rounded up its opponents and held them as hostages to induce society's good behavior. Then, as economic conditions worsened and social pressures mounted, it released them, hoping to gain a respite of goodwill. This usually provided a breather, but as hopes of reform inevitably plummeted, the cycle was repeated and again more hostages were taken.

Such patterns of political and social life, often intuited by much of the nation, were sometimes hard for foreigners to understand. To establish the mixture of putrefying Communism and idiosyncratic Polish romanticism required digressions and counterpoint. The social landscape was dominated by often tragic though sometimes ludicrous paradoxes. Almost everyone in Poland knew that what was economically necessary was politically impossible, that what was required was forbidden. The government knew this, the party knew this, the nation knew it. From Western perspectives, framed in pragmatic traditions, it all seemed static and hopeless and mired in impasse. But Poles have lived with paralyzing powerlessness for centuries. They have reconciled seeming contradictions in their everyday lives: anarchy and totalitarian rule, piety and atheism. Today Poland is one of the most uniformly and demonstratively Catholic of nations, yet it lives under the rule of proclaimed atheists, and the preferred means of birth control remains abortion. It is a place where even atheists hope for miracles if they do not pray for them. Poles cannot live on what they earn so they spend more than they make. How? Well, it is hard to explain.

Often I envied many Polish writers and journalists who very naturally and normally slipped into absurdist allegory to mirror social realities. My friend Ryszard Kapuściński, for example, has achieved international recognition with his surrealistic depictions of collapsing absolutism by ostensibly writing about the fall of rulers in Iran, Ethiopia, and Uganda. Another Polish writer once explained to me that he was not an absurdist like Ionesco, to whom I had compared him. "I am a realist like Zola," he insisted. "It is just Poland that is absurd." He is right. It is absurd; and much more than anywhere else I had served, it strained the normally useful and appropriate conventions of daily newspaper journalism.

When, for instance, I would write about the party's decline, I was fully aware of how ludicrous the situation was, yet I failed to adequately reflect the essential silliness. Here was the dominant organ of social control that under law held a monopoly of power. It offered its members real privileges such as higher pay, normally unavailable goods, and foreign travel, yet it was so discredited that no one was joining except the most cynical and corrupt. In my mind, I saw images of Polish mothers, crying and praying in churches that their infant sons never join, or of a poorly dressed drunk who stiffly informs the boss who has been trying to recruit him that he has thought it over, but family honor precludes his becoming a candidate member of the Polish United Workers

Party. By the time I wrote the stories, they ended up referring to the party's serious problems of cadre formation. That was the point, all right, but the proper tone of insanity was missing, as was the ever-present subtext of honor and shame. Or else, soon after Gorbachev took office as the Soviet first secretary, there came the spectacle of watching those who had once curbed free expression turn rhetorical somersaults to praise something they called "democratization."

I faced a related problem in dealing with Poland's history, which was simultaneously known in minute detail by almost all Poles and completely unknown and ignored by all foreigners. Poles were vibrating sympathetically to hundreds of echoes that had to be explained in digressive notes. Americans and West Europeans who were certain to recognize allusions to the Italian Renaissance, or the French Revolution, or fin de siècle Austria, were ignorant about Poland. Many of the foreign visitors I met in Warsaw could not clearly distinguish between Poland and Russia in the past or Poland and the Soviet Union today. Some saw the nation in terms of bigoted stereotypes or jokes and some, I learned, had condensed Poland's complex past into the simplistic view that Poles were, are, and forever will be nothing more than anti-Semites.

But in fact, more than almost any nation, the Poles continue to live in their history. While few Americans can name a Polish king, or identify any Polish writer, painter, or musician, the Poles shield themselves with a living past. The stanzas of dead poets are more meaningful to ordinary citizens than the declarations of contemporary political leaders. Held so long under foreign domination, the Poles eased their humiliation by building and reinforcing their national culture as a fortress. Practically every public event stirred images and episodes of the past that needed explanation. Writing from France, I would not have had to explain who Rousseau was, but in a dispatch from Poland I would have to tell who Adam Mickiewicz, the nineteenth-century nationalist poet, had been, and yet it is unquestionable that Mickiewicz has far more relevance for Poles and Poland today than Rousseau has for Frenchmen and France.

Finally, there was one other source of my journalistic frustration. I was taking things personally. Far more personally than I had when I lived and worked in Africa, India, Canada, or anywhere else. I had spoken Polish since childhood. I understood Polish ironies and nuances. My mother had told me the stories of her sisters and brothers whenever I lay sick as a child in New York. At that time those sisters and brothers and their children were being forced into ghettos and sent to their deaths. They were Jews, but like me they spoke to their mothers in Polish, not Yiddish. During my stay, I found traces of their lives, and put up stones to mark their slaughter. My family tree had died out in Poland, but before the Holocaust it had taken root there over centuries. Like so much of European Jewry, my ancestors had lived longer among Poles than among any other peoples and complicated, rich cultures were shaped in the sometimes tense symbiosis. I tried to take in the momentous sweep of tragic history and too often found it overpowering. There was too much of it, too much testimony, too much irony, too much passion, too much paradox, to permit tidy allocations of blame, shame, and folly.

For a while, I tried to cling to journalistic distance, but in the end, I was swept away by people in resistance to oppression, people who became my friends. They dealt daily with the moral ambiguity of Polish life. They opposed evil and repression and went to prison. Like Poland itself, they were constantly endangered but never fully defeated. Bravely, they were developing a conspiratorial society of honorable men in which grace was held to be the highest of virtues. I was finally captivated by this civil society that was spreading above and below ground. I came to know and admire men like Zbigniew Bujak, Bogdań Borusewicz, Jacek Kuroń, and Adam Michnik, gaining respect for their thoughts and actions, which were advancing liberty in an age of dehumanizing bureaucracies. And it was fun to be with them, to drink with them and hear their stories of risks and flights, their noisy fantasies. It was uplifting to sense their loyalty to each other, their commitments and acceptance of sacrifice. They befriended me and I felt honored.

This book, then, has come from these compounded frustrations. It is an attempt to evoke the often maddening atmosphere of a contradictory Poland that is still at the heart of a changing Europe. To make explanatory digressions into the often weighty echoes of Polish experience. To respectfully acknowledge my intertwined Polish and Jewish roots. To pay homage to my friends.

TWO

━━━━━━━━━━━━━━━━━━━━━━━━━━━

INTO CONSPIRACY

DECEMBER IN GDAŃSK is mean. Baltic winds whine through the narrow streets of the quaint, reconstructed old town and darkness falls soon after lunch. Giant cranes at the downtown shipyard loom like snatching claws against the skyline. In the streets, men coming home from their shifts hunch into gusts, their reddened fists jammed into padded denim jackets. Others stagger out from bars where dusty velvet curtains barely cut the draft. On December 12, 1981, Bogdań Borusewicz walked the streets of his hometown full of angry thoughts. That afternoon he had met with friends, workers who shared his fear that the leadership of the Solidarity free trade union was growing increasingly autocratic. Though he never gained the recognition of his less modest colleagues, the thirty-two-year-old Borusewicz had, in fact, been more instrumental in establishing the union than anyone else. For more than half his life he had advocated democracy and challenged Communism, first with rocks, then with leaflets, and ultimately by encouraging workers to form unions. From the small group of dockhands and shipbuilders he first recruited in 1976 had come all the men who two years later brought Solidarity to the attention of the world, among them Lech Wałęsa.

Borusewicz had been the first to recognize and promote Wałęsa's political skills, and he had been at Wałęsa's side when at the end of August in 1980, the mustached head of the then burgeoning union signed the breakthrough agreement with the government establishing the right of workers to form unions free of Communist Party and government control. But in recent months, he had increasingly differed with his old friend and protégé and he gradually withdrew from union activity. On that December day, as he walked off his irritation, Solidarity was winding up a two-day national convention at the same shipyard where it had scored its most dramatic victories. Several hundred union delegates were attending the meeting, but Borusewicz stayed away.

Over the previous year, as the union grew in membership and as its strikes multiplied, alarms were raised that the Soviets were preparing an invasion to smash Solidarity and end the popular clamor it had generated for economic change and expanded political rights. Just a few weeks earlier such fears were renewed when Moscow reported that military training maneuvers near the Polish border were being prolonged. Like most Poles, Borusewicz discounted the reports as psychological terror, and as he walked alone he was much more concerned with what the union was doing to itself than with any risk of attack from the outside. Three years later, while he led a conspiratorial resistance from hiding, he recalled in detail the thoughts he had that evening, oblivious of the last-minute preparations that the police and army were then making for a nationwide attack on the union and its backers. "I had effectively pulled out of everything," Borusewicz said. "Old friends, who had sacrificed when free unions were just flimsy ideas, were being shunted aside as yes-men and cronies took over. I simply did not see much sense in struggling on. I was disgusted to see people change when ambition went to their heads—how modest and decent friends became bosses who savagely destroyed their opponents. I saw that success does not have to change people for the better, that society's success, the nation's success, had stopped being my success. As a movement, it was obvious we had won, but that evening, I felt I, personally, had lost."

Borusewicz, a deceptively soft-looking man with a beaky, Irish face, was troubled then and is still upset by how rapidly Solidarity had evolved into what he saw as a parody of Communist rule. Since he joined a student protest in 1968, Borusewicz forged links between students and workers; between Catholics, like himself, and former Communists; between fragile clusters of originally timid activists from Gdańsk, Warsaw, and Lublin. He found it painful that as the union swelled, so many people who had once made common cause were growing increasingly insensitive to each other's political traditions, backgrounds, and legends. "The movement was developing all the negative traits of the ruling system: intolerance for those who think differently or act differently, contempt for criticism, primitive chauvinism," he declared in recollection. "I could not imagine a candidate for union office standing up to say he was a nonbeliever. After all, there were all sorts of people among us, Catholics and atheists. Still everyone felt it necessary to hold the cross up high in the same way that party people wrapped themselves in Lenin."

Sometime that night, as he called on friends, Borusewicz grew aware that there were too many police trucks moving around the streets. Something ominous was apparently under way. He had learned from taxi drivers that some hotels and the Solidarity offices in Gdańsk were being ringed by uniformed men. He could not find out how many people were being arrested or what was happening in the rest of the country. He was heading for the home of Alina Pieńkowska, who was expecting him. Pieńkowska was then a thirty-one-year-old widow, a slight woman with long prematurely silver hair. She worked as a nurse at the clinic of the shipyard where her father and uncles had spent their working lives. Six years earlier she had joined the group that Borusewicz had put together to put out a mimeographed journal called *The*

Coastal Worker. She had contributed articles about accidents caused by overwork. She was in the original handful that formed the Free Trade Unions, the organization that preceded Solidarity. She is a modest, almost timid woman, but in 1980, her soft-spoken voice was credited with turning the Gdańsk strike into a national movement.

The government had agreed to terms to end the shipyard strike and Wałęsa had announced that the occupation was over. The workers were rushing out to join their wives when Pieńkowska mounted a barrel and shouted them to a standstill. She told them that other, smaller plants were still striking and that if the shipyard crews went back to work, these efforts would be crushed. In that moment she persuaded the workers to redirect their strike for economic conditions into one of solidarity with all workers. This impassioned plea provided the name for the union then being born. After that moment she stepped back out of the limelight, continuing to work for the union anonymously. In the process, she and Borusewicz fell in love.

Borusewicz noticed the police cars parked on the street and warily entered the housing block from a back door. He was on the staircase when he saw the uniforms. He jumped out a window in the corridor. As he ran to a nearby wood, he heard two shots fired at him, but the footfalls of his heavily booted pursuers died away. When the police returned to the apartment Pieńkowska tried to read what had happened from their faces, but their expressions were impassive and they said nothing as they led her away. A neighbor took care of her daughter. She was to remain in detention for a year and she did not know what had happened to Borusewicz until some months later in a *gryps* she heard he was alive and conspiring. After her release they were married by a priest in an underground wedding and then, when their child was baptized, Borusewicz evaded the attentions of the secret police by dressing as an old, bent woman. The man who had been described in government dossiers as "a born conspirator" even had his hand kissed by an unsuspecting Wałęsa.

But on the night when he fled from shooting police, he had no clear idea of what lay ahead. Once, when he was eighteen years old, he broke away from police who had arrested him at school for printing leaflets. At that time, after he had been fired upon, he spent five days hiding out and eating roots in the hills around Gdańsk before surrendering. Of his second escape as martial law descended, he would recall, "I knew enough not to go home." For a while he thought he should make his way to the shipyard where he assumed workers must be preparing an occupation strike to protest what then appeared to be stepped-up harassment. "But I didn't think I had to hurry since, after all, I no longer had a union post. I knew the leaders in the shipyard despised me for my conflicts with Wałęsa and my associations with intellectuals. Some of them suspected that if I was not actually a Jew, than I was certainly a liberal, and definitely not a worker."

Everywhere, moments of awe are kept fastened in memory by intimate, frequently banal, details of personal experience. Ordinary people recall where they were and who they were with when they learned that a war ended or that a leader was killed or that men walked on the moon. For Poles, who have more painful days to remember than most nations, December 13, 1981, was such a time. All men and women old enough to have been aware keep in mind just how they learned that martial law had been declared. Stark images such as an apartment door splintered by police crowbars, or a tank parked by a churchyard, or an anxious face in a paddy wagon, encapsulate appreciations of the momentous fact. Even now, almost a decade later, people making conversation on trains or at wedding receptions will ask each other where they were and how they realized what was happening when General Wojciech Jaruzelski sent out armed forces in a surprise attack on the union and the nation that built it.

Often, the recollections are sorrowful, with men and women lamenting the passage of what is widely recalled as a time when hope and democracy raced through the land in a happy contagion.

But there are some, like Borusewicz, who, in hindsight, think back on that December day with grudging gratitude. They realize that the tanks and troops sent out to catch and silence them served instead to drive them into the longest-lasting and widest-reaching conspiracy in Poland's long history of patriotic conspiracies. For more than five years those who slipped through the dragnet of martial law and those who they later enlisted and trained were able to form and maintain an underground society. They mounted a nonviolent resistance unprecedented in any Communist police state. In the process, the influence of Solidarity, though it was destroyed as a union, outlasted that of Brezhnev, Andropov, and Chernenko, and in some measure, paved the way for Gorbachev and his policies of reform. A clandestine resistance, incorporating romantic elements of honor and shame, so long familiar to all Poles, managed to endure, and in many ways, to prevail.

It is still debatable whether Jaruzelski acted out of patriotic motives to deflect what he regarded as the inevitable Soviet intervention, or whether he issued his order as a loyal ally of Kremlin leaders, intent on smashing those whom he and they regarded as counterrevolutionaries, incidentally easing the burdens of his Soviet mentors. What is obvious, however, is that whatever his true motives, by ordering his army into the streets and factories, the general set out to do what Soviet troops had done in Budapest in 1956 and in Prague in 1968—that is, to foreclose hopes of political reform, crush dissent, and restore the monopoly powers his party had yielded under the pressure of popular expectations and the threats of strikes.

His battle plan for the assault had been assembled over months, but its exact timetable was known only to a handful of officers, including one, Colonel Ryszard Kukliński, who had been working as an American spy and who had been whisked to safety in the West earlier that winter. As the weekend began, all military leaves were canceled and police units were suddenly ordered to muster at special encampments. Late on the night of the twelfth, a Saturday, all over Poland slow-moving convoys pulled out of rustic compounds and headed for nearby cities. Just before midnight all Telex communication was cut, and soon after all civilian phones went dead. About the same time, police couriers drove to gas stations, ordering attendants to lock fuel pumps and turn away customers. All these measures were applied throughout the country, but in the first stage the focus was on Gdańsk, where so many Solidarity leaders had gathered. The idea was to seize them all and leave the ten-million-member union to twitch in headless agony until it toppled like a sapped dinosaur.

The operation, bureaucratically designated "the wall," began smoothly. In the five hotels where the delegates were housed, teams of policemen went from room to room leading out startled and sleepy men and women. They were placed in large blue trucks and driven off to internment camps. The senior party officials of the Gdańsk region came to the Wałęsa apartment in a large housing development. They said they had an invitation for the union leader to fly to Warsaw to meet General Jaruzelski. It was three in the morning and Wałęsa had by that time heard of the hotel raids. Angrily he told the party figures that there was nothing to talk about while his friends and associates were locked up. The party men left but they returned minutes later with policemen carrying crowbars. Danuta Wałęsa, then pregnant with their sixth child, stalled them for as long as she could, leaving the party people and the police standing in the cold stairwell for hours. But as dawn broke her husband finally left with the men who had come for him, to begin what turned out to be a year's confinement spent mostly in isolation.

Not only union leaders and sympathizers were being seized. There were writers who had criticized the government, high school and university students who had voiced democratic sentiments, professors, clerks, and housewives, some of whom still remain puzzled by their inclusion on police lists. Within twenty-four hours close to ten thousand people were in police custody. All Solidarity offices in every city were raided by police who seized records, equipment, and cash before padlocking the doors and posting guards. In the morning an austere General Jaruzelski appeared on television saying that martial law was in effect. On the streets tanks guarded roadblocks and soldiers patrolled with fixed bayonets to enforce a curfew. To add to the impression that the military was now entirely in command, sketchy television newscasts were delivered by men and women in army uniforms.

But contrary to what such appearances were meant to convey, not everything was proceeding as the general had hoped. As Borusewicz later recalled from hiding, "An unsuspecting union was attacked by an unprepared government force." He said that though the authorities later tried to present the attack as a super-efficient operation, it had all the elements of "the usual socialist confusion." He said the lists of those to be seized contained names of people who were long dead. "The only reason the police and army looked as good as they did was that we were so bad. As it turned out the handful of us that got away caused the authorities years of deep concern and heavy problems. Can you imagine what would have happened if two thousand had escaped?" Borusewicz thinks that could have been possible if, for example, people had been instructed before the raid not to open their doors to the police for at least ten minutes. "That would have slowed down the searches and given more people time to flee or hide."

One of the names that headed the police lists was that of Zbigniew Bujak, the twenty-seven-year-old president of Solidarity in the Warsaw region, who had almost as much authority with workers as did Wałęsa. It turned out that while tens of thousands of uniformed men were looking for him, he was in the heart of Gdańsk, unaware of the raids and carrying a portfolio covered with large red Solidarity stickers. During the five years that followed that night, Bujak would develop impressive conspiratorial skills, resorting to disguises and regularly switching false documents, but at the beginning, he acknowledges, he was saved not by guile but by luck.

Bujak was one of those authentic Polish workers churned into prominence by Solidarity. These were young men who seemed to reject everything about the communist system in which they were raised except for its repeated insistence that the working class was important, that manual workers, in fact, had the most important role in shaping society. Three years earlier, he had been an electrician at a Warsaw tractor plant, frustrated by deadening work practices. He was bored and anxious, looking for some challenge. At home he read history and began going to the theater, though he was afraid to tell his fellow workers about these outings, fearing their ridicule. He thought of joining a sports club or organizing weekend excursions for workers, as he had done for the paratroopers with whom he served in an elite unit. He had heard that some intellectuals were putting out underground newspapers dealing with workers' rights and went to ask his parish priest for help in contacting such people. The priest, Father Leon Kantorski, was well-connected, and from that point events moved very fast.

At first Bujak distributed the mimeographed papers and collected contributions from his co-workers, speaking in whispers at the plant. Within months he was confidently addressing tens of thousands through microphones and negotiating with factory directors. When the agreements legalizing free unions were signed in Gdańsk, he registered Solidarity's Warsaw branch in the courts and was chosen its leader. For many police, Bujak was considered even more dangerous than Wałęsa. He was younger, more impetuous, and less closely tied than Wałęsa to the sometimes restraining influence of the church. Moreover, he was reaching out to wider groups of intellectuals, reading the books they suggested and concerning himself with issues that went beyond union activity to question how totalitarian control in all spheres could be lessened. He was also interested in establishing links to dissident activists in all the countries of the East bloc and in the Soviet Union.

Bujak's entry into conspiratorial life was even more spontaneous and accidental than his rise to union leadership. "I read somewhere that when bizarre things happen once, that is accident, when they happen twice, it is coincidence, but when they happen more often, well, then you have to say that it starts to get interesting," he said when I first met him. Like Borusewicz, he was then a fugitive and had spent three years on the run. "It proves that God loves the innocent." The day before the arrests began, Bujak received a call from Wiktor Kulerski, his second in command at the Warsaw union federation, who reported that Communist party organizations were quietly forming groups of thugs to disrupt a solemn memorial planned to take place five days later. The observance was to have marked the killing of workers shot eleven years earlier as they protested food price rises in Baltic ports. Bujak said he would come back to Warsaw as soon as he could to alert workers to the threat of provocation at the rally. However, when the last gavel sounded, he felt very tired and he suggested to his best friend, Zbigniew Janaś, that they overnight at a hotel and then take the morning train to Warsaw. Janaś was the worker at the tractor factory with whom Bujak had gone to the priest to obtain underground newspapers, and the two worked closely together. Janaś insisted that they had to go back on the train that left at three in the morning, that his wife was expecting him.

The two friends went to eat and stayed late at a restaurant, nursing several brandies. Around two o'clock they wandered to the depot and while they were on an elevated platform, they saw that police vehicles were surrounding a nearby hotel. "Probably a raid on black marketeers," Bujak told Janaś. A man they recognized as a convention delegate approached them to say that the police had also arrived in force at other hotels where union people were housed. Bujak and Janaś noticed that some of the police cars were pulling back from the hotel. They set off to investigate, still clutching the portfolios with the incriminating Solidarity stickers that had been distributed to all convention participants.

The doors of the hotel were locked but through them they recognized a tall blond woman they knew only as Joanna. She worked as an assistant to Janusz Onyszkiewicz, Solidarity's national press spokesman. As they knocked, she surreptitiously gestured them to leave, but emboldened by the brandies, they continued hammering at the door until a cleaning woman sleepily let them in. In quick and hushed sentences Joanna told the men that they had to leave, that everyone had been arrested. "What, are they completely crazy?" said Bujak. "Don't the police realize they are simply forcing our hand? If they arrest well-known people like Onyszkiewicz we have no alternative but to call a general strike." The woman kept shaking her head and wiped her tears as an apparently tipsy Bujak railed on.

She was the British-born granddaughter of Marshal Józef Piłsudski, the founding father and military strongman of prewar Poland. A graduate architect, she had come to Poland two years earlier, drawn by the drama of Solidarity's rise and impelled by patriotic feelings. She had started working as a volunteer, drafting releases for foreign newsmen, and had fallen in love with Onyszkiewicz, a mathematician. More than a year later she would marry him in the warden's office of the prison to which he was eventually taken after his arrest that night. She had evaded arrest herself, presumably because of her British passport, or because of who her grandfather was. Piłsudski is officially ignored by the government but he remains the most revered Polish hero and his busts and portraits are prominent in countless apartments.

Again she tried to communicate urgency and danger to Bujak and Janaś. Everyone, she repeated, had been taken. All the union officers were removed from the hotel in handcuffs. In addition, she said, enunciating slowly, there were at that moment dozens of policemen on every floor of the hotel going from room to room checking the documents of all guests to make sure that they had not missed anyone.

"God's wounds," said Bujak, swearing like his peasant ancestors. With Janaś at his side he raced down the lobby stairs thinking he would kick in the glass and crash through in a parachutist's roll if the doors were locked. This time, however, the cleaning woman was ready with her keys. The two men ditched their Solidarity portfolios and split up, each heading to hide out with friends until they could find out what exactly had happened and begin to make their way home. For a week, as patrols all over the country searched for him, Bujak stayed put, and then, wearing the uniform of a railway conductor that had been obtained for him, with glasses he did not need, he took a train to Warsaw and life in the underground.

Bujak was eventually joined in that life by Janaś and Kulerski, the man he had left behind to take his place in Warsaw. Kulerski is a very careful, fastidious man who always wears a tie and a jacket. He had been Janaś's high school teacher and when by his own route he came to head the Solidarity teachers' union, he quickly came to Bujak's attention, taking on the role of his confidant and tutor. At fifty-four he was old enough to have childhood memories of the war years, when he lived in a Warsaw suburb under a false name with false papers. At the time, his father served in the Polish exile government in London as secretary to its leader, Stanisław Mikołajczyk. With greater vividness as well as greater pain, he recalls his high school years in the Stalinist fifties when his father, by then returned to Poland, was sent to prison for nine years, accused of espionage and treason. It was a time when he was shunned by classmates, some of whom wore the red scarves of Pioneers. As vice president of the Solidarity unions in the Warsaw region, Kulerski was responsible for all educational, cultural, and informational programs. These included literacy programs, historical lectures, worker newspapers, cultural tours, and art classes, which, in the words of a Polish saying, were sprouting like mushrooms after a rain. During Bujak's trip to Gdańsk, Kulerski had stayed in the office day and night reviewing proposals and appeals that had streamed in from union locals.

Sometime after ten o'clock on the night of the twelfth, he decided to go home. He routinely called contacts at the major factories and found everything normal. He told the overnight secretary that he would be in early the next day. He caught the last bus to the same wooded Warsaw suburb where as a Boy Scout he played conspiratorial games. But before he went home to his wife he gave way to a nagging feeling that he should call the office for one final check. The Kulerskis had no phone so he went to a coin-operated booth. The pay phone was broken. Almost six years later, after he had surfaced under the terms of an amnesty, he reconstructed those critical moments with a sense of wonder. "I usually hate phones and I knew that everything was all right but still I had this compulsion that I had to call." He went to another phone booth several streets away and it too was out of order, as was a third. He then went to a nearby hospital to use the phone of a friend who worked as a doctor. The secretary at the union office told him that everything was quiet, but as he was saying good night she suddenly asked him to hold on, that something curious had just happened. After a pause she came back on the line to say that while they were talking both of the Telexes in the office stopped chattering, as if they were cut off.

Kulerski had bucked an optimistic tide within the union and had for months warned Bujak that a repressive attack was inevitable. From the doctor's office he called his father, a man who is confined to a wheelchair with the rheumatism, emphysema, and blindness he contracted in prison. "Well, it begins," said the old man. "May God keep you." Then the phone went dead. As Wiktor Kulerski spent the next weeks hiding out in freezing huts and stables, he repeatedly turned the events of that night over in his mind. He concluded that if any of the inoperative pay phones had worked, he would have contacted the office before the Telex lines were cut and thus would not have been alerted to what was happening. He would have gone to bed and been captured. If, on the other hand, he had called a minute or two later than he did, he would not have gotten through because by then all phone communications were severed. Broken phones are quite common in Warsaw but still Kulerski is not certain whether he was saved by coincidence or providence.

He ran home to tell his wife he would have to leave immediately. She urged him to rest and asked what was so urgent. He told her something terrible was happening, but that he did not know the details. She asked him when he thought he might return home. "I told her I did not know. All the time I was thinking whether I should take some warm underwear and whether I should pack the fur-lined boots my brother brought me from Sweden. I took the boots and kissed my wife and left." Two hours later Mrs. Kulerski was awakened by police who searched the apartment looking for her husband. As it turned out, Kulerski did not return home until five years later.

Two other prominent Solidarity figures—Bogdań Liś of Gdańsk and Władysław Frasyniuk, the head of the union in Wrocław—also escaped the manhunt that night, slipping into stealthy resistance. Liś, along with Borusewicz and Wałęsa, had been an early member of the free trade union group that paved the way for Solidarity. An ambitious, streetwise mechanic, he had been one of those who signed Solidarity's historic agreement with the government with its twenty-one guarantees of union rights and expanded free expression. In the union power struggles, he tried to bridge the rivalries. He was on good terms with Wałęsa and he had the respect as well of those who were criticizing the federation president as dictatorial. The tensions of mediating had exhausted him and as soon as the final session ended he went home to sleep. He was soon awakened by two shipyard workers who came to tell him that the hotels were being raided and that the regional offices were surrounded. They urged him to leave with them. "Baked chicken," he cursed, using the Polish euphemistic substitute for "fucking whore," and he sent his friends away. A few minutes later they returned and this time Liś reconsidered and went with them.

Frasyniuk, the tough and athletic former truck driver who had risen to head the Solidarity union in heavily industrialized Wrocław, was, like Bujak and Wałęsa, high on the most-wanted list. Like them he was indisputably—and for the authorities, embarrassingly—a worker, a graduate of a technical school and a child of people who had come to the city from farms. For generations, Communists had talked wishfully about the advent of Socialism's new man, and when the Solidarity movement began, some of them must have been haunted by the thought that the prototype had indeed evolved. But instead of wearing red sashes and Lenin buttons, the awaited mutation appeared as self-confident, bold and well-spoken young workers who seemingly came from nowhere to condemn Communism. At twenty-seven years of age, Frasyniuk, a man trained to drive and take apart heavy diesel machinery, was leading an amalgam of unions with more than a million members. One reason that the police were particularly concerned by him was that Wrocław, like Gdańsk, was not only a tough workers' city, but one in which anti-Soviet feeling ran even higher than elsewhere. The old German populations of what had been Danzig and Breslau fled or emigrated after the war, when Poland's border shifted westward, and in their place came settlers from the eastern areas of prewar Poland, regions that were taken over by the Soviets. In these cities, grandparents raised grandchildren on family stories of Soviet brutality, referring to those who took their holdings not as Russians or Soviets but as "Red Ones," "Bolsheviks" or "*Kacaps*," all terms used as derisive epithets.

Frasyniuk and his delegation left the shipyard meeting and took the first train home without realizing that anything drastic was in the air. When they changed trains in Poznań a waitress told them that martial law had been declared, using the Polish term that literally translates as "state of war." Later Frasyniuk would recall that he discounted her report, assuming it to be government-inspired rumor intended to induce hysteria. Like other union leaders in Gdańsk he had considered the possibility of Soviet intervention, but he admits he never imagined that Polish forces would act on their own. A single policeman at the platform repeated the information and said, "Now we will settle your hash," but he made no move to detain the men. One of the workers shouted back, "Don't worry, you whore, we will still be able to deal with you." Frasyniuk told him to shut up. Back on the train, a conductor informed Frasyniuk that he knew who he was and that the police were waiting for the whole group in Wrocław. He urged the union delegates to get off at earlier stops. Frasyniuk said no, that they would go to the end of the line, but that they would jump off before the train pulled into the platform. The conductor shook his head, but a few kilometers before it arrived at Wrocław, the train slowed and stopped just long enough for the men to leave safely and unseen.

None of these men was prepared for conspiracy. Some weeks earlier, Frasyniuk had, in vague apprehension, withdrawn several million złotys from the union's account to keep funds in easy reach in case of emergencies, but neither he nor any of the others had moved to secure printing equipment and supplies against the risk of confiscation. Liś was planning to meet with some people in a week's time to discuss how best to hide presses and paper. In the first days of hiding, Bujak scourged himself for being so unsuspecting that just a week earlier he had deposited several thousand U.S. dollars that had been sent to his union from foreign backers. In their separate hiding holes the men were unable to learn who else was still at large. They had no previously arranged system for reaching each other.

For the most part their only knowledge of clandestine practice came from family legends of wartime resistance, or from tales of earlier risings and insurrections in Polish history. In that history, conspiracies advanced the nation's dreams for far longer periods than did the intervals of autonomy and democracy. Despite the obstacles, the links that the fugitives forged and the resistance they eventually mounted worked well enough to thwart any hopes of repeating in Poland what Soviet forces had accomplished in Budapest and Prague. Within a year after Soviet troops had entered Hungary and Czechoslovakia, both those countries were reduced to cultural and political wastelands. There, the champions of change were completely silenced. In Hungary, hundreds were hanged, thousands were sent to jail and tens of thousands fled. In Czechoslovakia, the reformers were purged and imprisoned or banished to little towns and paltry jobs. And in both countries, the pall of intimidation that fell still has not fully lifted. In Poland, the dreams and ideas of Solidarity were never erased by the tanks. They were sustained by hundreds of clandestine groups that rose to echo conspiracies ranging back more than two hundred years. And if today a Polish government is increasingly using the language of reform, it is in significant degree simply responding to a persistent underground, reckoning with ideas it could not squelch.

THREE

BEARINGS

BY THE TIME I arrived, almost two and a half years had passed
since the sweeping arrests. In the interim, most of those who had
been detained that night had been released, though some seven
hundred people, including some of the most prominent opposition figures, were still in prison. Wałęsa had been freed and had
been awarded the Nobel Peace Prize. Still he was shadowed by
teams of detectives as he went to and from his job repairing
electrical motors at the shipyard. The fugitives who escaped the
surprise attack had organized their own clandestine networks and
an underground culture was spreading. Tens of thousands of
people were regularly involved in producing illicit newspapers,
magazines, and books. As many as a million people were reading
the publications and passing them on. Some groups had built
portable radio transmitters and used them for illicit broadcasts.
Solidarity members at factories maintained illicit contact with each
other, continuing to collect dues and pass the money to the underground. Throughout the country, in schools, hospitals, and
offices as well as plants and mines, those who remained stead-

fastly with Solidarity commanded respect and retained personal authority.

A provisional directorate, loosely linking conspiratorial networks in all regions, had been established by Borusewicz, Liś, Frasyniuk, and Bujak. They maintained contact with each other, sometimes arguing over strategy and criticizing themselves for failures to shape regional strikes into national protests. Their joint declarations, put out in the name of the TKK, or Temporary National Committee, were widely circulated, inspiring many and embarrassing the Jaruzelski regime. Frasyniuk was captured after running loose for ten months and on June 10, 1984, the day I arrived, Liś was seized at a secluded lake outside Gdańsk, betrayed by a drunken watchman. Their places on the loosely structured national council of the underground were immediately filled by others rising through the growing ranks of conspiracy.

As I settled into my own duties as correspondent for *The New York Times*, I very much wanted to meet the Solidarity outlaws, and over the next three years, I did eventually come to know most of the prominent resistance figures and dozens of their more anonymous colleagues. Some I met while they hid and others after they emerged from cover or prison. But in those first months, lacking access to those who were dodging the police in disguises or those who were in jails, I tried to find my bearings on the surface.

The weather that summer was splendid and much of the country was very green. The strawberries and cherries were plentiful, and on street corners, squat peasant women sold large baskets of the sweet fruit. Meat was rationed, as it has been for almost the entire life of the Polish People's Republic, but the shelves of stores were no longer completely empty as they had been during martial law. There was always good bread and even some Bulgarian wine; however, ordinary goods kept suddenly vanishing. For some months there was no toothpaste and then underwear disappeared, to be followed by a shortage of light bulbs and cheeses. Toilet paper and many medicines were always hard to find. The stores that had merchandise also had lines. To make a reservation for a train journey required hours of waiting. To acquire an apartment took up to eighteen years of inching up lists. I remember watching an old woman at a flea market as she stood patiently all morning holding up the only merchandise she was offering, a pair of used pink plastic beach slippers from Hong Kong. I noticed other old men and women trying to supplement their pensions as they sat on benches charging the equivalent of two pennies to have people weigh themselves on rusted bathroom scales they carried to parks. Yet in all sections of Warsaw people lined up to pay high prices for fancy cut flowers and everywhere people emerged from buildings of tiny apartments to walk sleek, large, purebred and presumably carnivorous dogs: Great Danes, German shepherds, Irish setters.

Increasingly, the five hundred days of Solidarity's eclipsed ascendancy were being referred to with nostalgic irony as "the carnival." Still, echoes of the democratic giddiness maintained their sway, at least in private spaces, in living rooms and churches. In these intimate and secure confines, the story of the union was being filtered into national mythology to be spliced with earlier legends of resistance and hope. *Man of Iron* and *Man of Marble*, the films by Andrzej Wajda that described the union's birth, were no longer shown in public theaters but they were regularly shown on home videos. People still wore Solidarity insignia in their lapels, or on chains under their shirts, though the emblems were becoming smaller and more discreet. One man wore just a tiny little dark metal S in his lapel. He pointed it out to friends who would otherwise not notice.

On the surface, much of public life involved a stylized battle over symbols, with the government and party authorities using great energies and expensive resources to stamp out even the most modest emblems. One morning, early in my stay, I awoke abruptly before dawn and wandered streets new to me in jet-lagged excitement. Occasionally a drunk staggered out of my way. Polish drunks, like Polish dogs, I was to learn, tended to be timid.

31

In a residential neighborhood near the Vistula, Warsaw's wide and shallow river, I saw a group of five men smearing patches of yellow paint on a building wall. They were not painting the wall but covering over the *Solidarność* signatures that had been scrawled there in approximations of the movement's characteristic logotype. The men were members of the government's anti-graffiti squad. I stood and watched them until their leader asked me gruffly what I was looking at. I shrugged my shoulders. "Get stuffed," he said, and I walked on.

Over the next three years, I would see the work of such teams all over the country. The strange splotches of new-paint-covered walls and bridges called attention to what lay hidden. Often the overlay followed the pattern of the masked letters with the yellow coat adhering closely to the contours of the characteristic stylized S.

At first it occurred to me that the government painters were doing useless work. After all, the young people who wrote "Solidarity" on the walls did so to convey the notion that the movement still existed and had followers. Obviously, the telltale yellow paint left by the graffiti censors did exactly the same thing, proving that there were still people willing to take risks to proclaim their allegiance. Somewhat later, when I developed a more Polish way of looking at things, I even considered whether it was possible that at least some of the yellow splotches covered nothing but were painted by the Solidarity activists themselves in a sort of semiotic shortcut. In a similarly calculating vein, I decided that for the police who supervised the anti-graffiti operation, the point was not to eradicate the illegal name of the illegal labor movement but to demonstrate graphically that the organs of state had the power to rub it out.

Actually the police obsession with Solidarity symbols had effectively changed the face of the city, closing off the main square. There, just after martial law was declared, old women had placed flowers, flags, and union badges to form a large cross at the central parade ground by the Tomb of the Unknown Soldier. The women, like my housekeeper, Pani Kasia, would walk alone or in twos and place their flowers to start the floral cross. Younger people followed, raising their fingers in the forbidden V-for-victory gesture of Solidarity. They would shout Solidarity slogans and chant the names of Wałęsa and Bujak. Then the water cannon would roll in spraying torrents and the Zomo riot police would clear the square with their clubs held high and cocked. And hours later, when the old flowers lay kicked and tattered in puddles, another old woman would start the process again, coming from behind a tank with her carnations. To parry the old women, party authorities ordered the main square to be repaved, and fenced in the entire area. Work on reconstruction was to drag on for four years, a long time even by Polish standards.

Often such absurd rituals of social conflict and the openness with which people complained led Western visitors to regard Poland as a sort of second-class police state, unconsciously comparing Warsaw life to that of Moscow, or Prague or Bucharest. After all, they would meet Polish college students who would openly boast of how they taunted the riot police or climbed lampposts to steal red flags on May Day. No ordinary people boasted of party membership and very few even admitted to it, while cab drivers blurted out their scorn for the government, the generals, the system, and the Russians, without any encouragement from the backseat. But none of this changed the most basic quality of the Polish People's Republic, which is that it is a police state. It may be an idiosyncratic, sloppy police state and its leaders even like to cultivate the impression that they want to rule less rigorously, if they only could, but it is nonetheless a police state and those same leaders are kept in authority by police power which is sovereign. My first awareness of the sloppiness of Polish authoritarianism came literally as I arrived at the airport, where a pudgy customs inspector sighed in self-pity when I told him I was carrying books in my baggage.

"Eighteen inspectors on duty and you had to come to me and then you had to tell me you had books," he lamented as he set about writing down the titles of the forty-seven volumes which he then confiscated for the police to review. Several weeks later they were all returned. On my second day I saw a male transvestite in high heels and a short skirt walking past uncaring policemen. Clearly, I thought, this was not the Soviet model of efficient repression and submissive response. In a ritual frequently repeated after church services, I watched old women in kerchiefs as they walked slowly past ranks of helmeted Zomos saying, "We forgive you. We understand. We know you need the extra money, but think, how does your mother feel?" Meanwhile younger people threw coins at the riot police and taunted them with shouts of "Judas." Behind their plastic masks some of the Zomos clenched their jaws, but they kept their rage under discipline.

Whatever the level of repression, obsessions with police themes dominated the Polish imagination, complemented by Catholic motifs of sacrifice. Practically every novel published and every movie released had central scenes of arrest, interrogation, and imprisonment. Pani Kasia, my housekeeper, would, over breakfast, tell me of police outrages. In the sixties her late husband had been arrested. The charge was bootlegging, but as she told it, there was some political angle I could never quite understand. One of her sons, Krzys, had been imprisoned for beating up a policeman while drunk. A second, Jurek, had recently left prison under an amnesty after serving one year of an eleven-year term for Solidarity activism. When she referred to the police she used the term *glina*, a slang word that literally means clay. It was from her I heard my first Warsaw joke. "Why do policemen here walk in threes?" she asked. The answer: "Well, the first is there because he can read, the second, because he can add, and the third, to keep tabs on the two intellectuals."

In addition to the movies and the literary emphasis on police themes there are three former prisons in Warsaw that are now museums commemorating those who suffered within their walls under the czars, the Nazis and the prewar Polish government. Most Polish heroes of the last two centuries have spent years either in prison or in Siberian exile. In Polish, the word *conspiracy* has absolutely no negative connotation. A Pole will say "I was a conspirator," in the same way a Frenchman might say, "I was with the wartime resistance." But Warsaw also has two other monuments erected to men widely seen as jailers and torturers. In 1986 the state quietly unveiled a huge marble bas-relief in honor of the secret police, who were known by the initials UB, for Security Bureau. A few days after the statue was put on its pedestal, cab drivers were pointing it out with ridicule, calling it "the UB-elisk."

The second police monument, a statue of Feliks Dzierżyński, the Polish-born founder of the Soviet secret police, is even more widely despised. His likeness stands on a pillar outside Warsaw's city hall in the middle of a square that now also bears his name. During the Solidarity period young men would sometimes climb the statue to paint its hands red, but later police kept guard through the night. There is a joke that tells of a child on a bus who notices the statue and mentions to her mother that in school she has been taught that Dzierżyński was very fond of children. "Yes," says the mother, "it is just adults he could not stand." In another story, an old peasant visits the statue, crosses himself, and tells a passerby that Dzierżyński was one of the greatest Poles who ever lived. When the stunned stranger asks why, the peasant tells him, "Because he killed more Communists and more Russians than vodka and winter," a reference to Dzierżyński's role in Soviet purges.

The jokes and the tug-of-war over symbols were amusing and bolstered morale but they did not soften the harsh brutality of police efforts to obliterate Solidarity and subdue the union's supporters. Terrible things had happened and were happening. Fathers and mothers were taken away from young children. The health of many suffered from the hard beds and soft food of prison regime. Old friends stopped seeing each other because of suspicions that one or the other had talked to the police. Union activists were thrown out of work and blacklisted with so-called wolf tickets. Marian Jurczyk, the leader of the Szczecin strikers, learned in his prison cell that his son and daughter-in-law had apparently killed themselves in circumstances that left some people doubting the explanation of suicide. Piotr Bednarz, a Solidarity leader from Wrocław, did try to kill himself after weeks of uninterrupted interrogations, but he was saved by prison doctors. Jacek Kuroń, the ideological patriarch of the resistance movement, learned in prison that his wife had died of cancer; he had never been fully informed of her deteriorating condition. And Grzegorz Przemyk, the nineteen-year-old son of a poet supporter of Solidarity, died of internal bleeding after being taken in good health to a police station.

More than twenty thousand people attended the boy's funeral in May of 1983 and the gathering had turned into an angry antigovernment demonstration. More than a year later, several weeks after my arrival, two policemen, two doctors, and two ambulance drivers went on trial in the case. I was given permission to cover the final day's session. All the seats in the front two thirds of the courtroom were filled by men in business suits who flashed police identification cards to the uniformed guards at the door. Przemyk's family and some thirty friends and supporters crowded into the back rows. Among them was an eighty-year-old woman who had been the boy's teacher in elementary school. She carried a scrapbook with poems the youth had written. The police in the front glowered at the people in the back.

In his summation the chief judge went over what had been definitely established about the case. The youth had been drinking wine in the old town square to celebrate the end of high school exams. When he refused the request of a policeman to produce the *legitymacja* that all Poles must carry, he was taken to the police station. Two days later he died in the hospital, to which he had been taken from the police station. The accused policemen had testified that as they talked to the boy, he complained of feeling ill and that they summoned the ambulance. They said he walked out of the police station on his own. The boy's closest friend told the court that he had been in the station house and had seen the police beat Przemyk with clubs. The dead boy's mother, Barbara Sadowska, a well-known poet who had championed Solidarity, said her son had told her at the hospital that he had been beaten by the police.

The judge said that "the truth is sometimes impossible to determine." He said the testimonies of the mother and the friend were not credible. Meanwhile, the prosecutor, who technically at least was supposed to be bringing the case against the accused, declared that the statements by Przemyk's mother "led to the peculiar idea that beating up of detained people is a daily occurrence in police stations." There was no jury and it was the judge who fully exonerated the policemen. The men in the front of the court looked to the back rows, smirking. One after another the people in the back rose and left in silent protest before the judge finished. The doctors were given a suspended sentence for negligence, having failed to properly diagnose the youth's injuries, and the ambulance attendants were given two years for carrying the youth without a stretcher and dropping him on the floor of the clinic.

As a recently arrived observer I found the charade of due process and heavy-handed overkill to be jarring. Even if the outcome was politically predetermined, why was it necessary to pack the courtroom with scowling policemen? Why did both the prosecutor and judge have to attack the bereaved mother and offer extraneous praise for the police? Why was the lawyer chosen by the dead boy's family prevented from coming to court? Why the thuggish tone? Polish friends patiently explained what to them was as obvious as pain. The trial, they said, was intended, above all, to serve as a lesson on police power. Like painting over the Solidarity slogans, the trial was meant to show that police have the strength to cover up what they want and that those who object will always fail. The crudeness was considered necessary to make sure that the message was most widely understood.

Such strutting by the police is not an affectation of the system but lies at its very heart. The first few times I was stopped on the street and asked for my identification, I bristled as policemen wrote down my name and the time of our encounters, apparently for no reason. Gradually, like most Poles, I shamelessly accepted the inquiries as normal aspects of street life, like litter in New York. That, in fact, was the point of the exercise, to wear me down and make me accept their authority. Soon after telephone service was restored in the martial law period, callers were advised by recorded announcements that their conversations were being monitored. Clearly, most Poles realized that even the swollen police force lacked the manpower to listen to every single call. But that was not the object of the message. When the recorded voice was saying, "Warning: This conversation is being controlled," it was once again advertising the police as being ubiquitous and omniscient. Through such intimidating details the authorities have tried, and in some measure succeeded, in aggrandizing the dominion of the police and convincing many Poles that whatever happens, the police are behind it. That, in fact, every historical change has been the result of police infiltration, manipulation, or provocation. According to the police view of life, social movements do not take place because people are unhappy or yearn for freedom but because some cabal pulls the strings of an unwitting puppet. Or, because police consciously suspend vigilance or throw firecrackers into a crowd.

The best-informed disinterested student of police power in Poland is Władysław Bieńkowski, a former education minister who was expelled from the party in the late sixties for his examination of how power ebbs and flows under Communism. An intellectual loner, the small eighty-two-year-old sociologist has spent three decades tracing the cycles of police repression that he explained to me over glasses of dark tea. His basic thesis, which he first framed in an essay entitled "The Motors and Brakes of Communism," contends that under Communism, police powers to forbid, repress, and stultify expand unchecked by any force such as a free press or an independent judiciary or an established guarantee of due process. In Poland there are no normally existing countervailing forces to challenge or curb police authority. The result is that even without any political guidance the police will simply clamp down on more and more activity. This leads to what Bieńkowski calls a period of petrification. Eventually, the pent-up pressure of social yearnings and impulses for efficiency lead to eruptions and upheavals. At that point, state authority, which is identical to police authority, retreats. A thaw sets in and people act with increased freedom. But this only lasts for a relatively short period as the police consolidate their powers and increase their repression anew. Society's creative forces dissipate. Bieńkowski said that the cyclical process he described has been demonstrated with the major eruptions of 1956, 1970, and 1980, each giving way first to relaxation and then to tightening police control.

I asked the pugnacious scholar how the cycle might be broken. He said it would help to dismiss a great many policemen but he acknowledged this would be troublesome. For one thing, if, as he assumed, there were at least 350,000 police and, if, as was likely, every policeman were a party member, then policemen and retired police could represent as much as one seventh or even one fifth of the membership of the Polish Communist Party, which had suffered massive defections since Solidarity's rise. Theoretically, the party could chastise the police, but if it tried, it faced the real danger that the police might chastise the party.

On the street, where the Martian-masked Zomos were simply seen as Jaruzelski's praetorians, deterministic theories of police power, however elegant, were less useful than good running shoes. Some time after my visit with Bieńkowski, but still quite early in my stay, I was standing on a corner across the street from a group of fifty people who were keeping a silent vigil at a floral cross in front of St. Anna's Church. Men and women were kneeling. A few held hands aloft with two fingers spread in the outlawed gesture. The cross was dedicated to the memory of the Przemyk youth, and in addition to blossoms and candles it contained Scout badges and letters written to the boy. More than a year later I met a former captain in the riot police who had been fired for his Solidarity sympathies. He told me that this cross had originally been started by the police themselves as a diversion to lure the old women from the strategically more important central square. The former captain said he thought it was sadly ironic that what began as a police tactic eventually grew into a display of homage for a young man widely believed to have been killed by the police.

As I stood and watched the vigil two uniformed men approached me and asked for my identification. I showed them my Polish press credential issued by the foreign ministry. They took the card and after asking me to come with them they drove me with roof light flashing and siren wailing to a police station. I was left on a wooden bench in the day room, where for three hours I was apparently forgotten, or, I suspect, left to stew and worry. It turned out to be my only arrest in Poland and it was much more educational than heroic. For as I had nothing to do but observe, I watched streams of plainclothes operatives as they reported in from tours of duty.

Until that moment I shared in the conceit of reporters around the world who feel they can spot cops either by their hats, or shoes, or their cynical and tired looks so similar to those of newsmen. But in the Polish precinct house I was surprised. Old women in their sixties with shopping bags came in to whisper that they were "on the job." They were followed by professorial-looking men in wire-frame glasses and carrying briefcases, men and women in grimy work clothes, drunks with either real or well-simulated staggers, girls and boys with school bags who seemed to be teenagers. They came in one at a time, a few minutes apart, and checked in with the desk officer. A few of the younger men carried little leather purses, presumably to conceal their weapons. Tadeusz Konwicki, Poland's ironic novelist, says he spots secret policemen by these purses, which he calls "narcissist pouches" since he assumes they were made for people who do not want

the lines of back pocket wallets to mar their silhouettes. Sometimes he calls them "pederast bags." As I sat and watched the
traffic, I tried to absorb the fact that this, too, was Poland. That
in addition to the rebels, the underground activists, the prisoners,
the dissidents, the martyrs, the strugglers, and the victims, there
were also little old ladies who were probably proud that they
could so well conceal their police identities.

I was finally taken upstairs to be interviewed by an inspector
in civilian clothes who was watching a television program. It
turned out to be an American-made serial about a two-fisted priest
in the American West. He told me it was one of his favorite shows
and that he did not want to miss this installment. To make conversation I said that the star of the show had been a well-known
American football player.

"Ah yes, American football, it is such a brutal game," said the
officer.

I asked him why I had been detained. He asked me why I
spoke Polish so well if I had only been in the country for such a
short time. "It is not such a hard language," I lied. Again I tried
to learn why I had been arrested since I understood that my
credentials entitled me to cover news. Would I give him the film
from my camera? he asked. I replied that since I was in a police
station under his authority he could take my film but I would
not give it to him. I suddenly suspected that he might be concerned because some of the people I had photographed at the
vigil were in fact undercover police like the people I had seen
below. I told the officer that I would have no way of identifying
the occupations of the people who had been praying. He smiled
and asked, "Do I have your word?" I said sure. He shook my
hand and wished me an interesting stay in Poland. "American
football, it really is a terrible, brutal game," he said as I left.

I was released in time to get to St. Stanisław Kostka Church,
at which Father Jerzy Popiełuszko was expected to urge people
not to vote in upcoming municipal elections. A few days earlier
I had met the thirty-seven-year-old priest at the home of an ac-

41

quaintance. Four months later, when he was beaten to death by three secret policemen and his trussed body was recovered from a reservoir by frogmen, the details of his life were illuminated and publicized by his martyrdom. But when I met him, he struck me only as a modest, serious man with a great many obligations. He was thin and slight. I thought of him as a sad-eyed farm boy, vulnerable in the city. At the church there was an overflow crowd and some ten thousand people gathered on a plaza outside to hear the priest. In cryptic but unmistakable terms he noted that the Polish word for election was also the word for choice and that the word for voting was the same as that for giving voice, and that therefore it seemed to him that if people were unhappy they had the choice to stay mute, or withhold their votes.

After the sermon, the mass continued and when bells were rung, people around me began to kneel. I did not want to offend anyone, but I am not a Christian and I am not a believer. I have a bad knee. I had my notebook out and I thought that would mark me as a foreign journalist and exempt me. As the crowd fell to its knees, I looked around at the few people still standing. I tried to catch their eyes but they looked away from me. I thought to myself that they must be police and immediately, I knelt.

FOUR

LEGENDS

I WAS ON my way to visit Tadeusz Konwicki, the novelist, when in the courtyard of his apartment house I noticed a group of children at play. The smallest, a boy in shorts, was whining, "I don't want to be Jaruzelski again, I want to be Bujak." The older children kept insisting that the small boy order the troops out on the street so that they could get on with playing martial law. Moments later, Konwicki was telling me about his own childhood, how, in the suburbs of Wilno, a few years before the Second World War, he and his friends would reenact Piłsudski's defeat of the Bolshevik Red Army in 1920. Then during the writer's dreamy adolescence, first the Germans invaded and occupied his home ground and then the Russians came. Games gave way gradually and imperceptibly to life. At war's end he and his friends were living in the forest, attacking and being attacked by inchoate bands of deserters, killers, patriots, and survivors. He and his comrades darted in the Lithuanian forest among Germans, Russians, Lithuanians, Ukrainians, and frightened Jewish stragglers, certain only that they were going to die for Poland. In his knapsack, Konwicki kept a tattered book of Mickiewicz's poems,

43

and he was sure that even if he died deep in the dark wood, history would note his sacrifice. Many of his friends did in fact die and others were deported to the Soviet Union. At eighteen, the writer, today so much admired for his surreal imagination, was tracking down, facing, and shooting to death neighbors whom the underground had condemned for their collaboration.

At the time I was visiting Konwicki, I had been in Poland for several months. I was progressively coming to view the conspiratorial details of ordinary life as impressive but hardly rare aspects of the social landscape, like sand dunes in the Sahara or ice crags in the Arctic. I had some time earlier established contact with a former steelworker, whose real name I never learned though we were to meet regularly for three years. To call him something, I called him Maciej. He would telephone me in the style of a drunken Pole to praise President Reagan and ask me to convey his thanks to the White House in the name of the entire Polish nation. That would be my signal to meet him two days later. I would drive around a large housing project until I saw him. He was my *kolporter*, a term that meant bootlegger of illicit publications. When I first heard people telling me that they were waiting for their *kolporter*, I imagined that the expression referred to Cole Porter and I playfully speculated whether there might be Polish cultists who revered the sophisticated songwriter as an avatar of enviable capitalist decadence in the way that some Asian hill tribes worship Victor Hugo. In fact, the word was simply imported from the French, in which it means hawker or peddler.

At our meetings, Maciej would deliver shopping bags of illegal publications that included factory newspapers, regional weeklies, literary monthlies, women's magazines, two different children's magazines, audiotapes, videocassettes, photo albums, posters, and books from a dozen underground publishers. In the beginning some of these materials were poorly produced, mimeographed and stapled together, but the quality improved considerably to rival that of official government-censored publications. In a police state where paper was rationed and printing

44

equipment monitored, the volume was remarkable. Unlike most of those involved in underground publishing, Maciej was a professional who made his living from the commissions he earned by distributing the materials. He said it was about as much money as he used to earn stoking a steel furnace.

One of the first items I bought from him was a pamphlet called "The Small Conspirator," a manual for clandestine activity that declared on its front page that it was prepared by "people who are at the moment free." The foreword added that if readers carefully studied the first section, entitled "How to Plot," they might find the subsequent section on how to deal with police and prosecutors to be superfluous. The booklet, which became an often reprinted best-seller, urged people to establish their own autonomous "firms" and to conspire in whatever ways they thought best. Some groups, it noted, were specializing in servicing printing equipment or securing apartments for fugitives or obtaining false identifications. Others were organizing clandestine unions at factories, sending radio bulletins from mobile transmitters, monitoring police radios, and trying to penetrate party and police circles.

The booklet offered concrete advice on how to select places for meetings, how to build and use networks of couriers, and how and where to establish "boxes," apartments or offices where messages could be left safely in the event that normal links of communication were cut by arrests. Novice conspirators were advised to keep things simple. Tricky codes should be avoided and people should not carry address books with them. The instructions noted that the pressures of secrecy can be punishing but it urged people to resist confessional temptations. If, however, people simply had to boast or unburden themselves, that should be done only with the most trusted friends in the safest surroundings. The booklet cautioned people to be constantly wary, keep phone conversations to a minimum, look out for shadowing agents and maintain vigilance even in churches. "Remember, the church is an open house, which means that it is also open to the police."

The final chapter consisted of mock interrogations to be used to prepare people for the eventuality of arrest. The authors suggested that people should refuse to make any statement, or to simply deny all charges and cling to that denial. "The Small Conspirator" also gave advice about how best to serve time in prison. "As with everything, sitting in prison has to be learned," wrote the authors. "There are people who are wonderful comrades in struggle, work, and play, but who are terribly tiresome as cellmates. To endure in the closed world of the cell, people have to lower their emotional register, become calmer and less ardent. You need to show more tact and less emotion than do people at liberty. As inmates we have to carefully plan our day. We have to force ourselves into a corset of our own making so that we are not strangled by the corset of prison regulations or by social pressure from fellow prisoners who we can never fully trust. In letters to your family you should never write what or who you are worried about since, remember, the letters are being read by prosecutors."

The pamphlet was intended to both inform and inspire. It was being read by high school students as well as workers and for the young readers warnings of hardships such as this one were also implied tests of courage. "People are most frightened of pain and isolation. Physical pain can be imagined. All of us have had experiences such as broken bones or visits to the dentist, but in these cases the pain is not of our choosing and all we can do is simply to bear our lots. But whether to accept the isolation of prison and torture involves matters of choice and raises questions that each one must answer on his own. Still, we should remember that sympathy for the weak and compassion for the suffering should not serve as a blanket exoneration for capitulation with the excuse that none of us know how we would act when they tear out our fingernails. There are many people who never had their fingernails extracted, but who poured everything out during a single police interview because as they later explained to themselves, they had a wife and children. Well, we should always recall that we are in solidarity with people who also have wives and children."

Though the booklet carried no authors' names, it had, in fact, been compiled mostly by an outspoken and combative architect named Czesław Bielecki. Despite a height of six feet five inches and a personality that even his friends regard as belligerently provocative, Bielecki was able to thrive unobtrusively while the police searched for Maciej Polecki, the pseudonym under which he wrote. He set up an underground publishing house called CDN, an abbreviation that stands for To Be Continued, which produced "The Small Conspirator," among other works. According to reports he will neither confirm nor deny, he even produced a clandestine Solidarity newspaper for the army. When he was finally captured while visiting his two young sons, he followed the advice of his own manual to set records for prison obstinacy. For eleven months he held to a hunger strike, forcing his captors to feed him daily by pouring gruel into a bit clamped in his mouth. Within a week of his release in the amnesty of 1986, Bielecki was telling concerned friends that they should not have worried about him. "I knew exactly what I was doing," said the man whose weight dropped to 120 pounds. "I am a political creature and I will always make politics with whatever tools are available. In prison the only thing I had with which to fight Communism was my alimentary canal. But it worked. I knew I had them when the nurses started taking electrocardiograms three times a day. I could see that the guards were worried I was going to die and that cheered me tremendously. 'Look,' I told them, 'there's only one thing you can do and that is cut off my head, otherwise you should know that I have a radio transmitter stuck up my ass and every night I am reporting my condition on the Voice of America. Face it. You are through.' "

His pamphlet and dozens of other similar materials evoked all the images and symbols of Polish valor, from the anti-czarist uprisings of the nineteenth century to the resistance of the Second World War. From childhood, Poles are nurtured on legends of daring deeds and tragic hopes: Tadeusz Kościuszko leading a rebellion in 1794; Romuald Traugutt, hanged in 1864 at a czarist fortress after heading an insurrectionary government from hiding. Both Bujak and Jaruzelski had learned about Traugutt from their fathers. Both cited the hanged man as among their greatest heroes. Piłsudski emerged from that same Warsaw fortress to put out a clandestine newspaper called *The Worker*, to rob trains, and to recruit armed legions to prepare for independence.

The Second World War and its aftermath offered yet other parallels and symmetries. There were the guerrilla bands of the AK, or Home Army, which like the group Konwicki ran with, exchanged fire with Germans and Russians. And there was the Warsaw uprising of 1944, when for nine weeks a poorly equipped citizens' army of a secret state fought house to house and street to street. As the battle raged, Soviet troops stopped their advance long enough to allow the Germans to punitively raze the city and force surrender on the pro-Western fighters. In the postwar period there were yet other failed champions, men imprisoned for their Westernized taint or those who again formed futile armed bands in the forests. Still later came the protesting workers, among them the scores who were killed in Poznań in 1956 and on the Baltic Coast in 1970. Now in countless homes the stories of the Bujaks and the Borusewiczes and Bieleckis and hundreds of others were being woven into the Polish tapestry of resistance.

Nowhere else have I felt the constant awareness of history and tradition as I did in Poland. Quite early in my stay I met a university lecturer who had just returned from his first visit to Western Europe. He told me he was struck how the thick atmosphere of history he breathed in Poland thinned out as he moved away. "Everywhere else, people think history is something that happens to strangers, while here it is what happens to our mothers and fathers and what is happening to us and our friends." In the same vein a woman I know insists that there is a specific Polish emphasis on time, particularly on the past. "You foreigners live primarily in space, in geography, but for us time is the most important dimension." And once a priest told me that like Napoleon's soldiers, who held the destiny of France in their knapsacks, every Pole is raised to keep the fate of his nation in his heart. At first I thought he was being ironic, using a mock-heroic tone, but I realized he was serious.

Just how family legends of suffering, loss, and sacrifice blend with the drama of national destiny is most glaringly expressed every November 1, on All Souls' Day, which despite officially endorsed atheism, is a national holiday. The smoke of millions of memorial candles fuses in a pall that by early afternoon hovers over the capital city like a canopy of lamentation. Every Christian grave is illuminated. In addition, there are fresh flowers and ribbons on all the thousands of monuments and memorial tablets acknowledging the deaths of known and unknown heroes of named and unnamed wars, with most of the commemorated blood spilled in the last fifty years. On the sidewalks, before the plaques that mark sites of Nazi executions, rows of tapers flicker in ostentatious respect. Eventually the funereal cloud dissipates but the ashy smell of the candles settles and lingers for some days. In the thickening smoke and unavoidable smell, private grief melds into national mourning, and once again, in the words of the national anthem, Poles "attach themselves to the nation." It was clear that in their struggle to close the Solidarity chapter and "normalize" the situation, General Jaruzelski's government and police had to contend with the grandmothers and grand-fathers who kept the archives of family legends, both real and embellished. Government efforts were being blocked by barri-cades of romantic sagas. This was a force I knew long before I ever came to Poland, but I was to feel its impact most intimately when, after my first year in Warsaw, my then eighty-two-year-old father came to visit me.

In February of 1935, my father, Adam Kaufman, jumped bail in Poland after what was to be the last of his many arrests. Carrying skis he did not know how to use, he slid and stumbled down Carpathian slopes into temporary sanctuary in Czechoslovakia. He was thirty-three years old and had spent nine and a half years in prison as an organizer for the then illegal Communist Party of Poland. By the time he left he had been expelled from the party but he was being pressured by prosecutors to bear witness against old comrades.

In the half-century of his absence, Poland's borders had shifted some two hundred miles to the west as eastern areas of historic Poland were absorbed by the Soviet Union, while in compensation formerly German lands were rendered Polish. My father's ethnic and religious kin, the Jews of Poland, were gone, either killed by the Nazis or set to flight. In his day it was Communists who were hunted and imprisoned as dissidents and now, as he returned, a Communist government was hunting and imprisoning others. Polish society had changed radically and the landscape of his native land had been altered by war and time, yet there was very much in the conspiratorial and romantic culture of Poland that my father found movingly familiar.

From an intimately subjective perspective, my own involvement with Polish dreams and fantasies began on a subway train in 1946 when my parents and I were returning from visiting friends in Brooklyn. I was eight years old. That evening I heard my father use the Polish verb *to sit* in ways I never heard it used before. "Yes, I sat with him," he said, or, "I sat there for two years." On the subway ride home, I timidly asked him if that meant that he had been in jail. Very gently, he said yes, that in another time and in another place, he had been a Communist revolutionary. At that time I regularly listened to the radio program "Gangbusters." I believed that bad people went to prison and that good people put them there and here was the best man I knew, a man who had saved me from occupied France and the furnaces of war, and it turned out that he had been imprisoned many times. In that instant on the train I received my Polish patrimony, which in large measure includes an awareness that in this world the good often go to prison.

There is a Polish poet, Tomasz Jastruń, who while interned

under martial law wrote a short poem called "The Chain," which
established these links of Polish experience:

> His grandfather sat
> for Poland
> which did not exist
> His father sat
> for Poland
> which arose
> Now he sits
> for Poland
> which no longer exists.

Jastruń, the son of a poet of the wartime resistance, was inspired
by the family tree of a cellmate, Wojciech Kulerski, the brother
of Wiktor Kulerski, Bujak's assistant in the Warsaw underground.

Over the years, after that moment on the subway train, I came
to know many of the details of my father's early life. Once, when
he was seventy and I was thirty-five, he gave me a hundred-page
typescript spelling out as dispassionately as he could the details
of what he did and thought in the years before 1938, when I was
born. As I prepared to welcome him to Warsaw, I reread this
account of trials, interrogations, betrayals, hunger strikes, suicide
attempts, and illicit flights across borders. What had seemed dis-
tantly romantic and dated when I first read it in New York felt
almost contemporary amid present Polish realities.

From the very first hours of his month-long return, both of us
were absorbed by the often uncanny symmetries and striking
ironic twists. One of the first people that my father met in Warsaw
was Barbara Szwedowska, the girlfriend of Adam Michnik, who
was at that time still in prison. My father had hoped to meet
Michnik, whose father had been one of the codefendants in his
last trial and a cellmate. He greatly admired the thirty-eight-year-
old Michnik's antiauthoritarian essays, and he respected the courage of the man whom many in the opposition consider to be their

most articulate champion. He greeted the young woman, a former prosecutor, with almost courtly respect. He told her that his wife, my mother, who had died in New York five years earlier, had once waited a total of eight years for him and that her sacrifice, which had been for love, had turned out to be more fruitful than his own, which had been made in the name of dogma. When she, in response to his question, told him the specific charges that her lover faced, he nodded. "In my day it was Paragraph 102." He recited from memory: "Membership in an illegal organization that has as its aim to abolish much of the existing social order." He added, "Then it meant Communists, now it means Solidarity."

There were more echoes. The last time my father was charged under that law was when he stood trial with nineteen other men, among them Michnik's late father, Osjasz Szechter. That trial was held in Lwów, then a Polish city, now Lwiw, a city of the Soviet Ukraine. It was 1929. All the defendants were members of the Communist Party of the Western Ukraine, an autonomous part of the Polish Communist Party for those Polish provinces with Ukrainian populations. My father, at twenty-seven, headed the party as its secretary. He was the principal defendant in that trial and eventually drew the longest sentence, four years.

Szwedowska asked my father about his first impressions. He told her that there were many, but that one struck him as particularly ironic. He said that when he was a young organizer in the 1920s, people in Poland had many ways to explain and account for their unhappiness and dissatisfaction. "There was a pluralism of blame," he said. "A worker might blame the factory owner, some anti-Semites blamed wealthy Jews, Jews said the problem lay with anti-Semites, and the peasants resented wholesale merchants. Others pointed to Germans or Ukrainians as the source of trouble. Meanwhile, we Communists, a small group, ran around saying no, it's not a question of individual grievances, it is the system that is to blame. Now, after fifty years, I come back and what do I see? The whole nation knows perfectly well that the problem lies with the system, and only the leaders are saying no, the difficulties are the fault of individuals, former leaders, mistaken politicians, or, as during the anti-Semitic purges of 1968, Jews."

Szwedowska laughed. She then described for my father how she had nursed Szechter during the year he was dying of cancer. At the time his son, who uses his mother's name, Michnik, was also in prison, held in the aftermath of martial law. She said that the old man had some years earlier actively turned against Communism, and that he even had participated in protest hunger strikes in Catholic churches he had once regarded as bastions of obscurantism and repression and bigotry. My father replied with his own fifty-year-old recollections of her fiancé's father, who, he said, had been one of his political enemies, siding with the most ardent pro-Muscovite faction of the party. There had been constant arguments over tendencies and approaches that my father said he now finds absurd and ludicrous, like obscure points of medieval theology: "All that remains important to me now are the people, and I remember Szechter best for teaching me a song called 'A Letter to Mother,' by the Russian poet Sergei Yesenin. It was at a time after I was expelled from the party and no one else would talk to me." It turned out that many years later, Szechter had also taught the Russian song to Szwedowska, and in my living room she and my father sang it together.

> Are you still alive,
> my little old woman
> I am also alive, and
> I send you greetings.
>
> May the unutterable evening light
> float slowly over your small hut.
> They write me that while you hide your
>   anxiety
> You ardently grieve for me

Walking often to the road
in your old-fashioned fur.

And in the bluish dark of evening
you see the same apparition,
Someone in a drunkard's brawl
plunges a Finnish knife into my heart.

Pay no attention, my dearest. Be calm,
It is just delirious raving.
I am not such a total drunk
to die without seeing you again.

You need not teach me to pray.
There is no return to the past.
You alone remain my consolation.
You alone offer the unattainable light.

My father then told why the memory of Szechter teaching him the song was important to him. It happened after the Lwów trial. He had not only been sentenced for four years but the Polish Communist Party, which had dispatched him to work in the Ukrainian organization, expelled him for "Polish patriotic aberrations." The resolution expelling him specifically condemned him for having told the court of his service as a volunteer in Marshal Piłsudski's victorious army in the Polish-Bolshevik war of 1920. He was also assailed for having mentioned two "bourgeois" Polish authors and for addressing the court in Polish, which the resolution described as "the language of the oppressor," instead of Ukrainian, "the language of the oppressed."

In retrospect, the expulsion from the party probably saved his life, because it spared him from being summoned to Moscow and liquidated when a few years later Stalin first purged and then dissolved the Polish Communist Party for its nationalistic taint. However, with years of his term left to serve, my father, a veteran of more than a decade of party life, fell into despair. He had been the leader of the party commune, and then old friends and former acolytes turned away, scorning him as a pariah. He tried to kill himself, slashing his wrists and neck with a hidden razor blade. He was saved by prison doctors and after some time in an isolation cell, he was placed in the same cell as Szechter.

"We were political enemies but he was human and kind and we did not talk too much about party matters," he recalled for Szwedowska. "He taught me the song and I believe I indiscreetly told him how disillusioned I had been with the Soviet Union when I visited Moscow during the 1928 Comintern Congress." Szwedowska told my father that in the days and nights when she had talked to Szechter before his death he had told her that his first doubts about Communism had arisen in a cell in Brigidka prison, in Lwów, when he spoke with a man who had been in Moscow as a guest during that Comintern meeting, and she said that he must have meant my father. My father is very tough and he does not cry easily, but after she said that he sat still for several long minutes, his eyes shining with emotion. Later, when he was freed from jail, Michnik confirmed that story for me, but he added that though his father had always cited my father as arousing his skepticism, back then in the cell he may have been soliciting my father's confidences to report them to party superiors.

Not all the memories stirred by my father's return to Warsaw were flattering. Just after he arrived he asked me to take him to the area where he had lived when he was a poor university student, studying law. That street has been replaced by a park that runs along a riverside highway just below the Old Town. The area is now near the tourist center of the capital, with horse-drawn carriages carrying visitors over quaint cobblestone streets. The sight stimulated old feelings of guilt. This is how my father described it in a journal I asked him to keep during the visit:

"We passed through streets with familiar names: Freta, Długa, Kościelna, where I lived during my first year at Warsaw University. It was the winter of 1920 and I was very poor, permanently hungry. In spite of this I was exhilarated. I ran to lectures and I ran to the library writing down everything I could not understand.

I went to Parliament and listened to debates and returned home at ten or eleven at night. But even then the streets were full of people, selling, buying, talking, quarreling. Who were these people? Intellectually, I knew that in the narrow, teeming streets of the Muranów district there were hundreds of thousands of very poor, very helpless, very weak and tired Jews, carrying out a desperate daily fight for the necessities of life. Emotionally, however, they were outside of my consciousness. Years later, when these people were among the millions who were gassed and had their bodies burned to ashes, I reproached myself that as a boy of nineteen I had so little sympathy for my miserable neighbors and instead joined the party of Polish industrial workers who did not need my help.

"I regretted this, and I felt humiliated, but with time the remorse settled into my subconscious. Then, after walking the streets of Old Town, this old regret returned, evoking a sickening feeling, a mixture of nostalgia, mourning, and pity that the 368,000 Jews of Warsaw have gone and that only the names on the streets remain the same."

There were many more ironic echoes raised during my father's visit. There was the day that Janusz and Joanna Onyszkiewicz came for lunch. Janusz, the Solidarity spokesman, had been released from prison and was back at the university teaching mathematics. Joanna was learning to be a Polish housewife and a mother, coping with shortages. The fiftieth anniversary of the death of her grandfather, Marshal Piłsudski, was marked earlier in the year in churches all over the country. Old copies of his out-of-print books are highly coveted and his whiskered image hangs over tens of thousands of sofas. Though schoolbooks, movies, and state television ignore him, General Jaruzelski has hoped to capitalize on the marshal's popularity to justify his own military rule. During my father's prison years, Piłsudski was his hated nemesis, the authoritarian leader, with whose police, courts, and prisons he had to contend. In those years he had, perhaps daily, scorned and cursed the marshal, and now, in an irony he was enjoying, he was sharing lunch with Piłsudski's granddaughter, cooing with delight at the robust infant son she held in her lap.

"You know, we called him a fascist," he said of the marshal, "but we did not know then what fascism really was. No one could then imagine the totalitarian regimes of Hitler or Stalin and the horrors that lay ahead." He stopped short of praising the villain of his youth, but later he told me that in every way Piłsudski was better than all those who have followed him as Poland's leaders.

Onyszkiewicz, who was a delegate to the university senate, was explaining over lunch how academic freedom was being threatened by legislation that would have required teachers to swear loyalty to the prevailing system. Once again my father was reminded of an old experience. He recalled that his first arrest, on a charge of conspiracy, took place in April 1924, just a month before he was to have graduated with a law degree. He ended up spending three years in prison on the charge, but after his release, one of his professors, whom he met casually, suggested he return to his studies. A panel from the university senate asked him only whether he had ever received pay from a foreign power, and when he replied no, he was readmitted. My father wondered whether a student jailed for Solidarity activism would be treated in the same way. In fact, students had not been dismissed for Solidarity activity: There were too many of them. But teachers had been fired. Bronisław Geremek, a medieval historian with an international reputation and a key adviser to Wałęsa, was dismissed from his post at the Academy of Sciences because of his political views.

In our Warsaw conversations, my father several times recalled that in his day there had been brutal repressions. Once in jail he was forced to lie down with four other men in a tiny crawl space and kept near suffocation for forty-eight hours. He was on occasion beaten and he had seen and heard others being tortured. He had friends who had been in Bereza Kartuska, a prewar concentration camp for political prisoners, where conditions were very harsh. Still, in some ways, he thought, there may have been more tolerance then. For one thing, political inmates were, by and large, kept together in prison. They had access to books, and they maintained study groups. Once, my father recalled, he was given permission to make a May Day speech to fellow inmates. Furthermore, in contrast to contemporary trials where judges muzzled and evicted defendants such as Michnik, my father remembered how he and others would be permitted to use the prisoners' dock as a political pulpit. At one of his trials he was even complimented by the judge on his rhetorical skill. Though honor and shame were still important in Poland, Communism had devalued some chivalrous gestures.

In our search for echoes, my father and I visited the czarist Citadel, where the cell occupied by the young socialist Piłsudski lies near the ones that held Dzierżyński and Rosa Luxemburg. I showed my father the paintings of Siberian exile that are tucked away in a corner of the museum. They are the work of Aleksander Sochaczewski, a painter who died in 1923 and is hardly known to Poles. His canvases are large studies of people in chains, enduring exile, and dying in snowy wheelbarrows. Sochaczewski, it turned out, had been a rabbi's son who while an art student in Warsaw was arrested for distributing underground leaflets during the uprising of 1863. He was sentenced to death but because czarist law barred execution of those under twenty-two years of age, he was kept in the Citadel and then sent to Siberia. He was released in the amnesty of 1880 and spent the rest of his life painting brutal scenes from memory, showing manacled men who had half their heads shaved and their faces tattooed to thwart escape. He willed the paintings to the museum in Lwów. The paintings seemed to me to be very rare representations of suffering not of saints but of ordinary people, comparable to Goya's "Horrors of War." I can only imagine that at the end of the war, they were found by a curator who did not know what to do with the images of Russians whipping Poles. I am grateful that he did not burn them. Somehow, they made their way to Poland, and though they are not cited in officially published anthologies of Polish art, they hang quietly in the darkened corner of the old prison to be examined with interest by schoolchildren on class trips.

We also went to another prison that is now a museum, one that my father had known well. It was at Łodź, Poland's second largest city, where we stopped first at the house at 17 Piotrkowska Street, where my father was born and where he lived his first ten years. With great nostalgic joy, he pointed out the balcony where, according to family legend, his mother shielded him with her body when during the failed revolution of 1905, he came out to watch Cossack troops firing from Schultz's textile factory across the street toward striking workers scattering in the courtyard below. He was very moved by the streets of his childhood, streets and houses that were clearly recognizable except that now, he said, they were cleaner and populated by much better-dressed and healthier-looking people. He was surprised that the open sewers and rats of his youth were gone, while I was surprised that so many city dwellers still had to use outdoor toilets in courtyards.

We went on to the Museum of the Revolutionary Movement, which is housed in the jail in which my father on three occasions spent the better part of a year. A sign on the door said it was open to visitors, but a uniformed guard snarled that we could not come in. A young Polish friend who was with us said, "Of course, he has a uniform, so he has to say no." I came close to losing my temper and remarked that three times in this old man's life, when the building was a prison, he had not wanted to enter but had been forced to, and now that it was a museum, he was being barred. I said that this was Poland, a country where it is easier to go to prison than to a museum. A young official overheard us and invited us in. My father was not much moved nor was he upset. He noted that we were the only visitors and that he assumed that the place was kept open mostly for school groups or shepherded tours of workers. The appearance of three people coming in from the street must have astonished the staff. We tried to find the punishment cell where he had almost suffocated but it was gone. Instead there were the display cases of clandestine periodicals with names such as *The Worker, Struggle,* and *Independence,* all looking and sounding quite similar to materials being printed by Solidarity groups. There were letters in tiny script that had been smuggled from jail, such as he had written and such as were still being written, and there were photographs of illegal strikes.

My father was less moved by all this than he had been at his old house, but when among the photographs of people he had known and worked with he spotted the face of Jan Tennenbaum-Jelski, he breathed in deeply. "Naturally, it doesn't mention that he was finished in the Soviet Union by Stalin," he said pointing to the face of the man who had been his mentor and model as a revolutionary. My father had told me about Jelski, whom he still admires greatly for his physical and moral courage. Once in Wronki Prison, Jelski spent a year in an unheated cell, and wore only underwear rather than accept prison clothes. Later he escaped in handcuffs from a Warsaw trolley while being transported from one prison to another, and made his way to Moscow.

His memory sparked by the photograph, my father recalled his last meeting with Jelski in Moscow in 1928. "He told me that Stalin was going to murder all of us, and I remember his saying that it was better to sit and teach in Polish prisons than to vegetate in Soviet bureaucracy." He grappled with his thoughts about Jelski. As we walked in the weedy, sprawling Jewish cemetery on a fruitless search for family stones, my father returned to thoughts of the man. "He had great courage and character, but now I realize that his intelligence was limited by political faith and submission to party discipline." How could so many decent people have accepted such idiotic positions, he wondered, recalling particularly the time before World War II when the party line insisted that both " 'fascism' and 'social democracy' were equivalent sins." I think he was approaching self-recrimination.

"I see now that it was inevitable that I became a communist," he said as we walked in the cemetery. "I was poor, Jewish, and hungered for answers. The Russian Revolution took place during my adolescence, and Poland was reborn. I wanted desperately to enter into the wonderful romantic sweep of Polish history. One way would have been conversion to Catholicism, which for me was impossible. Another way was the party. It was inevitable but still a moral mistake."

My father's retreat from party life had been painful, leading to attempted suicide and flight. After his expulsion, he was arrested again and faced with the impossible choice of either testifying against old colleagues or standing mute and facing yet another long sentence. My mother pawned her inheritance to raise bail and arranged my father's flight across the mountains to Czechoslovakia. From there he eventually made his way to Paris, where I was born just before the war.

For me there are several, essentially Polish, burdens to his saga. In adolescence, in New York, I tormented myself by wondering how I would ever know and prove my worth if no one ever took me handcuffed from a trolley car. How would I act when someone passed a red-hot poker in front of my face, asking for the names of confederates? Could I go weeks without food, days without water to advance any cause? Was I prepared to sacrifice without any chance of victory? More simply, would I ever be a hero? Eager for testing, I held my hand over candle flames and carved girls' initials into my arm with straightened, heated paper clips. In self-detestation, I flirted with betraying the man whose dramas oppressed me with unattainable standards of the grace I sought. It was the time of McCarthy and witch-hunts, and my father, living and working as a resident alien, had his own fears of official summonses and renewed interrogations about who he may have known and what he may have thought in a different land at a time before the galaxy shuddered. I denounced him to my girl-friends, telling them he had been a jailed revolutionary communist, hoping to wrap myself in his myth.

Once, I mentioned such things to Jacek Kuroń, the patriarch of the Polish resistance, soon after he returned from prison. He told me that his own deepest fear as a seven- and eight-year-old child was that the Second World War would end before he would have a chance to conspire in it. He also told me that his father urged him never to smoke, "because it would cost me when I went to prison."

FIVE

IMPASSE

As a journalist trying to understand the tug-of-war between state and society I was concentrating largely on underground dramas and police chases, but I knew, of course, that most Poles were neither in resistance or security forces, much less prison. According to my housekeeper, Pani Kasia, they were, in fact, either standing in lines or moving slowly from bureaucrat to bureaucrat with pleas and unsolved problems. The dreary pattern of everyday life was often mired in impasse and gridlock. No one was visibly starving and there were no beggars on the streets, but the struggle to maintain customary levels of drab existence was, for people like Pani Kasia, becoming harder and more time-consuming. One day the rolls she liked disappeared and when she asked the baker about it he told her that some inspectors came and ordered him to use his flour only for bread, which was price-fixed, rather than for rolls, which were not. The heat and water in her apartment house had been cut off and no one could tell her if the repairs would be completed before the really cold weather came. She could not buy the space heaters that were on display in the department stores because they were reserved for

63

young married couples. One of her sons had been released from prison for Solidarity activism, but he had trouble finding a job and the police had confiscated the car she had purchased for him with money she saved while working as a maid for a Polish diplomat in New York.

Every morning, as we spoke over breakfast, Pani Kasia would sigh and blame her woes on the system, the Red Ones, and Jaruzelski. Like so many others she focused on the long lines and unavailability of goods to describe a pervasive sense of decline and decay. She would tell me about her unsuccessful search for arthritis medicine in five drugstores and she would complain about the rudeness of the clerks. At times she would nostalgically recall the chocolate she bought before the war from the Wedel store. It was better, she said, than any chocolate she has since tasted. I later learned that as a poor girl from the country, she had bought the chocolate only twice. But what was most disturbing to her was that the Wedel store was nationalized, that now the long lines of customers who queue up daily can buy only hard candies. The chocolate has gone, and in the mind of Pani Kasia it was killed by Communism. Everywhere I went I heard such stories. All over the country I found that the most common topic of conversation was not sex or politics, not even consumerism, but frustration. People often sought to outdo each other with tales of inconvenience and bureaucratic strangulation.

Many of the accounts involved variations on the catch-22 theme. A man who sold two kinds of neckties was fined because by displaying his limited wares in his shop window he had violated an ordinance requiring pleasing and artistic window dressing. Another man I knew kept seeking a doctor who would be willing to fraudulently diagnose him as an asthmatic so he could obtain a telephone. I met a divorced couple who, two years after their legal separation, still shared a one-room apartment because neither had anyplace else to go. Acquaintances would sometimes ask me to bring them things from abroad. They often needed items desperately. They would ask for medicines and one man begged me to bring an intrauterine device, but some wanted video recorders, digital watches, and cosmetics. I had a very good friend who one day noticed a bunch of bananas in my kitchen and sheepishly asked if he could have one. He said he loved them but had not had one in three years. His wife recalled that once, when he returned from a police interrogation, he told her that during his questioning, he fantasized that he would be offered a banana to talk about friends and colleagues and he wondered if he would weaken. After his wife told the story he laughed and added, "Fortunately bribing people with bananas is beyond the means of the government and I easily withstood the usual threats and promises."

Often, people set aside regular days each week for *załatwianie spraw*, which means taking care of such tasks as repeated visits to police stations to apply for passports, obtaining or updating dozens of forms such as ration cards, establishing proofs of residence, even searching for foreign fountain pens to present to surgeons in order to speed admission to hospitals. One woman spent every morning going to a large store hoping to spot a piece of simple Scandinavian-style furniture that might have arrived overnight. Once she went four months without seeing anything she wanted. After more than a year she managed to furnish her apartment and at the party she gave to celebrate the achievement she admitted that she had devoted ten times as much time and energy to the project as she expended on her editorial job at a magazine, and, she added, "a thousand times more interest and motivation."

I also met a woman who spent every Friday buying as many rugs as she could find. She was an energetic worker who cleaned the apartments of several Polish writers. Her employers, most of whom earned foreign income from published translations of their work, paid her well. She earned about thirty-two thousand złotys a month by working four days a week. What this amounted to in any international currency is hard to say. It was practically impossible to exchange złotys for dollars in a Polish bank, but if one were exchanging dollars in the state bank, the official rate at that time was two hundred złotys for a dollar. However, taxi drivers as well as men who changed money openly on the street just outside the doorway of the bank were offering eight hundred złotys for the dollar. What this meant was that a Pole whose aunt in Chicago mailed him forty dollars a month could quite easily convert that into the same thirty-two thousand złotys that the cleaning woman earned. However paltry the sum might seem when tabulated as dollars, as złotys it was roughly twice a steel-worker's monthly pay, which in turn was 25 percent higher than the salary of most doctors. The woman's husband also earned a good deal of money as a mason and bricklayer building private dwellings and summer residences for the small but growing number of entrepreneurs.

Their problem ironically was that they literally did not know what to do with their money. They had a house and a car and as much land as they could legally own. They kept only a portion of their earnings in the state bank, which they mistrusted. They did not know how to speculate in gold or silver or dollars and they feared the risk. Still, they had three children and they wanted to leave them something. So once a week, the woman would tour shops to buy woolen kilims which she stacked from floor to ceiling in a room of her house.

Signs of economic imbalances and institutionalized inefficiency were as common as potholes on Warsaw streets. I once asked a Polish friend why there were women caretakers sitting idly at tables in every public toilet. "Because," she explained, "for one thing, that is how we maintain full employment, and for another, can you devise any other system that would keep people from stealing toilet paper?" But, why then, I asked, were the toilets so dirty? "Look, if you had a terrible job that required you spend eight hours in a toilet, would you want to clean them too?" she answered with only partial irony. In Gdańsk I found a hotel full of hundreds of Filipino workers who were being paid U.S. dollars to work on Swedish ferries in the Polish shipyard. The Swedish contractors had taken over the multimillion-dollar project when the Poles failed to meet work deadlines. The managers from Stockholm determined that they could demand hard work only if they paid hard currency and they were quite willing to pay dollars to Polish workers. But the Polish party bosses said no. They feared that to have some Polish workers receiving dollars and other Polish workers receiving złotys for similar work was a prescription for unrest. As a result the Swedes were getting their ferries, the Filipinos were sending dollars home, and the Poles, as far as I could tell, were getting nothing.

During my explorations I called on the office of price control, where an administrator greeted me with candor. He said that his staff set close to 80 percent of the prices charged for goods. The process was essentially one of mediation between producers and consumers, with attention paid to vaguely defined notions of general welfare. The true cost of inputs, he said, had less bearing on prices than political ideas about the social usefulness of products or the group for which they were intended. As an example, he explained that the price of notebooks has been fixed at a small fraction of their production costs because it was deemed right that all schoolchildren should have them. The result, he went on, is that speculators quickly buy up all notebooks and either resell them at a steep profit, or convert them into paper for sale to what I gathered were printers of underground publications. Meanwhile, many children had trouble getting the pads. The official said that what was true of tablets was equally true of hundreds of other items in the chronically unstable market.

I thanked him and said that from his explanation, it seemed that the Polish economy was a madhouse, only I used the Polish idiomatic equivalent of madhouse, which is bordello. Without smiling he replied, "Oh, no, you could not run a whorehouse like this, a whorehouse requires real order and real discipline." A few days later I heard a radio interview in which an official

67

from the ministry of finance defended a putatively illegal black market. "Let's face it," he said, "without the black market how would we ever know the real values of things?"

There is a Polish saying that describes how a Tartar has a Cossack by the throat while the Cossack keeps the Tartar in a headlock, the point being that it is often hard to tell who, in fact, is dominating whom. As a motto expressing Poland's prevailing political culture, this rhymed bit of folk wisdom is as valid as *e pluribus unum* is for the United States. Like two wrestlers, state and society have for a very long time had each other in painful grasps. They circle and stagger, but neither has any chance of decisively pinning his adversary or freeing himself. The government and party cannot imprison or deport the nation. The nation cannot overthrow the authorities while Soviet power looms so near. One result is that a sense of unavoidable impasse permeates almost every human activity. "What is necessary is impossible," a university lecturer lamented as he tried to tutor me in the system. "What is required is precluded." Later, others would often use the simile of squaring the circle to explain why a vast and longstanding network of interlocking absurdities cannot be rationalized.

During a boozy afternoon I once spent with Konrad Bieliński, another mathematician and an underground fugitive, he kept insisting that any reform, no matter how minor, would if pursued to the end inevitably lead to the collapse of Communist control, the one thing Poland's leaders and their Soviet mentors could not permit. In the syllogism he offered, Poland's Communist leaders knew that to stimulate greater efficiency they would have to introduce greater liberty. But they also knew that greater liberty would bring greater public accountability, and that, in turn, would topple the leaders who were ostensibly backing reform. "The problem is that to change anything, the party has to saw off the branch on which it is standing," he said.

For those brought up in pragmatic Western cultures, a system that accepts stalemate as the best possible substitute for success seems like a Wonderland absurdity. Yet, all over Poland, I was to find factory workers, farmers, teachers, office employees, and government officials who deeply believed this. Partially these feelings were the result of forty years of an imposed Communism. But there is also a purely Polish component. After all, whereas other national anthems make claims to God's glory and nature's bounty, the Polish hymn modestly attests that "Poland is not yet lost while we are alive." If stalemate is less than victory, Poles intuitively understand that it is also better than defeat. In the factories and schools and farms, administrators and those they administered limped from one patchwork compromise to another. No group was strong enough to win outright and only a relative few were so weak that they could be swept aside for good. Might met right, and the result was often half right and half might, or, what was more likely, two-thirds might and one-third right. Similar compromises papered over clashes between good and evil, truth and lies, efficiency and wastefulness. Management pretended to manage and, sometimes, in exchange, workers pretended to work. Prices rose and then wages rose, at least those wages of those workers who were most likely to threaten disruption. The highest salaries are not paid in the most productive plants but in those that have the most workers, where strikes would be hardest to conceal. There, increases are dished out as hush money.

And while Polish society lay enmeshed in a tangle of impasses, General Jaruzelski was also clearly paralyzed by interlocking standoffs that reflected the grappling of the proverbial Cossack and Tartar.

During much of 1983 it was not at all clear whether the government and party controlled the police or if the security forces had the upper hand. In many party councils, particularly at the regional and local level, policemen and retired police formed majorities or powerful cliques that favored harsh crackdowns on all dissent. Sometimes these police dropped hints that they had powerful Kremlin allies. The general could not ignore these critics and he could not suppress them. He could only hope that the economy would improve and that this would win him time and support. The economy, however, was moribund and failing steadily. Throughout the country, building projects started with Western credits obtained in the seventies under the leadership of Edward Gierek remained unfinished, their unclad girders rusting in the country's exposed poverty. The importation of vital raw materials dried up. Jam factories had fruit and sugar but they lacked paper to print labels needed to sell the preserves abroad. Reconstruction work on the major bridge over the Vistula in Warsaw stopped for weeks because no screws were available. After the bridge was bombed in the war it had taken less than a year to rebuild; now it was to be closed for three years just for repaving. Mountains of coal accumulated at Silesian depots awaiting freight trains that were immobilized by a lack of spare parts. Export earnings could not provide the money needed to pay off just the interest on the $36 billion owed to the West, while cuts in goods and services were reducing the already low standards of egalitarian dreariness at home.

The toothpaste shortage was characteristic. For many years, the country's major toothpaste factory paid lower-than-average salaries. During the Solidarity upheavals, when employees gained both confidence and mobility, two thirds of its workers simply quit. This caused the first drop in production. Then, as lines of foreign credit were erased, the central bank withdrew allocations that were earmarked for imported chalk needed in toothpaste manufacture. Poland has chalk deposits but these were not being mined because construction of a chalk processing plant, approved many years earlier, was running three years behind schedule. The central planners had anticipated the shortfall of toothpaste supplies and they tried to accommodate consumers by bartering within the Communist bloc for tubes of Bulgarian toothpaste. However, when those shipments arrived, they were impounded because Polish health authorities found they contained levels of saccharin that exceeded Polish limits. Wherever one looked there were similar problems, and they were growing in number and complexity.

As early as the winter of 1983, General Jaruzelski's economic advisers were telling him that he either had to seek relief from the West or accept greater economic integration with the Soviet Union, an option that some Poles referred to as "becoming the sixteenth Soviet Republic." Most of the economists wanted the restoration of Western investment but this remained a chimera as long as political prisoners were in jail. There were about one thousand such detainees, but in effect the impasse centered on twelve men being held in two groups at Mokotów Prison on Warsaw's Rakowiecka Street. It was these men whose names were raised regularly by Western diplomats in conversations with Polish officials and it was their cause that was most prominently taken up by international human rights organizations.

The first group included four activists who had come to Solidarity from KOR, the eclipsed Committee to Defend Workers. In it were Kuroń; Michnik; Zbigniew Romaszewski, a physicist who had set up Solidarity's clandestine radio network; and Henryk Wujeć, another physicist who was also associated with the Club of Catholic Intellectuals. They were facing a military trial on charges of attempting to overthrow the established order. The other eight, all well-known union officials, had been confined without indictments since martial law was declared.

Month by month, the dilemma of what to do with these men mounted into a bizarre test of strength. When it ended it was very hard to declare a clear winner. Going through with a sedition trial would predictably thwart the government's hopes of reestablishing links with the West. But simply to let the men go after they had been detained for two years would amount to a public admission that the charges were fabricated. An idea for a face-saving exile of the twelve men had occurred to some church leaders who viewed it as a humanitarian compromise that would end the suffering of those imprisoned while it removed an embarrassing obstacle to economic recovery. They discussed it with government authorities and a few weeks before Christmas the offer was conveyed in great secrecy to the imprisoned men by General Czesław Kiszczak, the minister of interior.

On his honor as an officer, General Kiszczak promised that if the men agreed to leave Poland for a period of at least five years, they would be given free passage to the West. If they did not accept these terms, he told them, they would stand trial and they would certainly be given long terms. Either freedom on the Riviera with the support of Western labor unions or many years in Polish cells. Take it or leave it.

Kiszczak grew up in the army and in accordance with the decorum of party and military life, he had kept his personality and passions pretty much to himself. To much of the Polish public he appeared as another gray functionary, reflecting party loyalty, army discipline, and a show of bureaucratic efficiency. His pants were always neatly pressed and he regularly kissed the hands of women callers. Once in parliament he scorned the underground fugitives as self-styled cavaliers who trifled with the affections of the women who hid them. But Kiszczak, in fact, also had a Polish legend of which he was proud. At the outbreak of the war he was a fourteen-year-old son of a steelworker who had been fired for Communist sympathies. During the occupation his father was forced to work in German factories on the Baltic coast while young Kiszczak was press-ganged to work in Nazi factories, first in Wrocław, and then, after he was seized in a roundup, in Vienna. There he delivered messages for a conspiratorial group organized by a fellow worker, a Croatian Communist. In 1945, soon after his return to Poland, he joined the Communist party. With his peasant and worker background, Kiszczak fit what was then regarded as the ideal profile for Communist leadership. He was singled out for ideological education in the party school and he moved steadily through the ranks. He led combat units against anticommunist, anti-Soviet bands fighting in several parts of the country.

In 1946, one such force, known as *Ogień*, or Fire, attacked the home of his parents near Katowice. In a rare, laconic, but revealing interview he gave to Polish journalists, General Kiszczak recalled that the group "robbed whatever was valuable and took all my documents and personal photographs, even those from my holy communion. My father was beaten, and my mother had to plead for his life." Years later he learned the names of the attackers, "but I have done nothing to repay them. In the interim several amnesties were passed that erased more serious crimes, even murder, from memory. I was unable to take justice into my own hands and I did not want to do it."

Since he took over the ministry, which runs the police and prisons, the general has tried to convince Poles that his hands were cleaner than those of his predecessors. Specifically, he has staked his honor on the way he behaved in the early 1950s, when scores of army officers were purged, jailed, and some even sentenced to death on falsified charges of espionage. The wave of arrests, which began in 1951, ensnared officers who served in the prewar Polish army, or who spent time in the West during the war, or who fought with the international brigades of the Spanish civil war. In the wake of Tito's apostasy in Yugoslavia, the quest to expose imagined spies and traitors turned into a rabid inquisition. At the time, Kiszczak, a junior officer, was assigned to the army's counterintelligence command. He recalled that "rather early I recognized that the cases were not very clear. I was then a young officer and I did not know all the details of the investigations since they were surrounded with secrecy. Still from the information I had, I formed the impression that the matter was too smooth to be credible." He knew and admired some of those accused. "Disoriented and full of doubts, I decided to move myself to the side and to look at the situation from some distance. To the surprise of my superiors and my colleagues I asked to be sent to any duty outside Warsaw."

He was transferred to a unit in Silesia, serving as chief of counterintelligence. There, he discovered that five men in his command had been labeled in Warsaw as suspects. "I can confirm that nothing happened to any of these people," he said in the interview. The general believes that his unwillingness to join in the purge cost him early advances in his career but he also feels the decision established his honor and today still validates his moral authority.

Michnik, the man who was about to engage General Kiszczak in a duel attacking that sense of honor, was then thirty-eight years old. Since the age of twelve he had boldly questioned authority, that of his family, of schools, and ultimately that of totalitarian Communism. He had been regularly interrogated by police since he was fourteen. At fifteen he was identified by name as a public enemy in a secret speech made by Gomułka. He had been thrown out of the university and ordered to work for two years at a light bulb factory. He had been beaten by thugs who invaded public meetings. Unlike some of his imprisoned colleagues, who agreed to discuss and explore Kiszczak's offer, Michnik refused even to leave his cell to talk about the proposal with priests or with a representative of the United Nations who came to Warsaw. As he explained, his own sense of honor simply precluded any negotiations with jailers. In part this is because what he demands is justice and not charity, but his attitude was also shaped by his awareness since childhood of what happened to his father in the city of Łuck in 1931 and 1932.

Michnik's father, Osjasz Szechter, had by that time been released from the prison where he recited poems with my father. After a short period of freedom, he was seized along with three hundred other clandestine Communists, betrayed by a man who had turned informer. All the suspects were brought to Łuck, where they were systematically tortured to sign confessions. One of those detained, a man named Boiko, died during torture and his body was thrown into a river. One woman was stripped naked and interrogated by a noseless man who told her he was a syphilitic and threatened her with rape. The most prevalent torture was called PPG after initials that stood for Polish Rubber Industry.

It involved beating trussed people on the soles of their feet with hard rubber batons. Another practice, called Paraguay, consisted of pouring cold water into the nose of a victim to induce the sensation of drowning. During three years of pre-trial detention, Michnik's father was subjected to such practices and to one that prison guards called "a Chinese conversation." He was shackled and beaten on the testicles with a rubber truncheon. In the course of one such session, Szechter was told by the man who was beating him that he had been beaten in exactly the same way in a Soviet prison across the border.

After two years of interrogation fifty-two of the suspects were tried, Szechter among them. He received eight years for antistate activity. At the proceedings, the defendants showed their defiance by singing revolutionary hymns on the way to court. Nevertheless they and the other suspects who had been rounded up in the case were suspended from party membership because their superiors judged that they had breached party discipline by admitting their party affiliation under torture, thus opening the way for their questioners to ask about who else was in the party with them. The brutality of the Łuck interrogation was unusual enough to gain attention of human rights groups in France. Eventually, questions were asked in the Sejm, Poland's parliament, and some of the police officials involved were dismissed. Osjasz Szechter was freed in 1935 under a special amnesty for all the Łuck defendants.

Nearly fifty years later as a Communist minister offered Szechter's son an amnesty and exile, Michnik fought back with wit, irony, and a small pencil. He also had enough familiarity with the Polish prison system to enable him to smuggle messages to the outside. Beyond the walls, others would know how to disseminate his words further through foreign radio stations and the underground press. Normally he writes slowly but here he was impassioned. He made sure that the *kapuś* or stool pigeon in the next cell was sleeping as he began his open letter to General Kiszczak. At the top of his letter he identified himself as "Adam

Michnik, son of Osjasz," thus following the prescribed form of official prison correspondence and paying tribute to the father who had died a short time earlier.

Michnik noted that apparently the minister of the interior had insufficient powers to deal with his earlier complaints about his books being confiscated. "You did, however, have the power to present me with a somewhat curious choice—that either I spend next Christmas on the Côte d'Azur or else I go on trial and face many years in jail." Michnik scorned the offer with irony. "Your soul is as generous as the Ukrainian steppe," he wrote before offering his summary and analysis of the deal.

> 1. You admit that I have done nothing that would entitle a law-abiding prosecutor's office to accuse me of 'preparing to overthrow the government by force' or 'weakening the defensive capacity of the state' or that would entitle a law-abiding court to declare me guilty.
>
> I agree with this.
>
> 2. You admit that my sentence has been decided long before the opening of my trial.
>
> I agree with this.
>
> 3. You admit that the indictment written by a compliant prosecutor and a sentence pronounced by a submissive jury will be so nonsensical that no one will be fooled and that they will only bring honor to the convicted and shame to those who convict.
>
> I agree with this.
>
> 4. You admit that the purpose of the legal proceedings is not to implement justice but to rid the authorities of embarrassing political adversaries.
>
> I agree with this.
>
> From here on, however, we begin to differ, for I believe that:
>
> 1. To admit one's disregard for the law so openly, one would have to be a fool.
>
> 2. To offer a man who has been held in prison for two years the Côte d'Azur in exchange for his moral suicide, one would have to be a swine.

3. To believe that I could accept such a proposal is to imagine that everyone is a police collaborator.

I know very well, General, why you need our departure—so you can besmirch us in your newspapers with redoubled energy as people who have finally shown their true faces, who first executed foreign orders and then were rewarded with capitalist luxuries. So you can show the entire world that it is you who are the noble ones and we, the spineless wretches. So you can say to the Polish people, Look, even they gave up, even they lost faith in a democratic and free Poland. So that, above all else, you can improve your own image in your own eyes; so that you can proclaim with relief that after all, they are no better than us. Because the very idea that there are people who associate Poland not with a ministerial chair but with a prison cell, people who prefer Christmas under arrest to a vacation in the south of France, unsettles you profoundly.

I cannot foretell the future and I have no idea whether I will yet live to see the victory of truth over lies and of Solidarity over the present antiworker dictatorship. The point is, General, that for me, the value of our struggle lies not in its chances of victory but rather in the value of the cause. Let my little gesture of denial be a small contribution to the sense of honor and dignity in this country that is being made more miserable every day. For you, traders in the freedom of others, let it be a slap in the face.

For me, General, prison is not such painful punishment. On that December night it was not I who was condemned, but freedom; it is not I who am being held prisoner today, but Poland.

The impact of the letter on Poles lay in its audacity. Its tone immediately evoked Polish traditions of eloquence framed in duress and difficulty, the defiance of the condemned and exiled. After two years of virtual solitary confinement, a far from chastened Michnik was giving moral instruction to his oppressors. He openly called them "scoundrels" and "vindictive, dishonorable swine" and revealed their weakness. He rejected the offer and hurled his own challenges. From his prison cell he had gone on the offensive.

Once smuggled out, the letter was heard by much of Poland as it was broadcast by the Polish services of the Voice of America, the British Broadcasting Corporation and Radio Free Europe. It was reprinted in most underground journals. It inspired many and amused some but it also was also effective as a key to open prison gates. In July of 1984, five months after it was written, all the charges against Michnik and the eleven other remaining prominent detainees were dropped. But Michnik played his role to the end. When he was told he was to be freed he declared he would not willingly leave his cell. He demanded a trial, saying that the state that had seized him on a whim could not simply release him on another one. What was at issue was due process and democratic rule. He said he wanted a trial and the acquittal justice demanded and not an amnesty. He was, in fact, shouting that he wanted a trial when the guards came and forcibly carried him from his cell. Michnik resisted just enough so that the world press would write about it and embarrass Jaruzelski. He was making politics with what he had. But in the end, he was free, not in France but in Poland. At least for a while.

SIX

UNDERGROUND CIVILIZATION

THE AMNESTY WAS proclaimed on July 22, 1984, the fortieth anniversary of the day that a provisional council was installed in Chełm, behind the advancing lines of the Red Army. That council had been appointed in the Kremlin and it was never recognized by any other government. Still its formation is now celebrated as Poland's national day, marking the flimsy origin of Communist rule. In the last few decades it has often been observed with amnesties. The one that was announced in 1984 was broader than most such decrees. Its provisions extended not only to some seven hundred political prisoners and thirty-five thousand common criminals but also to fugitives active in a nonviolent underground. Those conspirators who surfaced and renounced their clandestine activities would have all charges against them dismissed. Less than a dozen generally unknown people did report to police stations to be shown on television stammering unconvincingly through tales of their disillusion. Several of them spoke awkwardly of their desire to return to their families. Zbigniew Bujak and Wiktor Kulerski, who by this time were coordinating an extensive network of underground "firms" in the Warsaw area, never considered the offer and thought it a chump's deal. "It was as if someone were urging the Rockefellers to declare bankruptcy," said Bujak. "There was no point to it, everything was going fine."

Indeed, it did appear that the underground was thriving. Practically every day, I had contact with some clandestine "firm." The Theater of the Eighth Day, a group of politicized actors, would invite me to see a production of anticommunist and anti-Soviet skits performed for workers. Klemens Szaniawski, a world-renowned logician and the former rector of Warsaw University, would be lecturing on Polish resistance during World War II to a mixed group of workers and students. Jacek Federowicz, once Poland's most popular television star, displayed his satirical drawings and delivered humorous commentary on the party and its leaders. The country's best writers, Tadeusz Konwicki and the poets Zbigniew Herbert and Czesław Miłosz, who was in exile, shunned official publishers and offered their works to underground publishing houses. None of the country's better-known writers, artists, filmmakers, or journalists joined the government-sponsored associations that were meant to replace the forcibly dismantled independent groups that had arisen in the Solidarity period. *Tygodnik Mazowsze*, the four-page weekly of Warsaw's underground Solidarity, had not missed a single issue. It was being printed in six different underground shops with a press run of about fifty thousand copies. The ninety-sixth consecutive issue contained an assessment of the amnesty by Bujak and Frasyniuk.

Frasyniuk, the Wrocław Solidarity leader who had been one of the twelve prominent detainees who spurned exile to France, shook the security detail that had tailed him as he left prison and, before heading home to his wife, he dramatically and defiantly met with Bujak, Poland's most notorious fugitive, who was heading the Warsaw conspiracy. In their statement the two men declared that the amnesty was welcome, but that the freedom it granted was a right and not a matter of government compassion. They deplored the threats of renewed arrests that accompanied its announcement and they rejected any suggestion that the underground structures be abandoned. "In this climate Solidarity must continue to struggle for the restoration of union pluralism and the pluralism of thought. We have to act to advance respect for liberty and the dignity of individuals. Solidarity has to exist so that Poland can become a free country."

In addition to what might be called cultural projects, the underground was also involved in political and civil-rights activities. Election boycotts were organized. Money was collected and distributed to the families of those who were in jail or who were fired for union activity and given "wolf tickets" that blacklisted them everywhere. Groups of doctors were organized to provide medical examinations for people coming out of prison. Money and printing materials were smuggled in from the West where representatives of Solidarity had set up offices and strengthened ties to labor federations. Lawyers loosely associated with the underground formed committees to monitor civil rights abuses and published details of the most suspicious cases. Other lawyers defended people accused of possessing *bibuła*, the term for contraband publications. At one point an underground insurance fund was created to replace automobiles confiscated from people accused of transporting unsanctioned publications. The fund was financed with premiums from the dozen or so underground publishing houses. NOWA, the oldest of these enterprises, was employing two hundred editors, printers, binders and bookkeepers on a full-time basis, paying salaries that compared favorably to those offered by official publishers. In addition to books and periodicals, NOWA was also producing audiotapes of Solidarity songs and historical lectures and videotapes unapproved by any censors.

New firms were sprouting and mounting initiatives in many directions. Wałęsa often uses the metaphor of a river to describe both the Solidarity movement and Polish history. He likes to say that both have at times roared like torrents in flood and then disappeared from the surface to run their courses underground. Wałęsa also points out that like a river, the flow of Polish destiny has been fed by countless streams of many traditions and experiences. In a similar period, a decade earlier, KOR, the Committee to Defend Workers, had mobilized intellectuals to provide money, medical care, and legal assistance for workers. Men like Kuroń, a former Communist, had joined forces with Catholic activists such as Henryk Wujeć and democratic socialists such as Jan Józef Lipski to battle for justice. Old divisions faded as the people of KOR mounted hunger strikes in churches.

At one such strike, Bujak met Kuroń. Kuroń was only fifty-six but for Bujak, as for so many others, he was the old man, practically a historic figure, who showed them their own possibilities. He had spent a total of nine years in prison since he first challenged party rulers in 1956. He had been Michnik's scoutmaster and he had provided Borusewicz with shelter and guidance when the union organizer was still a student. More recently at another church Kuroń met a university graduate named Jacek Czaputowicz who was looking for his own ways to challenge Communist power. Inspired by his elders, Czaputowicz, along with friends, organized Freedom and Peace, a group that was emphasizing disarmament issues and pacifism. Some of its members were refusing to take the oath of induction as soldiers because of a phrase that obliged recruits to support the interests of Poland's allies. While some went to jail, others held demonstrations and made contacts with West European disarmament and ecological groups, the very people whose sympathies the Soviets were trying to enlist.

In Wrocław a group of theater students were swept up in the movement and eventually they developed into the Orange Alternative, a group that used Dadaist imagery and guerrilla theater to underscore the absurdities of Communist rule. On the National Day of Women its members distributed sanitary napkins, a rare commodity, to women on the street, for which they were arrested.

At Christmas they sent Santa Claus out on the town and when he was arrested, they ringed the police station with a few dozen other Santa Clauses who danced around the building demanding the release of what they said was the real Santa Claus.

One of the videotapes illicitly distributed by NOWA was a movie called *The Interrogation*, which had been banned before it was released. Still, it became the most talked-about film of 1984 once it was rescued from limbo by the long reach and ingenuity of the underground. The movie was directed by Ryszard Bugajski, a thirty-five-year-old protégé of Andrzej Wajda, Poland's best known filmmaker. During the "carnival" Wajda had quickly made and released films like *Man of Iron* and *Man of Marble*, which extolled the rise of Solidarity. But when martial law descended and rigid censorship was restored, Bugajski's film was still awaiting release. The censors banned it and all copies were seized.

The movie is set in the 1950s and tells the story of a flighty cabaret singer who is imprisoned in what she at first believes to be a mistake. Gradually she realizes that her questioners want to know about an old lover. She refuses to cooperate and despite graphically brutal tortures, her resolve stiffens. She learns that her husband has denounced her. She is confined in a chamber where water is pumped in until it covers her nostrils. At the last second before drowning the water stops and she is removed. She is kept awake for days. She is threatened with rape and beaten. Throughout the ordeal, she clings to her simple belief that it is wrong to betray a friend. Meanwhile, one of her harshest interrogators, a devout Communist who survived a Nazi death camp, begins to waver in his faith as he fails to break the woman. "How can you hold out when you speak for no one, when you have no one behind you?" he shouts at her. He is drawn to her and in the end, it is he who breaks. He fathers her child, arranges her release and then kills himself with a pistol.

When the film was formally banned, its director was in jail along with the thousands of other martial law detainees. Just after he was released he was fired from the studio where he worked because of the film. For eighteen months he eked out a living writing for the underground press and eventually he took the government's offer of a one-way passport and emigrated to Canada. But even as he was packing, his film was being widely seen thanks to the cassette version made by NOWA.

Bugajski, who lived around the corner from me, told me that by the time he got out of prison, all the copies of the film had been confiscated as ideologically incorrect. He had been told that one major objection was that the security men's uniforms used in the film were similar to those worn today, thereby sowing disrespect for the ministry of the interior. All the copies were destroyed except for one that was turned over to the archives of the ministry of the interior. Bugajski was told that this film was to be used for training purposes, to show old methods of control and interrogation. Apparently it was this film that was copied by NOWA to generate the hundreds of videocassette versions that circulated throughout Poland.

How, exactly, it came to be "borrowed" from the ministerial archives remains a mystery, but this was hardly the only instance in which the bastions of party and government were infiltrated by Solidarity sympathizers. For example, the first Warsaw meeting of the TKK, the Temporary National Commission of Leading Solidarity Fugitives, took place in the apartment of one of General Jaruzelski's closest associates. The man's daughter told her father that some of her friends were coming to hold a group therapy session and that they did not want to be bothered. The daughter of Jerzy Urban, the government's chief spokesman, married an underground printer, while Monika Jaruzelska, the general's only daughter, dated a fellow university student who wore outlawed Solidarity insignia. Leaks of embarrassing party documents were common. Many of these were to be reprinted in the underground press, revealing the party's cynical trade in favors and privileges.

As the boldness of the underground grew, so did its technological capability. The few mimeograph machines that had been stashed away after martial law had been replaced by offset presses. Bujak and Kulerski were using an imported computer to develop a program for election boycotts.

One evening I was taken by some people I knew to the Warsaw suburb of Legionów. They said they wanted to show me a surprise. Legionów is, like so many urban settlements, an area of relatively new eight- to ten-story buildings arrayed around dirt and grass plots. In the summer there are usually borders of flowers by each house and there are usually splotches on the façades where patches of stucco or cement have worn off. As in many Polish residences you need keys that look like bottle openers to get into the tiny elevators, a precaution to prevent children from playing in them. Once in the apartment, I was placed before a television set and offered hot tea in a glass that was set in a chrome holder, one of the few Russian affectations that have taken root. Soon after the seven o'clock television news began, a printed legend, "Solidarity lives," flashed quickly but legibly over the head of the announcer. After a short interval another message appeared saying, "Listen to Radio Solidarity in half an hour" and giving the frequency that would be used for the broadcast.

My hosts, who were members of the firm that sent the signal, were proud of the skills that enabled them to literally break into television. They explained that the slogans inserted into the news program could be seen within a mile radius of the mobile transmitter that their friends were using. A few thousand families probably saw it. The idea, they said, was mostly to startle and cheer the audience with the underground's audacity, but they added that television was a less hazardous way of alerting people to the shifting frequencies of illegal radio transmissions than dropping leaflets in public places. Even before the explanation was fully finished, we could hear the sirens of many police cars and from the windows we could see a blue truck go by with a small disc direction-finder on its cab. "It's driving the police crazy," said one of my hosts. "They can't believe we can penetrate their television. They are trying to pinpoint our transmitter, but they won't find it."

All of this—clandestine lectures, unsanctioned performances, unofficial art exhibits, the publications, and the media conspiracies—at times appeared to be almost normal activity. They shaped the commonplace conversations of dinner parties. "Have you seen *The Interrogation?*" one guest would ask another, or, "That was an interesting interview with Zbigniew Herbert in *Independent Culture*, wasn't it?" Sometimes the material would be mentioned casually by government officials. I had to remind myself almost continually that the illicitly produced books, magazines, and films, innocuous as they might appear by Western standards, were without parallel in the East bloc. In Russia unsanctioned gatherings of stamp collectors or car enthusiasts, let alone social activists, were until quite recently subversive acts likely to bring denunciation and immediate harsh penalties. Nowhere in Communist Europe except in Poland were groups of people doing so many things independent of party or state. In Prague, the leaders of a group of jazz enthusiasts who sought to distribute a mimeographed newsletter about contemporary music were sent to prison for years and their publication was suspended. Other young Czechs risked arrest when they lit candles for John Lennon, whom they hold in reverence. I was with the Czech playwright Vaclav Havel when security policemen forcibly prevented him from entering a cemetery to place a wreath on the coffin of his close friend, Jaroslav Seifert, the Nobel Prize–winning poet.

In Hungary, which in the West is often regarded as the most liberal Warsaw Pact country, I saw leather-jacketed police stop a sixteen-year-old girl from placing red and white flowers on the statue of a hero of the nineteenth-century national revolt. In Budapest, on the thirtieth anniversary of the anti-Soviet uprising of 1956 the only observance I could find was a sad little gathering in which twenty people defied police warnings and turned out in a private apartment. They lit candles in silence to commemorate those who fell under Soviet tanks. A few days later, at a church in the suburb of Warsaw, I stood with more than a thousand men and women who came to unveil a plaque inscribed in Polish and

Hungarian which celebrated the heroism of those who resisted Soviet tanks in 1956. The underground published a book of poems in both languages that lauded Hungarian hopes and courage. Today in Budapest, the more than two hundred people hanged for their role in those street battles still lie in unmarked graves. Their colleagues who sometimes come to the site are turned away or arrested by secret police who hide behind trees.

What was happening in Poland was that a multifaceted massive resistance movement was evolving more or less spontaneously. Taking its inspiration from Solidarity, this broad movement experimented in different forms of challenge. "Once resistance had meant taking up a gun," said Bujak. "Now, people instinctively took up typewriters." Gradually, the fugitive leaders came to see their primary role as one of stimulating, supporting, and coordinating the self-motivated activities of the many groups that were forming. And by the time the 1984 amnesty was proclaimed, their daily routines more closely resembled the lives of executives or bureaucrats than those of insurrectionist outlaws.

Every few days, associates would come and move them separately to new quarters. Usually, these were rooms in large buildings with many entrances where the presence of strangers would not be noticed by janitors or neighbors. Bujak often moved about in theatrical disguises stolen by acting students at the dramatic academy. Once he sat next to one of his sisters on a tram and she did not recognize him. Kulerski preferred to stay indoors. Outwardly, he was calm, but for three years he was unable to sleep until he heard the rattling bottles of milkmen that told him that the chances of a nighttime raid had passed. Then he would sleep for two or three hours, always waking to the same realistic dream of police knocking at his door.

Each man had his own "bureau." Bujak supervised all union business in the Warsaw region while Kulerski coordinated activities involving the burgeoning independent culture and the underground press and radio. They did not actually visit their offices, which like the hideouts, were shifted regularly. Instead, links were maintained through couriers, men and women who knew only the location of the bureaus and whatever apartments the leaders were using. None of the messengers knew any of the others, so even if they were arrested they could not compromise the network. Their job was to pick up reports and requests for help or money from the many "mailboxes" and pass them along to yet other go-betweens. The messengers, who included grandmothers, office workers, and high school students, would also then carry back decisions and advice that filtered down through the network from the two leaders. For reasons of security the lines of communication were kept intricate.

The first time I was taken to see Bujak in hiding, I counted twenty people who were involved in bringing me to him. I was shuttled from guide to guide and driven on circuitous routes in three conspiratorial taxis. At one point I was told to run as fast as I could across the main train station following a fat man carrying an unraveling bouquet of daffodils. I thought we were being outrageously conspicuous but I assumed my escorts knew the conspiracy business better than I did. Bujak estimated that there were several hundred people like himself in full-time conspiracy while some ten thousand in the Warsaw area were devoting most of their time to clandestine enterprises. He said less involved, part-time activists probably numbered more than a hundred thousand. Such participation would mean that there were probably more people involved in conspiratorial activities in the 1980s than in the organized underground resistance to the Nazis of the 1940s. To be fair, the risks involved were far greater under the Germans.

Bujak would maintain written contact with representatives of former Solidarity locals that were trying to hold together as clandestine units, or, on occasion, he would meet these people. One issue he had to deal with daily was what former Solidarity people in different plants should do about the various worker councils and government-sponsored unions that were being established. People loyal to the Solidarity leadership wanted to know whether they and their fellow workers should boycott these organs while insisting on the restoration of their outlawed union or whether they should infiltrate the various worker councils, using them to advance Solidarity's goals. The advice from the top varied. In those factories where the new bodies were transparent shams run by the management and by party hacks they were to be shunned and ridiculed. But in plants where this was not the case, Solidarity people were urged to participate if only to wait for a time when they could openly ally such councils with the ideals, goals, leaders and name of Solidarity.

Other union business involved distribution of money that was being raised as dues or that was filtering in from abroad. The money included contributions from Western labor unions, the sometimes murky donations of foreign governments, and sums sent by emigrés through the Paris and Brussels offices. Bujak monitored the fund-raising and determined disbursements to various groups. He concentrated on the large Warsaw region but he also maintained regular contact with the underground leaders from other regions to coordinate a general strategy of resistance.

In the meantime, Kulerski corresponded with groups of teachers, doctors, and lawyers who all published regular underground journals. He helped clandestine editors in their constant search for paper and for places to store it. He helped arrange the lecture tours, the art exhibits, and the theatrical performances that were touring from churches to private homes, and he appointed librarians and archivists to keep track of all the publications that were being produced. Five years later, he said that he was still coming across titles and series that he never knew about. He helped coordinate two separate efforts to produce a Polish encyclopedia free of government scrutiny. His work, he recalled, consumed fifteen or sixteen hours each day.

After such days, as he lay down in yet another unfamiliar apartment, the meticulous Kulerski would marvel at the course that brought him to this point. He had, after all, been a high school teacher in the same school for twenty-two years. He taught art and biology. He had been a social rather than political activist, working with Scouts and leading a campaign to prevent alcoholism among the young. Once he had organized an exhibit at the high school about the Jews who lived in the area before the war and he led a group of mostly Catholic youths along the route of a death march in which Jews living in the Warsaw outskirts were herded into the Warsaw ghetto, with many stragglers shot along the way.

Since his adolescence, when his father was jailed as a spy for having served the wartime exile government in London, he had been disgusted by political life. But in 1976 he heard on a Voice of America broadcast that some people in Warsaw had formed KOR, the Committee to Defend Workers, and they were asking others to write to the Polish parliament to complain about the police who had forced striking workers in the city of Radom to run through gauntlets of policemen who beat them with clubs. One of those who signed this appeal was Józef Rybicki, a man then in his eighties. He had been one of the major commanders of the Warsaw uprising and in 1945 he helped form an anticommunist force called Freedom and Independence. Rybicki had spent more than a dozen years in prison, many of them in the same institution where Kulerski's father served much of his nine years. "When I heard that Mr. Józef was asking for citizens to do something, I knew I had to answer," said Kulerski. "I gathered a petition of people in my neighborhood and I brought it to the Sejm [Parliament]. I was attacked by the ministry of education. I was shifted from my school. I became more involved with KOR and after that one step led to another until I was hiding with Bujak and wondering where we might find or store printing paper."

Eventually, a third bureau was established to deal with such purely administrative chores as lining up apartments, cars, and false credentials as well as providing meat and gasoline ration cards for the conspirators. It was headed by Ewa Kulik, a woman who was trying to write a doctoral work on William Faulkner, and Konrad Bieliński, one of the mathematicians who, along with physicists, historians, and mountaineers, were noticeably prominent within the resistance movement.

Security, of course, was a constant preoccupation and Bujak had his own intelligence specialists working in what was euphemistically called Hygiene and Safety. These specialists checked out reports of provocateurs and infiltrators and inspected apartments to see if they would make suitable hideouts. They tried to monitor police activity and establish the patterns of raids. Still, despite their efforts there were constant arrests and the top leaders had many close calls. Once, the housing project in which Kulerski was staying for a night was encircled by two thousand policemen. From the windows he could see that squads of officers were entering each building to carry out an apartment-to-apartment search. Like all apartments in the developments, the place he was staying in was very small, offering no place to hide.

Feeling himself close to panic, he took his host's German shepherd for a walk in freezing weather, leaving the building as a unit of police approached. For five hours he and the decreasingly frisky dog walked back and forth on an embankment next to a train track that abutted the development. He returned safely upstairs only when the police left. A few of the police had winked at Kulerski and he assumes they must have thought he was one of them, a secret policemen assigned to canine patrol to make sure that no one escaped to the rail line.

Bujak tells of his own closest call almost with relish. It happened one night as police burst into the apartment where he, the most wanted man in Poland, was meeting with five associates. After he produced the credentials of a psychiatrist that had been altered to include his own photograph, everyone in the apartment was taken to a police station. There Bujak continued to claim he was a doctor at a mental hospital. The police then ordered him to accompany them to his apartment so that they could search it. He agreed though he had never been at the address. He knew that once at the door of the apartment he would be exposed as an impostor by the real resident whose identity he had appropriated. As he and two officers approached the building he suddenly tore away from them and ran through a series of linked courtyards. He had been a long-distance runner in the army and his adrenaline was pumping. He heard the policemen shout that they would shoot, but there were no shots, and after a minute or so the sound of their pounding boots receded.

My father had not been able to meet Bujak when he returned to his native land after fifty years. But in 1986, when he came once more to visit me, he met many of the opposition figures who two years earlier were either in jail or in hiding. My father was particularly impressed with Bujak, recalling that in his own conspiratorial days there were always gulfs between workers and intellectuals who were ostensibly struggling together for a classless society. Meanwhile Bujak kept asking my father what it was like to run and hide between the wars. He told my father about the moment when, as he said, "I knew absolutely that it was yes or no, now or never, win or lose, and that I had to act or perish."

In the years that followed martial law, the accounts of the risks taken by Bujak, Kulerski, and their colleagues echoed and fused with heroic legends of earlier Polish daring. As the tales spread with occasional embellishment, they gained the force of myths. But this time the conspiracy that these new myths served was turning out to be something new to Poland and indeed to Europe, a nonviolent challenge to repressive power. It proved to be the most effective use of nonviolence anywhere since the campaigns of Martin Luther King, Jr. in the American South and before that of Mahatma Gandhi. Few mentioned Gandhi in Poland, but clearly, in terms of tactics, the Polish underground movement of the 1980s had more in common with the Indian campaigns of noncooperation than with the many chivalrous, bloody, and often quixotic uprisings of Poland's past. This time there were no calls to arms, no vandalism or destruction of state property.

Instead, as Gandhi and Martin Luther King had done, the Polish opposition leaders encouraged ordinary citizens to take back control of their everyday lives where they could. In Montgomery, black people responded to King by riding in sections of buses reserved for whites, or they walked. In India, millions emulated Gandhi and made their own salt, thus bypassing and shortchanging the state monopoly on salt. In both countries, men and women were moved to court arrest and in the process embarrassed rulers of societies that prided themselves on being fair and democratic. Poland was a different case. Questioning the democratic self-esteem of leaders was not likely to shame people for whom power was more important than popularity. Moreover, the totalitarian organization of Poland made symbolic and focused protest difficult. Not just salt, but everything else was a state monopoly. In a sense everyone in the country was forced to ride in the back of the bus, and the sidewalks also belonged to the police. In theory, and sometimes in fact, protesters placed their jobs, their homes, their vacations and the education of their children at risk. Because of the constant police presence, demonstrations were broken up before they could grow beyond a few people. While the Indians and the followers of Dr. King could act openly and publicly to defy state restrictions and court arrest, most Poles had to be sneakier in their surreptitious brand of nonviolence.

But just as Gandhi had contested the British monopoly on salt, so Bujak's friends and associates were challenging the government's monopoly over information, history, and cultural life. No matter what its subject or content, every uncensored pamphlet, newspaper, and play that reached an audience was immediately understood to be a declaration that society had the right to organize itself spontaneously without petitioning anyone. People were reclaiming their past by writing about and talking about subjects they had accepted as taboo, and in the process they were saying that the stories told to them by aunts and uncles had greater validity than the pronouncements of commissars and ideologues, both homegrown and imported. And just as in the cases of Gandhi and King, each act of righteous defiance emboldened new people to define their oppression and challenge authority.

Strikes and boycotts were still rare, largely because of the fear of administrative reprisals, but people were willing to help publish some sheets, or go to church to see an anticommunist play, or hide some fugitive, or just happily read an uncensored paper that a few years earlier they would have been afraid to bring home. In the end, this incremental seizure of freedom of expression changed Poland and Communism at least as profoundly as Martin Luther King changed the United States and Gandhi changed India and colonialism.

This strategy was not obvious when in the first days of martial law, a few Solidarity figures were lying low, simply hoping to evade the police dragnets. As they found each other and realized they would have to do something, some turned to the Polish past, imagining insurrections, symbolic terror, and perhaps more suicidal uprisings. Kulerski recalls that he was paralyzed by the responsibility. Why me? he wondered. "People so much brighter, so much more experienced were in detention, but we were free, and it was we who would have to act. But do what? Where do you begin? Should we set fire to a police station? Should we flee to the West and work from exile? All I can say is that we were motivated by fear. Not the fear of getting caught but the fear of making some mistake. I did not want to make one false step that could have terrible consequences later. I simply kept asking, What should we do? What should I do?"

The first time Kulerski remembers raising the questions was on the day after martial law was declared when he found himself at the Ursus tractor plant. Among the workers who were building barricades of barrels and cardboard cartons to block the tanks already on their way, he spotted Jan Józef Lipski, the sixty-year-old historian who had been one of the founders of KOR. Kulerski respected the older man, who he knew had been wounded as a nineteen-year-old fighter in the Warsaw uprising. He asked him what he should do. Lipski told him, "Listen, I am an intellectual and all I know how to do in situations like this is to sign petitions and stand with workers when they get arrested. Also I have a weak heart. If you can't think of anything else to do then stand here with us. If, however, you think you might be more useful out of prison, then leave now." He left but for months afterward, he kept returning to the conversation, wondering again and again what he should be doing with his freedom while so many of his friends had lost theirs. "We knew there was a value in simply not being caught, but beyond that it was hard to envision any conspiratorial program."

Vague strategies emerged as he and Bujak moved from hut to hut, to church basements, to farms. Once, while both were being hidden by an old Jewish toolmaker who, though frightened, took them in because, as he explained, he too once needed to hide, Kulerski sent a letter to his father asking two questions—How did the old man think the situation would develop, and what kind of resistance made sense? By the time the courier brought the answer, Kulerski had gone on to a snowy village twenty miles from the capital. He had nothing to do but wait. Once, he saw the village children walk past his window, each one carrying half a split pig. He thought for a moment that he was hallucinating from idleness. It turned out that Polish soldiers had thrown the pork to the villagers from a freight train they were ostensibly guarding on its journey to the Soviet Union.

The response he received from his father was terse and unsentimental. The old man, whose life experience included dinners with Churchill as well as the years in Polish cells, wrote that "the government will try to tire people out. It will try to make daily life still harder than it is and in time this will isolate the underground from society. Ordinary people will be so preoccupied with the chores of living that they will regard you, at best, as entertaining Robin Hoods. When that happens, the authorities will pick you off, group by group, one by one. All you really can do is to try to delay the process. The longer it takes, the better it will be for society and the worse it will be for the government. In the meantime something may happen elsewhere, perhaps even in Moscow." He wrote that his son had only three choices. "You can surrender. You can use terror and violence. Or you can experiment with some form of nonviolent resistance." He made no recommendation.

As Kulerski and Bujak kept looking for the most effective forms of resistance, they had to deal with Polish society's glorification of passionate insurrections and conspiracies, most notably that of the underground state that operated under Nazi occupation in World War II. This clandestine state had a government in exile in London, and a military command on the ground, the AK, or Home Army. It organized schools and medical care and assassinated Nazi leaders. One wing provided some minimal help to the Jews, and its couriers to the West were the first to bring out accurate though barely believed accounts of the destruction of Jews taking place. The AK mounted the heroic Warsaw uprising.

Bujak recalled that "for months, as we talked and corresponded with people, the suggestion was made again and again: organize a secret state. I confess it was tempting. We would be allying ourself with the glorious past and our generation would be making its stand." As a child Bujak had heard his father's accounts of wartime experiences as a clandestine instructor drilling peasants in military exercises he had learned in the prewar Polish army. As the elder Bujak took his youngest son with him on moonlighting contracting jobs, he would talk about the times he was arrested by the Nazis, when, once, he was put against a wall and threatened with execution. He also told the youngest of his eleven children of the time toward the end of the war when a Russian soldier tried to pay him for some homebrewed vodka with a pair of military boots in which an officer's severed feet remained frozen. His father told of his anger when he watched Soviet soldiers destroy the library of wealthy farmers condemned as *kulaks* or aristocrats. At dinner, his father would speak of the nineteenth-century insurrections. All of it merged to spur an interest in history and when, at seventeen, Bujak received his first stipend from the vocational school where he was studying to be an electrician, he spent it all on a three-volume history of diplomacy.

Nevertheless, much as romantic tradition and Polish reflexes favored the proclamation of a new secret state, Bujak and Kulerski resisted. "It was no longer a time for sabers against sabers or pistols against pistols," said Bujak. "In Budapest and Prague we saw what happens when it is tanks against rocks or bottles. We no longer live in the countryside like Afghans, but in cities. Then, too, we had to face the fact that if we chose violence, we would be facing government forces that were better at terror than we were. Even if we managed to convert some army units to our side as some people were urging, that would not give us enough strength to defeat the Russians. Often I had to remind people that though all our Polish uprisings were noble and glorious, they had all failed."

Kulerski's objections were both moral and practical. "Solidarity had arisen in nonviolence and if we abandoned that commitment, we would be betraying the movement. We would also lose our credibility both here and abroad. Polish society had enough of terror under Hitler and Stalin. Over and over I kept arguing that to declare ourselves any kind of state would be usurping power. It is true that no one had elected Jaruzelski but no one had elected us to anything beside our union posts. I kept telling our friends that if we formed a state, sooner or later we would have to have our own laws and our own courts and I kept asking them if they were ready to carry out verdicts. Were they prepared to shoot those identified as collaborators or shave the heads of women who slept with Communists?"

Out of these discussions there finally coalesced a model of an underground society. "A state, we realized, needed bureaucracy, centralization, and coercion," said Kulerski. "Society, on the other hand, was by its nature decentralized and rippled with spontaneous and pluralistic associations. In the end we decided that the best thing we could do was to give people the courage and the resources to do whatever they felt like doing. We realized that it was a long-term strategy and we even called it the long march. We did not think that having dozens or even hundreds of groups printing newspapers, or organizing charitable help for those who are repressed, would bring Jaruzelski to his knees. But we felt that through such activity people would be learning how to be free and that this process would eventually prove irresistible."

In the late seventies, before Solidarity came into being, something like this approach had been favored by many of those who founded KOR. In 1976 Michnik wrote an essay called "The New Evolutionism," in which he disparaged old utopian formulations and instead advocated the creation of "a day-to-day community of free people." At that time the idea had been to encourage Poles to shed their fears and to act openly in the pursuit of basic freedoms. In short, to create a civil society. As they reviewed their options in the aftermath of martial law, Bujak and Kulerski decided to implant this concept underground. Not everyone agreed. Some predicted that voluntarism would dissipate into posturing and Boy Scout pieties. Others argued that without a tight central command, it would lead to catastrophic adventures and terrorism.

But the most detailed and troublesome criticism came from Jacek Kuroń in two articles that he smuggled out of the Białolenka internment camp. He was the patriarch of Polish resistance. Furthermore, he was one of the progenitors of the new evolutionism, practicing it in his daily life. When he was free he never hid and he never kept his door locked. He disregarded wiretaps and spoke openly on the telephone to inspire and instruct others to live freely. Still, as the undetained opposition was taking its first conspiratorial steps, he pleaded passionately with Bujak to drop the idea of a free-form, do-your-own-thing, nonviolent conspiracy in favor of a structured model with clearly defined lines of authority and command, which would, if necessary, strike out in violence.

In his smuggled letters, which were soon illicitly published under the title "The Way Out of a Situation With No Way Out,"

Kuroń declared that sooner or later there would have to be a compromise between Poland's Communist leaders and some representatives of a society that because of Solidarity was more unified than it had ever been. In theory, he wrote, Poles might be willing to simply await the collapse of the Soviet empire, but in reality most people would not accept or endure the decline in living standards that accompanies the process of decay. As things inevitably worsened, the Polish government, which he likened to an occupation force, and the Polish people would both want to sue for peace. But who, in this situation, was to speak for the people? What was needed, he insisted, was a disciplined and defined opposition movement, whose leaders the government would eventually be forced to recognize as partners in compromise. For this scenario to unfold, centralized control of the resistance was necessary. Someone would have to channel social energies and set an agenda of expectations, thus bringing pressure on the authorities for negotiations. For the government to agree to any talks, wrote Kuroń, it would have to be certain that Bujak or Wałęsa, or whoever, had the support of large, organized, and visible blocs.

Kuroń also expressed his doubts that a free-wheeling conspiracy could avoid fragmentation or violence. Addressing himself directly to Bujak and Kulerski, he asked, "On what do you base your faith that Poles will patiently withstand worsening economic conditions and constant government provocation without responding with terror? How can you ask people to join in a conspiracy without letting them know what goals are being sought? If you cannot tell them what tangible ends they are working for, then the only outcome will be eventual despair, frustration, and hatred, and from this hatred will come terror." Kuroń reminded his friends that he had been an advocate of just the kind of society of self-help groups that they were envisioning. But he said that at this time such organizing efforts would be a strategic blunder.

While he deplored the prospect of terror by small groups acting on their own, Kuroń was not as committed to forswearing all violence as Kulerski was. "You cannot build a program on the hope that the generals and secretaries will voluntarily agree to a compromise. You have to accept that force recedes only in the face of force and you have to say clearly that the movement will not categorically reject the use of force." Specifically, he urged his friends to proselytize within the police and army and to hit at "the occupation government" by every form of protest possible, from symbolic candle lightings to strikes and rallies.

Bujak and Kulerski were stung by these words. Kuroń had been in the vanguard of every struggle and skirmish since 1956. Still, they told themselves, the view must look different from prison. They were outside. "We saw what people were doing on their own, how much energy was involved," said Kulerski. "I kept thinking of my father's advice. All we could do was delay the Red Ones from wearing society down and hope that in the meanwhile something else happened to change the equation. We set our course for an underground society."

When, after his release in the amnesty of 1984, Kuroń was able to explore that society, he was surprised and acknowledged he had been wrong in his advice. The amorphous conspiracy was robust. People had not yet shown signs of despair or frustration. The only terrorism was that used by the police and it had not yet provoked a violent reaction. Negotiations for national reconciliation seemed as elusive as ever, but Kuroń had to agree with Bujak's assessment that things were proceeding well.

SEVEN

THE PARTY

SINCE THE IRON curtain first dropped, the Poles have had the most aberrant Communist party in Eastern Europe. Over the four decades of its rule it has made successive concessions to appease a hostile nation—and perhaps to assuage the guilt of leaders nagged by a sense of their illegitimacy. Early on, the party retreated from policies of aggressive atheism to the point where, in the eighties, Catholic churches were being constructed faster than state schools. Some ministers bent and kissed the ring of the pope when he passed before their receiving line. Agriculture was never energetically collectivized, and farmers continued to feed the nation from lands they owned. Jazz and jeans won official tolerance earlier than in other parts of the bloc, while relatively large numbers of people were permitted to travel in the West. Early efforts to suppress the nation's awareness of its history also eased and it even became possible to recall and glorify such once-forbidden subjects as the Warsaw uprising and the murders of Polish officers in the Katyn forest by their Soviet captors. There was a parliament that, though impotent and servile to the ruling party, was less of a sham than the assemblies that gathered in one- and two-day sessions in other Communist states. There were non-party ministers, a Catholic university, a major Catholic newspaper.

For the leaders of the East European fraternal parties, these departures marked the Poles as worrisome and suspect. The neighboring parties realized that such deviating compromises had been forced upon their Polish comrades by the steady resistance of a population that never accepted the ruling system. They understood this, but they never liked it. Now, in the aftermath of Solidarity, the persistent activities of a de facto opposition were transforming their forebodings into open fear. For several years, the state hotels in the other East bloc capitals had stopped selling *Trybuna Ludu*, the Polish party paper, for fear that even its highly censored reports might arouse curiosity and mimicry. Poland's Warsaw Pact allies even banned or limited tourist visits to stem threats of contagion. Three years after martial law, no Czech tourists were crossing the Tatras and, rather remarkably, ordinary Poles found it easier to get to Paris than to Prague. All over the bloc, party leaders were insisting that Poland had to be "normalized" as Czechoslovakia and Hungary were once normalized.

But, as the Polish party leaders realized, it was far easier to demand toughness than to demonstrate it, since there was really no one to do the normalizing. In Hungary and Czechoslovakia, it had been Soviet armed force that scourged the nations, purged the "revisionist" Communists, and replaced them with submissive people. In the absence of such intervention in Poland, the responsibility for putting things right obviously lay with the Polish party and, specifically, with the man who headed it. In Hungary, at least 280 people were hanged and some forty thousand were arrested in the punitive aftermath of the 1956 revolt. Could anyone imagine Polish forces imposing comparable rigors in their own country, which is more than three times as populous as Hungary?

In theory, the Polish party, just like the Soviet one, still ran everything. It was supposed to reign paramount, steering the fate of the state and nation. Its mission was to control the present, selectively record the past, and determine the future. In practice it was otherwise. The party was in morbid decay. Jaruzelski had not been able to reverse its sagging fortunes or restore its diminished authority.

There are and were only three possible approaches that any leadership could use to impose the kind of control over Polish society that their Soviet patrons, from Stalin to Chernenko, dreamed about. In theory, at least, the Polish party could try to terrorize and punish people into submission and productivity as Ceauşescu has done in Romania. This had been tried in the early fifties but it was hard to imagine how any Polish government could reimpose such rigors since so many Poles had been emboldened by their experience of Solidarity and the ruling party had grown so weak.

The second theoretical possibility involved the inspiration of great masses of people to work well and hard. What was needed for this was an ideology that promised Poles that their children would have a happier future in exchange for present sacrifice. To a limited extent this had once worked in East Germany. In Poland it was a patently absurd direction. Work crews still painted Marxist slogans on highway overpasses and billboards. But the fading phrases like "Workers of the World Unite, You Have Nothing to Lose But Your Chains," and "The Economy Is a Family Matter for All Poles," rang hollow, and often drew laughter. They were probably put up for visiting delegations of Soviet bureaucrats. Everyone knew that the most compelling mottoes came from other ideologies and value systems, phrases like "God Is Love," or "Coke Is It."

The final potential strategy to win the support or passivity of the nation depended on an offer of material well-being in exchange for good behavior. This was the pattern in Czechoslovakia, where many workers were effectively bought off with summer houses or cars. In Hungary, a similar pattern was called Goulash

Communism. In the period that led to Solidarity's rise, under Edward Gierek, the Poles had tried something of the sort, but the Polish economy simply lacked surpluses that could be distributed as hush money. Gierek had borrowed heavily from the West to fulfill the consumerist yearnings of workers but when the bubble burst, hopes were still thwarted and the West wanted its money back. There were not enough cars, no summer houses, few apartments, and no goulash to buy out anyone.

Without draconian prospects or credible slogans, and lacking cash, the Polish party was in no position to normalize the nation. It was doubtful whether it could ever normalize itself. The Polish army might, if ordered, break strikes, but it was unlikely to respond to crueler commands. Anyway, for traditional Marxists, overt military rule was an unacceptable heresy. That left Soviet military intervention, and this was what everyone had tried to avoid in the first place. There seemed to be no possibility of breakthrough, and Jaruzelski, whose specialty was tactics, limited himself to fine-tuning, to oiling the squeakiest wheel. Amnesties that appeased the West and the liberals were followed by attacks on universities that raised the spirits of the hard-liners. His occasional chastisement of those who called for greater duress was balanced by criticism of those who urged greater reconciliation.

The party had lost something like 20 percent of its membership in the years of Solidarity's rise, with the greatest losses coming from its younger and more idealistic adherents. In general, people were less likely to openly admit their party ties than to volunteer that they drank too much or beat their wives. I had a number of close friends who always sidestepped my questions about whether they were members or not, and one woman took me for a walk to tearfully tell me that she had not returned her party card because she was fearful that such a step would hurt her son's career. Her tone was that of someone confessing to a deep family shame.

In Wola, a large working-class district of Warsaw with more than a hundred thousand people, only seventeen new members were inducted into the party in 1986. At the universities less than 2 percent enrolled in the party's student wing despite the privileges that came with joining. The party's own, perhaps suspect, figures showed that in 1986 it had 2,129,000 members, a drop of 115,000 over the previous four years. But the demographic redistribution of that membership was more significant. In 1970, 11 percent of all party members were people who were under 24 years of age, while in 1986, that figure was just one percent. In 1970 14.2 percent of the party members were between 25 and 29. In 1986, only 5.8 percent were in that age group. Conversely, the percentage of older people, many of them pensioners, rose radically in the breakdown offered by the party. In 1970 those above fifty years of age represented 18 percent of the total, while sixteen years later that same category had swollen to 36 percent of the total. The sharp decline embraced all classes but the drop among manual workers was greatest; consequently, in 1986, 52 percent of the Polish United Workers Party (PZPR), a majority, were bureaucrats or white-collar professionals. More than 10 percent of the party members were listed as engineers, nearly 6 percent were teachers and 4.2 percent were economists and planners. The representation of peasants also dropped from 11.5 percent in 1970 to 9 percent of the 1986 total. There were almost half as many economic planners as there were farmers. In Poland, the dictatorship of the proletariat was becoming smaller and growing older, and it was less and less proletarian.

There were wives who left their husbands because the men had stayed in the party. They denounced their spouses for careerism. Once as I flew on a short visit to Moscow, I sat next to a man in his thirties who as we landed pinned on the Polish party badge he took from his attaché case. It was the only time I ever saw anyone wear the PZPR insignia. My traveling companion obviously thought it advantageous to flaunt it as he prepared to pass through Soviet customs, just as he understood that there was no point or advantage in wearing the thing in Warsaw.

Among the hundreds of thousands who turned back their party

credentials after martial law were people like Romana Granaś, an ailing eighty-two-year-old woman who had been a Communist since she was seventeen years old. She had maintained her allegiance even after her closest friends and lovers were killed in the Soviet purges of the thirties. She stayed on, making apologies for the Molotov-Ribbentrop Pact, saying that Stalin had to sacrifice Poland to buy the time he needed to arm for the inevitable fight with Germany. After the war she was in the Polish Central Committee and headed the party's ideological school. Later she directed a publishing house. But in December of 1981 she sent her party card to General Kiszczak, who had been one of her students. She attached a note that said, "After sixty years as a Communist, I can no longer be a member of a party that turns its guns on workers." When I visited her in the two-room apartment she had been issued in the sixties as a "prominent," she was lame and dying. She told me that her pain and isolation were retribution for her sins as a Communist. She promised that one day she would tell me how she had helped rig the 1947 referendum, which the Communists used to legitimize their seizure of power, but she died before she did that. "We old Communists are cursed unto seven generations," she told me in what I think was only half a joke.

Those who remained in the party had to face an embarrassing stream of revelations about party life that gushed regularly from the underground presses. A firm in Kraków published the top-secret testimony of Edward Gierek, the former first secretary, who was called before a party panel looking into allegations of corruption and abuses of power. Gierek kept telling his questioners that he should not be treated as "a crook," that he had always comported himself modestly as "a decent Communist." He complained that his grandchildren were being teased and tormented by their classmates simply because they bore his name. In the leaked transcript he was quoted as saying that he was ready to assume the role of a scapegoat and take blame for the conditions that bred Solidarity if the party leaders wanted that, but he asked that his family be left alone. He also said that he never knew exactly how much money had been borrowed from the West while he was in charge. Others who appeared with him before the so-called Grąbski Commission showed even less dignity and defended the use of party positions to obtain trips abroad, furniture, and summer houses.

In a best-selling underground book, *They, Stalin's Polish Puppets*, Teresa Torańska presented her collected interviews with people who helped introduce Communism to Poland after the war. Most of the recollections were suffused with self-pity and cynicism, as once-powerful figures tried to explain what it was like to rule in fear of Stalin's whims and pleasures. The book includes the angry self-justifications of Jakub Berman, who from 1947 until the mid-fifties had been among the three top figures who imposed Communist rule on Poland. Over and over, he kept trying to tell his interviewer that Stalin demanded submission, that to resist the Soviets would have been fruitless. Pathetically he tried to save his honor by claiming that if he had not accommodated Stalin, the Soviet dictator would have sliced Poland into a sliver by turning over the western lands the country had acquired after the war to East Germany. In the interview, Berman defended Stalin's 1939 attack on Poland and continually viewed the country of his birth from the point of view of Moscow's interests. He scorned democracy and the will of the people, saying that submitting to such "fashions" would have meant that those who ruled would have had to accept their own execution. "Who needs that kind of democracy?" he told Torańska as she prepared the book in 1980. "You know we can no more have free elections now than we could in 1948 or twenty years ago because we would lose. There is no doubt of that. So what's the point of such an election? Unless, of course, we wanted to behave like such ultra-democrats, such perfect gentlemen, that we took off our top hats and bowed low and said, 'Fine, we're going to get some rest, go ahead and take power.' "

In another, quite eerie, passage, Berman described how he and

Molotov danced with each other in the Kremlin in 1948. In the interview, Torańska thought he had made an error. "Surely, you mean Mrs. Molotov," she interjected. "No," answered Berman, "she wasn't there; she was in a labor camp. I danced with Molotov—I think it was a waltz, or at any rate something very simple, because I don't know the faintest thing about dancing, so I just moved my feet in rhythm. Molotov led. Actually, he wasn't a bad dancer. I tried to keep in step with him, but what I did resembled clowning more than dancing. Stalin did not dance. He wound the gramophone, considering it his duty as a citizen. He never left it. He would just put on records and watch. He watched us dance. Stalin really had fun. For us these dancing sessions were a good opportunity to whisper to each other things that could not be said out loud. That was when Molotov warned me about being infiltrated by various hostile organizations."

One Polish friend of mine said that reading about Berman and others made him feel as if he were "watching a geek bite the heads off live chickens—you couldn't quite feel sorry for the man but you wondered whether he knew that the whole thing was in bad taste."

Hurt by such revelations, its ranks pared, the party tried to regenerate itself. In the summer of 1984 Jaruzelski had been to Moscow, where an unsmiling Chernenko told him he had to do something to attract young people to the party and to limit the influence of the Church with its links to the opposition. The Soviet leader reportedly acknowledged that those who were twelve or older when Solidarity flourished had to be written off. But Chernenko urged the Poles to concentrate on those who were younger. The message was delivered as the Soviet Union, increasingly aware of its economic decline, was making what later appeared as a last aggressive surge into the third world. There had been costly and inconclusive investments in Angola, Ethiopia, Afghanistan, and Latin America. But it was Poland that was the sorest and weakest point in the empire. Chernenko's most fearful nightmares no doubt centered on crowds of Poles carrying crosses and praying in Polish factories, mines, and shipyards.

For Jaruzelski the task of attracting the young and curbing the church was an impossible assignment. Periodically, over the next three years, he tried to follow the pattern set by János Kádár. The Hungarian leader had after five years begun to lessen the most rigorous controls imposed after the Budapest uprising. Like Kádár, Jaruzelski tried to change the standard "If you are not with us you are against us" to one that declared, "If you are not against us, you are with us." "We do not ask where people came from," he declared, inviting former Solidarity activists to participate in the dozens of councils, assemblies, and associations that were being set up with high visibility and no authority. He had very few takers. The requirement that the newcomers denounce their old union activity and, by inference, their old colleagues evidently carried too high a social cost.

A special party commission was empaneled to study the question of youth. It came up with the obvious platitudes about the need to make the party organs more responsive and more open. Meanwhile the ministry of higher education set off to abolish the independent university student organizations with their links to Solidarity and replace them with representatives of the Socialist Youth Movement, a small minority on each campus. The ministry was also planning to reintroduce the mandatory courses in Marxist philosophy, Communist economics, and Russian language that had been ruled optional electives under the impact of Solidarity's rise. Prominent Solidarity supporters were fired from university posts. About the only signs that anyone in the party was forcefully thinking about youth lay in the steady increase in emigration and the sharp increase in rock concerts. Leaving the country, either to work for some time in the West or to resettle permanently, was a safety valve. It released the pressures of accumulated frustrations although it often deprived the country of the most creative and most daring people. Every few months, the office of public opinion research measured the attitudes of high school students. In these soundings close to 85 percent of those of high school age predicted they would most likely live abroad, either working to save money or as permanent emigrants.

The rock festivals were obviously not meant to enlist support for party or government. They were simply intended to divert the young, keeping them from either clandestine political or overt religious activism. The idea was not to win hearts and minds but rather to neutralize them. In the winter of 1984, the ministry of education sent out letters to schools asking officials to submit the names of what were described as "deviant" students to the police, and to maintain watch over youth subcultures. The letters specified that the lists should include young people suspected of membership in groups of "punks, hippies, fascists, drug addicts, and sniffers of narcotics." At about the same time, Jaruzelski had declared himself on artistic permissiveness. "One must finally draw the line between creativity and artistic trash," he declared.

In ideological terms, the greatest attraction for the young was the church. Each summer hundreds of thousands of young people left their parish churches and marched for days to the shrine of the Black Madonna in the central Polish city of Częstochowa, camping out and singing as they hiked. The sight of so many young people filling the roads and bivouacking in farmers' fields stood as painful proof of the church's influence and the party's ideological impotence. Those who were charged to come up with a youth strategy concluded that the best they could do was to cut into the processions with the help of heavy metal, and even antiestablishment punk. As some conservative churchmen saw it, the Communists were willing to tolerate and subsidize even Satanist bands and their followers to lessen the sway of the church. This may have been an exaggeration but it was clear that despite Jaruzelski's appeal for artistic standards, more and more government money was being allocated for festivals of often nihilistic and aggressive music and life-styles. Each summer since Solidarity's decline, the number of these music festivals grew.

There were blues festivals, rock festivals, country music festivals, and jazz festivals. Students and young workers spent much of the summer traveling by train or hitchhiking to rural areas from one musical gathering to another. Full-time students receive small year-round stipends and there is no tradition of summer jobs for students. With so much hidden unemployment, there is no need for summer workers. During one summer harvest, when Warsaw's Socialist Youth Organization appealed for volunteers to go out into the countryside and help gather in crops, less than ten students responded.

But, about twenty thousand young people would throng the village of Jarocin every August, among them many who had tattoos, shaven scalps, and safety pins in their ears, and wore metal-studded leather jackets. There were separate encampments of youth tribes reflecting adolescent pathologies familiar in the West. There were the so-called "gits," who corresponded more or less to British rockers, and there were heavy-metal people in black, and punk girls with shorn and dyed hair, and there were pale people decorating themselves with pagan images. The band names reflected the despair and hostility that characterizes a genre made famous by performers like Sid Vicious and Johnny Rotten, but they had their own Polish twist. There were bands called Pathology of Pregnancy, Sewage, Dissecting Room, Formation of the Dead, Delirium Tremens, Plutonium Execution, Doom, Shock, Crisis, Verdict, Shortage, Paralysis. The songs were similarly morbid and gloomy. "December Nights" deplored martial law. One woman sang about people who "hide behind dark glasses that conceal nothing," obviously a reference to Jaruzelski. "The Ape Factory" mocked education under Polish Communism.

At one blues festival in the northern city of Olsztyn, I met five men and women in their early twenties who were spending two weeks riding around the country. They were from Katowice in the Silesian coal-mining area and they talked of their roaming as blissful escape. They had all been in high school when Solidarity captured their imaginations. Two of them proudly claimed they had been interrogated by police about printing leaflets. "But that is all over," said one, an art student. "Now there is summer, music, traveling with friends, picking berries and trying not to think about tomorrow." That seemed to be what the party and government had in mind. There were rarely Solidarity symbols at the concerts, but other signs of rebellion were common.

"You know why I like blues?" said a twenty-three-year-old man I met at the Olsztyn gathering. "Because it was born out of drudgery and yearning and you should know that around Katowice we work like white slaves. As for yearning, all Poles are experts." At a country music festival where one performer sang a lyric that asked "How come Willie Nelson knows exactly how I feel?" four teenagers chanted their own adaptation of a Solidarity slogan. Instead of the call, "There is no Liberty without Solidarity," they quietly intoned, "There is no Liberty without *kompot*."

Kompot is the name for a derivative of poppy stalks that can be cooked up quite easily. Though weaker than heroin or morphine, it is quite addictive. After the method of production was first developed in 1974 by a university student, its use spread quickly and a decade later estimates of the number of users ranged as high as half a million. Poppy seeds are a Polish staple used to stuff and sprinkle pastries. The flowers grow on every farm and along the roadsides, where the dying stalks are available for the taking. As habits grew, the stalks were sold and prices rose, and a demimonde addict culture developed with its economy of minor crime and prostitution. A government report claimed that in 1982 there were two hundred thousand *kompot* addicts, almost all of them young. The party youth paper said addiction was spreading like a prairie fire among fourteen- and fifteen-year olds. Two years later the neurological institute claimed that a half million young people regularly took drugs other than alcohol. Police arrested users, but the government left anti-drug programs and rehabilitation of addicts to either church groups or to an independent treatment facility known as Monar.

Bujak was convinced that the government and party were at

least ambivalent about drug use among the young, if not actually encouraging its spread as an alternative to emigration. He once asked me, "In whose interest is it to keep large groups of people drunk or nodding, to keep them docile, dependent, and inactive?" The opium of the Polish masses, he said, particularly the young masses, was increasingly turning out to be opium. Kulerski, an anti-alcohol crusader of long standing , often pointed out that the government's single largest source of revenue came from the taxes on vodka. While the health ministry may have favored programs to cut alcohol consumption, the ministry of finance had to fear the prospect. One survey reported in the official press claimed that there were ten quarts of vodka consumed each year for every man, woman, and child in Poland and that there were more than three million alcoholics. A government economist reported that almost a third of an average family's food expenditures went for hard liquor. The empirical evidence of the problem was even more disturbing.

Several times friends of mine proved to me that they could get *bimber*, or bootleg whiskey, anywhere at any time. Janitors, cab drivers, hotel waiters would provide. Sometimes you could not get gasoline or meat, but you could always get bread and you could always get vodka. In every hamlet and city there are bars and restaurants where each Saturday and Sunday groups of young men gathered to get as drunk as they could as fast as they could. By two in the afternoon these places resemble wards of senseless men. There are rarely women present and there are no songs or banter to accompany the journey to oblivion. The drinking is always single-minded and purposeful. The men are usually young, and not badly dressed. Many seemed athletic. I sometimes wondered what it was they were trying to escape. At times I thought they were avoiding family or sex, that they were choosing drink to avoid women. When I suggested this to my friends they all told me I was crazy, that what was being avoided was everything, reality.

The drug users I met were different. They tended to be well-educated. Some told me that they had begun experimenting with drugs as part of their fascination with the West. They said they thought it was part of the package that came with jazz, jeans, rock, and images of freedom. Others, particularly those from provincial cities, said that the subculture of users offered excitement when there was in fact nothing else to do. But I was particularly struck by one young addict I met at one of the Monar treatment centers, a farmhouse near Białystok. A jazz fan in wire-rimmed glasses, he said that the lack of what he called possibilities for normal rebellion led young people to take the most dangerous risks. "I have never been in the West," he said, "but as I understand, in your country there are many ways in which young people can develop their own personalities and escape or withdraw from their parents, their families, their schools. I read about American students who work in the summer at hotels or ranches. They can run away from home. I suppose they can shout or argue with their parents. Here you cannot run away because without credentials you cannot live anywhere. You cannot get a job unless you are registered as living someplace. It is even hard to shout at your brother when you are sharing a kitchen with three other families or sleeping in the living room with four other people. You learn very quickly to hold everything in and just about the only socially acceptable form of protest and rebellion that we have is getting drunk, and, more recently, with drugs."

Beyond diverting or sedating, there seemed little that any Communist government could do with a youth policy. In an earlier time, party leaders might have considered a public purge, stripping away the most corrupt and tainted elements and encouraging new, younger people to take their place. After the defections of the Solidarity period, however, such a course would have meant cutting too close to the bone. As it was, the party was in danger of losing its critical mass and it could not afford any more losses. For the most part Jaruzelski concentrated on negotiating between rival tendencies and groups. Meanwhile, at party conferences, more and more discussions were taking place on "the problems of cadre formation," and "negative selection." These phrases referred to the issue of how the party was to find enough people to run things, and what kind of people was it likely to attract if the best educated, the most qualified, and the most honorable continued to shun it like something that smelled bad.

The process of negative selection had been first described and deplored by Solidarity. During union negotiations, sociologists and economists acting as union advisers pointed out that key decision-making positions everywhere were routinely filled solely on the basis of party loyalty, which meant that almost by definition leadership was placed in the hands of the incompetent, the cynical, and the corrupt. Efficiency, they insisted, was subordinated to patronage and a cycle of decay was set in motion. In virtually every office and plant and school, the most ambitious and the most cunning people used party membership as compensation for their inadequacies. If there were writers who were members of the party, they tended to be the worst and least-respected writers; party engineers were the worst engineers; party economists were the worst economists; party physicists the worst physicists; and so forth. The syndrome had permeated every activity. I even met a twenty-five-year-old woman who after identifying herself as "the deputy director of the division of soft drink acquisition," said her advance at the supermarket was blocked because all the higher jobs were reserved for party people. In Communist Poland titles proliferate madly. Intrigued by the one my acquaintance cited, I dropped in at the store to see what she did. She was a stock clerk stacking cases of soda. She blushed when she saw me but with proud grace she begged off work for a few minutes and bought me a cup of tea at a nearby café.

Under the system, the party was supposed to develop and administer cadres to fill several hundred thousand critical positions in industry, commerce, mining, services, and education. Collectively, those who held these jobs were the *nomenklatura*. The *nomenklatura* was supposed to include directors of factories, deans of universities, principals of schools, directors of theaters, foremost writers, artists, heads of television stations, and editors, to shape the leading role of the party. But as more and more competent people continued to avoid the party, the available pool of willing and capable talent was shrinking. The only growth area for recruitment was among young policemen. Most of them were country boys who had not done very well at school.

To make matters worse for Jaruzelski, the party, though shrinking in size and power, was also split with rivalries, each with its own tortured and convoluted traditions. The very name of the party, the Polish United Workers Party, was a euphemism patching together various often bitterly antagonistic antecedents. In fact, the party was established after the war by people who functioned as Stalin's agents. They had spent the war years in Moscow, where they survived the purges that had killed many of their fellow Polish party comrades from the prewar period. Presumably they had endorsed the Soviet invasion of their own country and had accepted Stalin's 1938 dissolution of the prewar Polish Communist Party in what appears to have been a sort of down payment to Hitler for the then still secret Molotov-Ribbentrop Pact. The party that Jaruzelski headed also sought to absorb the legacy of those Communists who remained in Poland during the war and operated in small, fairly autonomous partisan units. These people had been persecuted by those who had returned from the Soviet Union. Many of them had been imprisoned after the war, but once Stalin died their power increased. In addition, surviving members of the prewar Polish Socialist Party were pressured into a shotgun wedding with the Communists as the PZPR tried to appropriate the respect that people had for those Socialists who were once led by the anti-Soviet Piłsudski.

The point of all this is that the party's professed genealogy was a lie and its members and Polish society knew it was a lie. To admit the lie openly would mean admitting that their party had simply been put in power by the Soviets and that could mean giving up the right to rule. But in the face of the nation's knowledge of its past, it was impossible to completely deny the lie. It lay there on the conscience of the party and its leaders through all the cycles from repression to amnesty.

With so many conflicting impulses, rivalries, and traditions within the party, plots and vendettas were inevitable. However, since the skirmishing took place far from public view, it was impossible for even the best-informed observer to always know exactly which tendencies were rising and which were waning. Generally, and somewhat simplistically, the basic division was seen as one that separated party "liberals" from "hardheads." To a large degree the differences were matters of style and patronage, and of the way people related to the diverging aspects of the party's past. The hardheads, sometimes also called members of the "cement" bloc, stood for more law and more order. They favored strengthening and enriching the police. They were often people whose families had leaped up the social ladder since the war. They did not like amnesties of political prisoners. They did not like priests preaching about social issues. They generally hoped to roll back some of the concessions that had been made to the church. They tended not to like national minorities and generally drew on the prewar program of the National Democrats, who saw Polish national destiny as being forged only by Polish Catholics. Many had identified with Mieczysław Moczar, the one-time interior minister and top policeman who in 1968 launched an anti-Semitic campaign in his unsuccessful bid for power.

The liberals, on the other hand, hated Moczar. They yearned for acceptance by West European leftists and they wanted to be understood as being more realistic than the Solidarity opposition, whom they viewed as misguided romantics. They were generally more polished, better-read than the hardheads. They also wanted to roll back concessions to the church but they were likely to read underground publications or émigré journals. They were more likely to have been to Paris. They condemned Solidarity but they had been friends with many of the prominent dissidents. Many of them wanted the West to realize that they had supported martial law in order to prevent a Soviet invasion and the consequent rise to power of the hardheads. If the hardheads or cement faction saw their heyday in the period of Moczar's campaign for power, the liberals saw their genesis in the liberalization that followed the popular upheaval of 1956 when Władysław Gomułka came to power espousing a "revisionist" and "national" Communism. Privately, many of the liberals had cheered for the success of the Czechoslovakian thaw but publicly they endorsed sending Polish troops to douse the fever. Many had children who had emigrated to the West.

Jaruzelski was well aware of the faults, schisms, and booby traps that crisscrossed party terrain. By the time he returned from his talks with Chernenko, the general may have been reminded of his days as a young soldier assigned to reconnaissance duty and probing for mines ahead of the advancing Soviet army.

EIGHT

THE GENERAL

S OON AFTER POLISH security forces had moved to suppress Solidarity, Caspar Weinberger, the American secretary of defense, declared in an interview that Wojciech Jaruzelski was "a Soviet general in a Polish uniform." Jaruzelski saw a television report of the remark and he smoldered. For the next three years Polish diplomats were under orders to raise Weinberger's comments in every contact they had with U.S. officials. They demanded that Weinberger retract his words on U.S. television. Jaruzelski, they said, had felt himself deeply insulted and there could be no improvement in relations with Washington unless the injury was acknowledged. The Polish diplomats told their American counterparts that the general wanted Weinberger to know that his grandfather had suffered in Soviet exile, that his father had died in a Siberian camp and that he considered himself to be a Polish patriot.

In those first months after martial law was declared, most Poles were cheered by Weinberger's characterization. Almost everywhere in Poland Jaruzelski was seen and described as a villainous cat's paw and a treacherous marionette who had done the dirty work for his Soviet masters.

But as the third anniversary of his assault on the union neared, the views of the general were growing more complicated. They were being fleshed out with Polish paradox and thickened with still more family legends. Though most of my Polish friends clung to their contempt, some were conceding that in terms of the general's aberrational background, he was the most unusual figure ever to have taken power in any Communist country. Some even recognized that by accepting a man of his profile, the Polish party and its Soviet patrons were acknowledging that the system was at the end of its reserves. After all, for a party that had for so long stressed the symbols and categories of class origin, the general's emergence as a savior could only underline embarrassing ironies.

On one hand, the system that claimed to rule in the name and interest of the proletariat was being challenged by electricians and welders like Wałęsa and Anna Walentynowicz, who came out of a shipyard named for Lenin. In the face of this, it was being defended by a general with ties to the feudal gentry, a man whose heraldic crest was a blindfolded crow. Another element involved the party's abashed guilt at having a military man in charge. According to Communist doctrine, this is simply not supposed to happen. The army is supposed to serve the party, not run it. No Communist party anywhere had been headed by a professional general and to the more orthodox in the Kremlin and in the bloc there was something shameful, something decidedly South American, about having a leader who preferred to be addressed as "Mr. General" rather than "Mr. First Secretary." Jaruzelski had been scolded on this by Mikhail Suslov, the Kremlin's last prominent puritan, but then, not long afterwards, Suslov died. What was going on in Poland was obviously the Bonapartism that Marx and Lenin had warned against. There was also something about all of it that smacked of Piłsudski, something that evoked old Polish military traditions.

Jaruzelski is definitely not charismatic. Pink-faced, with a weak chin, his stiffness and reserve are accentuated by the corset he wears to ease the pain of war wounds. The dark glasses he uses to cut a painful sensitivity to light also play into the spiteful hands of underground cartoonists. His speeches at home were forged of banal phrases delivered in precise, well-spoken, but uninspiring Polish. He flustered easily. When he appeared on television with the pope, he seemed uncomfortable, like a lapsed altar boy who had just been given a heavy penance. A televised New Year's speech to the nation turned into a comedy of unintelligible squeaks after an incompetent director decided to hide the microphones under the table in order to try to make the general more folksy. At Polish party congresses, he assumed the role of the dutiful and disciplined loyal ally of Moscow, a man who spoke of doing whatever had to be done to save and improve socialism. He was often shown on television visiting factories, farms, and schools, rigidly formal and seemingly ill at ease as he accepted flowers from curtsying children. On these occasions he would, like the leaders who preceded him, deliver cheerleading addresses urging workers to work better, farmers to farm better, and students to study better. And yet when the same television showed him abroad at meetings of East bloc leaders, he seemed much more interesting than the other members of the satellite choir. Until the arrival of Gorbachev, he was the odd man out. At sixty-one, he was by far the youngest and the only one who ever wore a uniform.

As he extended his rule, wavering between policies of repression and amnesty, he was increasingly viewed as a poker-faced strategist who kept his real wishes and compulsions bound beneath his corset. Over dozens of dinner tables I heard speculative questions about him multiply. Was he, in fact, primarily subservient to Soviet interests as Weinberger's comment alleged, or did he have some cunning long-term agenda to strengthen Poland's independence? Had he declared martial law simply to save his Muscovite patrons from the dreadful costs of invasion, or had he acted to forestall a Soviet assault he knew would have been more devastating to Polish interests? Were the tactical concessions he was making to Polish public opinion changing the face of Communist totalitarianism? Was he, willingly or not, presiding over the dismantlement of the ruling system in Poland? Or was he trying to lull and wear down society before turning to harsher measures?

I can recall how some years after the amnesty, Wiktor Kulerski, by then surfaced and seeking employment, assessed the general, his nemesis, as a man who, quite fortunately, had never learned the lessons of Machiavelli. "He declared martial law but then he was not harsh enough. Now he is hated by the nation for doing what he did on December 13, and he is bothered and attacked by people like us whom he declined to finish off. He was too harsh to be loved and not harsh enough to be feared." In the absence of any confessional materials, almost all of the dining table debate on Jaruzelski's motives and plans was conjectural. A good deal of it centered on what little was known of Jaruzelski's childhood and adolescence, when as a sixteen-year-old boy he was deported to the Siberian labor camp where his father died.

Once I approached one of Jaruzelski's close confidants, Major Wiesław Górnicki, with a request that his chief talk to me about this period of his life. Górnicki is one of several journalists who along with army friends make up the general's inner circle. For many years he was a respected reporter and foreign correspondent for the party's liberal weekly, *Polityka*. He is only a reserve officer but ever since martial law he has worn his uniform with childish delight, even on his vacations. He wrote some of the general's speeches and advised him on approaches to the West, particularly to the United States.

At one of our meetings, I reminded Górnicki that Jaruzelski had spoken of the need to fill in the blank, censored pages of Polish history, and I suggested that a good place to start might be with the details of his own life. Górnicki listened sympathetically. He knew that an article in *The New York Times* about Jaruzelski's wartime tribulations in a Soviet work camp could only raise his leader's standing in Poland and the West. Unfortunately, he said, my request was still premature. "We have come as far as we could go," said Górnicki, implying that the obstacle lay in Moscow.

I had come to expect such explanations. They are often accompanied by a movement of the neck with the head thrust in what is presumed to be the direction of Moscow. It means "them." It is probably the most eloquent of contemporary Polish gestures, just ahead of the finger pointed upward that means "we are bugged," or the four-finger chop at the neck that connotes "I was drunk." Górnicki himself had written a terse four-page official biography of his boss as an introduction to a collection of the general's speeches published in London. "The formula we used was to say that in 1940 he found himself in the Soviet Union. Where exactly he found himself, why he found himself there and what he saw and experienced, are all questions that for now have to remain without complete answers."

Still, I managed to glean some details about this period from Jaruzelski's old acquaintances and some of his estranged and distant relatives. Before September of 1939, when Germany began the war with its attack on Poland, Jaruzelski was a sixteen-year-old attending the Marist Fathers High School in Warsaw. His father, who had retired from the army, worked as the manager of a large agricultural estate near Lublin, not far from the smaller holdings that belonged to the Jaruzelskis. The family was Catholic, patriotic and anticommunist. I once met an elderly woman who told me that in the late twenties she knew one of Jaruzelski's grandfathers. She remembered a day when the old man was told that the son of a well-to-do acquaintance had been arrested for communist activity. "I would rather my son die than to see him a communist," the woman quoted the old man as saying. Jaruzelski's other grandfather had taken part in the anticzarist uprising of 1863. For this he was sent in chains to Siberia, returning home after an amnesty in 1880. The Jaruzelskis were not rich, but they kept faith with the traditions of the *szlachta*, the privileged gentry. The future general, for example, learned to fence and to ride. His favorite subject was military history.

The role of the *szlachta* is one of the things that has made Poland very different from its neighbors. The gentry made up a higher percentage of feudal society in Poland than anywhere else and their influence was paramount for centuries. There has never been a period of bourgeois dominance in Poland as there was, for instance, in Czechoslovakia. Under partition and foreign domination, the gentry often led rebellions and uprisings. As urbanization and industrialization were advanced, to a large extent by Jews and Germans, the often impoverished rural-based aristocracy set standards of grace and behavior in ways that echo the life of the American South after the Civil War. Genealogical pride blended with patriotism. William Styron once told me that when he came to Poland to do research for *Sophie's Choice*, he was struck by how much the Polish countryside reminded him of his native Virginia. Similarly, Konwicki discovered when he visited America that the only things he found familiar were the hamlets and decaying mansions of Virginia. There he sensed the fraying gentility and decomposing values of his own childhood.

Until the Communists came, all of Poland's leaders and most of the heroes were from the *szlachta*. Kościuszko, Pułaski, and Piłsudski were all from this class. Even now, customs of this nobility are more deeply entrenched than the egalitarian gestures that Communist ideologues have tried to introduce on the Soviet model. Hardly anyone uses the term *comrade* in public, while virtually all men kiss the hands of women. Nowhere else in the world do men of all backgrounds kiss the hands of women. In Vienna, some aristocrats do it, but in Communist, ostensibly classless, Poland, every man does. Steelworkers, gas station attendants, mailmen, and staggering drunks kiss women's hands. What was deplored by leftist levelers as a feudal vestige has become a nationalist and patriotic custom. Instead of treating each other according to the imported forms of an invented "proletarian culture," Poles from all origins have very pointedly adopted the manners of counts and dukes.

In the autumn of 1939, as German tanks raced across Poland, Jaruzelski's parents fled, taking him and his younger sister to Lithuania. Two weeks into September, Russian forces seized the eastern half of Poland under the secret provisions of the pact that Molotov and Ribbentrop had signed. As Red Army units moved westward, they took Polish troops as prisoners, among them fifteen thousand officers. The bodies of four thousand of these men were later discovered buried in Katyn forest, each with the skull shattered by a bullet. The others have never been found. As the Soviets occupied their half of Poland, Red commissars and NKVD agents culled suspect Poles. The Jaruzelskis were among those arrested and sent east. Relatives say that Jaruzelski's father apparently died in a camp of illness and overwork in 1942. It is unclear whether his son was with him at the time. Jaruzelski's mother and his sister remained in the Soviet Union until after the war. For at least two years, Jaruzelski himself apparently worked as a slave laborer.

Nothing has appeared in print about the family's travails in exile but aspects of the experience can be inferred from the large library of memoirs by Poles who shared similar fates. For example, Gustaw Herling-Grudziński, a Pole taken to a northern camp, wrote A World Apart, which contained one of the first descriptions of life in the gulags to reach the West. In the eighties in Poland such testimony was not hard to find. One seventy-five-year-old woman I knew in Warsaw spent seven years carrying logs on her head in a camp near the White Sea without ever receiving a change of clothes or being told of the charges against her. A childhood friend of Konwicki's spent eight years in a mine, during which time he saw the sky only twice. When Hitler attacked the Soviet Union in 1941, most of the surviving captive Poles were mustered into two armies. The larger force, with ties to the London government, was deployed first in Iran and eventually fought its way bravely across northern Africa and into Italy. A smaller

Polish army, closely integrated with the Soviet command, was organized and committed to battles in the Ukraine, Poland, and Germany. This is the force Jaruzelski joined, turning up at a recruiting camp with his feet bound in rags and paper.

Bismarck once said that Poles habitually made politics of literature and literature of politics. In reference to Jaruzelski's life, the aphorism has uncanny relevance. A military leader whose father died in a Soviet gulag had through twists of circumstance risen to take over the leadership of the Soviet Union's largest, most important and most precariously combustible European ally. For Poles such details evoke obvious literary resonances. In the early nineteenth century, shortly after he was banished by czarist authorities, Mickiewicz wrote a narrative poem called "Konrad Wallenrod." It is set in the fifteenth century, when Poland came under persistent attack from the Teutonic knights. In the poem, Wallenrod is a Polish child kidnapped by the raiding knights. The marauders slay the boy's parents but take him back to their fortress and raise him within their belligerent order. Bold and intelligent, with a flair for strategy, Wallenrod rises through the ranks and eventually is chosen to head the militant and powerful crusaders. At the end of the poem he knowingly leads his legions into a Polish trap. He dies at the head of his forces as he avenges the murder of his parents.

Over many dinners, in many living rooms, I heard many people raise and dispute the parallels with Jaruzelski's life that were suggested by the poem. There was general agreement that the forced deportation of a privileged adolescent and the death of his father in exile must have left traumatic and permanent scars. But how Jaruzelski may have dealt with that trauma was a matter of animated debate. Some insisted that he simply repressed any passionate hatreds and vengeful fantasies beneath a veneer of pragmatic subservience. Others thought he might well be biding his time, waiting for the moment when, like Wallenrod, he could demonstrate his Polish patriotism fully.

My own intuition led me to suspect that whatever Jaruzelski

had seen and experienced in youth had convinced him that it was futile to resist Soviet power. I felt as if he was privy to some secret knowledge of the Soviets' potential for cruelty that went beyond what even most Poles assume—an awareness perhaps that Moscow was capable of once again deporting hundreds of thousands across the Urals. This was, of course, mostly conjecture on my part, but I mentioned my suspicions to a man who regularly met with Jaruzelski, hoping to provoke a reaction. He did not dismiss the point I was raising but answered elliptically that I should look into the biography of Kazimierz Zygulski, a sociologist whom Jaruzelski had named to be minister of culture.

A native of Łwów, Zygulski had been a leader of the wartime resistance to the Nazis and a representative of the London-based exile government. In 1944, as Soviet commissars moved into those parts of the Ukraine that had been Polish before the war and were to become Soviet after, he was arrested and tried for espionage. He was sentenced to fifteen years at hard labor. For eleven years he worked in a coal mine in the Komi Republic in the Urals. He returned to Poland a year later, where he specialized in studying the spread of artistic values. He never joined the Communist party. When asked about the years he spent in the mine, he would only say that while there he had worked in a clinic, analyzing blood and urine samples, and that as a scholar he was appreciative of what he learned on the job. Among Poles who knew his story there were many who thought Zygulski had been broken in the Soviet Union. They noted that as minister he increased the numbers of Soviet books to be translated and talked often of a need to counter Polish fascination with Western literature, art, and music.

For most of my friends from Solidarity the key fact about Jaruzelski was that he had spent his entire adult life in the Polish army. He had, they pointed out, become its youngest general at a time when that army was under the complete domination of Soviet officers. He was minister of defense in 1968 when Polish forces joined Soviet troops to suppress the Prague Spring, dispatching what in the prevailing Orwellian language was officially termed "fraternal assistance." Whatever his background, said the opposition people, this meant that he had clearly proved his loyalty to Moscow over and over. You could not, they repeated, rise through the ranks as he did without fully accepting the limitations of Polish sovereignty and the dominion of the Soviet empire. All of the Wallenrod analogies, they claimed, were at best misleading, and at worst bits of disinformation planted by police agents to win over sentimental Poles.

Furthermore, Jaruzelski's claims to "realistic" and "responsible" patriotism might possibly be understandable if he, like Tito in Yugoslavia, had commanded Polish armed forces to challenge rather than serve Soviet authority. For instance, the critics said that after quelling the strikes by force, he could have used the latitude he had won from the Russians to permit Solidarity to continue as a chastened but free union. He could have used the ground and credit he won from Moscow to maneuver for greater Polish autonomy. But he did not. First he suspended the union and then a year later he outlawed it completely.

Instead of comparing him to Wallenrod, they said Jaruzelski should more appropriately be likened to Slav janissaries of the Middle Ages. Though they were also often abducted, they nonetheless served loyally as mercenary field commanders for the Turks. Or, as a Polish student of American history once told me, the general should be seen as a "house nigger" taking on the views of his masters. Weinberger, the opposition critics declared, had it right. Once, after I had raised the Wallenrod metaphor in a magazine piece that was read in Polish translation on the Voice of America, I was attacked harshly. "What is this nonsense about Wallenrod? Why do you write about possible intentions?" said the man, a Solidarity activist who headed a committee aiding the families of those fired from their jobs and blacklisted. "What do his intentions matter? Maybe he really wants to bring us to the promised land? Maybe in his heart he wants to tear up Yalta, retake Wilno and Łwów? No one knows. No one can ever know.

But everybody knows what he did. We know he declared war on the nation and he crushed a free union. We know his police have killed people and forced them to lose their jobs. That's what a journalist should write about."

And once, when I noted in passing that the general had showed greater tolerance for the opposition than any other satellite leader, Michnik chastised me for sloppy thinking. "You are right that he has not ordered people shot, but do not think that this is socialism with a human face, it is Communism with a few teeth knocked out. He has not been even more repressive because society has not let him be more repressive. As for contentions that he is not as evil as he could be, I suppose there are people in Czechoslovakia who are saying that Husák is not Ceauşescu and in Romania, there may be some who find solace that Ceauşescu is not Idi Amin and in Uganda, they may have said that Amin was not Hitler. That road is a blind alley."

That the opposition despised and disdained the general was obvious. What was less apparent to Poles was that by the summer of 1984, Jaruzelski's Soviet patrons were also growing displeased with him for his failure to silence Poland's resistance movement and for what they considered to be his wishy-washy and ambivalent policies. Three years after taking over the party, Jaruzelski was facing yet another not unusual impasse of Polish political life: He was proving to be too much of a Communist to win the trust of Poles, but too much of a Pole to maintain the full trust of the Kremlin. General Jaruzelski had, of course, saved the Soviets from dreadful consequences when he ordered his tanks to roll to crush the free labor union. If he had not taken the initiative and if the Soviets had sent their own troops to Warsaw as they did to Budapest in 1956, Prague in 1968, and Kabul in 1980, their costs would have been excruciating. All chances of negotiating disarmament agreements would have collapsed. The cold war would have worsened. The Sino-Soviet rift would have grown wider. There was also a real chance that Polish workers might fight back and that Polish military units might join them. On that

December morning, Jaruzelski, though scorned by his country-men as a villain, was esteemed by Leonid Brezhnev, whom he had saved.

Nearly three years later, Jaruzelski was still regarded by most Poles as a Soviet marionette. At the same time his stock in the Kremlin was falling. All Chernenko wanted from Poland was stability and better economic performance and an end to the skirmishing between state, nation, and church that Jaruzelski was tolerating. The Soviet leader had spent much of his career in police work and he had his own favorites among the Polish hardheads who he felt might provide firmer rule than the general.

From the viewpoint of orthodox Communists, Jaruzelski himself was a quintessential and frightening example of negative selec-tion, not because he was incapable or corrupt, but because so much about him reflected qualities of the old order that Com-munists had so long sought to eradicate. For the orthodox, his presence at center stage confirmed nightmares of Communism's disintegration. His ascendancy suggested that the system's ben-eficiaries were making a last-ditch effort to save themselves by piling everything on the barricades, notably those old virtues they had once belittled as sentimental and archaic—patriotism, aristocratic tradition, military tradition, literary motifs, hints of anti-Russian feeling, and chivalrous honor. Not all of Poland's remaining Communists, and hardly any elsewhere, were over-joyed by the Jaruzelski profile or by the aimlessness of his rule. Only a very few saw his tenure as a transition to some hybrid system in which freer markets and some limited freedoms could be introduced without threatening the party's deciding role.

As I listened to such people—they usually identified themselves as Communist liberals—spin out their fantasies, it seemed that they wanted to share the responsibility for governing without giving up any of their power. A much larger group within the party supported the general on the assumption that he was pre-siding over a temporary tactical retreat. The general after all was a military man and they thought it was natural that after the debacle the party had suffered as Solidarity bloomed, it had to pull back, reassemble its forces, gather in the stragglers, and avoid costly battles. They assumed the general was biding his time, appeasing society, while planning some future counteroffensive that would restore the party's standing and dominance. They imagined that once the party regained its strength, more conventional leaders would replace Jaruzelski.

Then there was a third group—the hardheads, who believed that the general had already gone too far, that by placating the amorphous opposition he was placing the party in grave jeopardy. These people were only a minority, though it was always a significant minority. Nonetheless they held many of the lower- and mid-level party jobs, and in some party organs they dominated. The hardheads had never been happy with Jaruzelski, who, aside from his suspect class origins, seemed to them too puritanical, too austerely clean. They felt that the pattern of concessions had to be stopped, quickly and dramatically.

A few of these hard-line critics were ideologues who truly believed that each new freedom given to appease national sentiment only drove the party to the next concession. Vast areas of cultural life had been effectively wrested from party or government control. Now, plans for economic decentralization and expanded free markets were being drawn up. What then, the hard-line ideologists wondered, was keeping Poland Communist? They would grumble that in contrast to Communists elsewhere in the bloc, only Polish leaders were obsessed with such sentimental issues as proving their patriotism or justifying themselves before history, the nation, and who knew, perhaps even God. Did Ceauşescu in Romania, or Husák in Czechoslovakia or, for that matter, any Soviet leader before Gorbachev really care what people thought of him, or how history would deal with him? Communists were supposed to wield power and not play to the crowd. Still, this was Poland and, lamentable as it was for the hardheads, romanticism had even undermined the politburo.

There were even those who felt that if things continued as they were, the only thing Communists would have left to concede to the nation were their lives. In order to prove their Polishness, they would have to commit political suicide and vanish. The struggle for survival was, they reasoned, no longer a competition of ideas or visions of social organization. It was threatening the privileges of the ruling elite and eventually their existence. Some years earlier Konwicki had written *A Minor Apocalypse*, a novel in which a writer, a detached intellectual, is visited by two opposition gadflies who urge that he immolate himself before party headquarters in order to inspire the nation, shame the oppressors, and attain martyrdom. Now, as the hard-liners saw it, they were the ones being asked to make similar, unacceptable sacrifices. Whatever Jaruzelski was, they certainly were not Wallenrods. The party, they argued, was needlessly pursuing honor, legitimacy, and validation when it should be simply establishing its power. It did not need to inspire love or understanding, just fear.

The hardheads also had their more parochial differences with the general. Much of their strength lay in the security services and they were unhappy about the appointment of General Kiszczak to head the ministry of the interior. The cement people looked at Kiszczak as an outsider brought in from the army to clean house. He was disrupting old ways of doing things and interfering with old networks of patronage and privilege.

Some time after the sweeping amnesty these critics began spreading reports that Moscow wanted a change of direction, that the Kremlin was demanding that the Poles crack down decisively on all opposition and that they even aggressively confront the Catholic Church. The hard-liners, who had in general kept their silence while Moscow signaled its gratitude to Jaruzelski, were now smirking in the open.

My contacts with the rank and file of the cement faction were limited, but I did occasionally meet with a journalist who identified with their positions. He was particularly unhappy that Jaruzelski had surrounded himself with several journalists from the rival liberal weekly newspaper, *Polityka*. In addition to Górnicki,

Jaruzelski had appointed Mieczysław Rakowski, the editor, as his deputy premier, and he named Jerzy Urban, a provocative columnist who was not a party member, to be the highly visible government spokesman. In the late summer of 1984, my cement acquaintance gleefully predicted that "the liberals" would be out by winter and that Jaruzelski would either be forced into a hard-line stance by the Soviets, or he would be removed from office. To support his views he showed me a clipping from a Soviet newspaper that strongly attacked Bonapartism. Who else but Jaruzelski could be the target of such obvious Soviet displeasure? He was the only Bonapartist in the Communist world. The article, my acquaintance said, made everything very clear. Moscow was sick and tired of Jaruzelski's concessions. Even people at *Polityka* conceded that there were new pressures for more toughness. When the amnesty did not bring about the removal of Western economic sanctions, the Soviet hard-liners had gained leverage.

The Kremlin was not withdrawing its support of Jaruzelski, but in what had been a time-honored mechanism of control, it was simply restoring support to his rivals in the cement wing. The signals were clear and, according to the *Polityka* liberals, Jaruzelski would have to appease hardhead sentiment over the next few months, step up attacks on the opposition, resume arrests of dissidents, and mount an attack on the church. The liberals cautioned me not to make too much of this shift, saying that the general's commitment to reform would prevail. One of the *Polityka* people told me that he expected that things would move in sharp zigzags for the next year as the general sought to simultaneously appease the Soviets, the cement people, the Western powers, the Solidarity resistance movement, and the compulsions of Polish national history. "You have to remember," said the liberal journalist, "Jaruzelski's best subject at military school was always tactics."

NINE

A PRIEST
IS MISSING

S T. STANISŁAW KOSTKA is a white twin-spired building that, like many Polish churches, verges on the kitschy. Its façade is often festooned with hundred-foot-long diagonal ribbons. Red and white for Poland; or papal yellow; or pale blue, the emblematic color of the Virgin Mary, revered both as the Mother of Christ and the Queen of Poland. For many months a large blue letter *M* for Mary hung above a balcony announcing a period of special devotions to the Virgin. The church lies at the heart of Żoliborz, an area of Warsaw that has much more of a neighborhood feeling than most of the other homogeneous parts of the capital.

Żoliborz stretches up from the banks of the Vistula at the northern end of Warsaw and its name is a corruption from the French *Joli Bord*, or Pretty Bank. Across the street from the church is a Bauhaus-style block of prewar worker housing that, though spare and rectilinear, is far more inviting than the taller projects built since war's end. Down a small street are plaques listing the names of the first twenty people who were killed in the Warsaw uprising. Just around the corner is a rotary where many streets come together. Officially it is now named "The Square of the Paris Commune," but Warsaw residents, both young and old, usually refer to it by the name it had before the war, "The Square of President Woodrow Wilson." As with most Polish neighborhoods, manual workers, shop clerks, professors, and bureaucrats live in adjoining apartments, but there are probably more artists and intellectuals in Żoliborz than elsewhere. Andrzej Wajda, the internationally honored film director, lives there in his small but elegant private villa and there are a number of artists' galleries. A mammoth flea market takes place in the neighborhood on Sundays and there are several theaters and restaurants. The Citadel, a fortress and prison in czarist times, is now a museum that looms over the river's edge. Still, since martial law, the major landmark in Żoliborz, and perhaps the most compelling site in the city, was the Kostka church. It stood as the most visible and approachable symbol of national resistance, a shrine where the spirit of Solidarity continued to be regularly invoked and affirmed.

Almost every day chartered buses would arrive from the countryside bringing men and women with deeply lined faces and knobby hands. The largest crowds came on the last Sundays of every month, when special masses for the fatherland were celebrated. The church would be filled to capacity by some three thousand people, while as many as ten or twelve thousand more stood outside, often in cold or snowy weather.

The sermons at these masses were given by Jerzy Popiełuszko, a slight, somber, and frail priest. At thirty-seven years of age he had through those sermons become the best-known cleric in Poland after the pope and Cardinal Glemp, and the one who was most closely identified with Solidarity. Before the masses began, the out-of-town visitors would often walk through the fenced-in church grounds, stopping to examine plaques and monuments that testified to Polish losses. On the eastern outer wall of the church a large inscription proclaimed "For God and the fatherland." Beneath it lay a row of tablets listing the Nazi concentration camps where Polish citizens, among them Jews and others, were killed: MAJDANEK—500,000, TREBLINKA—750,000, DACHAU—

160,000, DORA—60,000, BUCHENWALD—240,000, FLOSSENBURG—81,000, MAUTHAUSEN—164,000, NEUENGAMME—95,000, CHELMO NAD NEREM—390,000, BELZEC—600,000, RAVENSBRUCK—132,000, STUTTHOF—120,000, SOBIBOR—250,000, PLASZOW—150,000, OŚWIĘCIM-BRZEŻINKA [AUSCHWITZ-BIRKENAU]—3,840,000, GROSSROSEN—325,000, ORANIENBURG-SACHSENHAUSEN—200,000, BERGEN-BELSEN—750,000. Among the memorial plaques were a few that commemorated men who had "died in the east," or at "Katyn," which all the visitors understood meant at the hands of Soviets rather than of Nazis. Usually, homemade banners with Solidarity symbols were hung on the church fence. They declared that clandestine union chapters from this or that region or city were keeping the faith.

For some years the Kostka church had been the most prominent political oasis in Poland. It was the one place in the capital where thousands of ordinary people could gather regularly in an open place to express the fused ideals of Polish nationalism, Christian sacrifice, and Solidarity's outlawed program. Like early Christians in the catacombs, they would raise their fingers in forbidden witness and sing old hymns, raising their voices at precisely those verses that the authorities found provocative, stanzas that Cardinal Glemp, the primate, had at the government's urging asked them not to use. For instance, in the hymn "God, who watches over Poland," the primate had ordered that only a new version be sung, one that included the refrain, "O Lord bless our Fatherland." But every Sunday, the crowds ignored the urging and obstinately sang the old line written as Poland lay dismembered, "O Lord, restore a free Fatherland."

Of the younger activist priests, only Popiełuszko had been able to withstand the pressures of church superiors, who wanted them to keep aloof from politics. Mieczysław Nowak, a priest who had worked closely with workers at Warsaw's tractor factory, found himself first admonished by the primate for his associations with Solidarity and then banished to a remote rural parish. Father Stanisław Małkowski, another outspoken critic of Communism and Communists, was forbidden to preach in Warsaw. Popie-łuszko had also been upbraided by Cardinal Glemp. In his diary he wrote that the primate had treated him more brusquely than the secret police as he condemned his activism. He wrote that after the reprimand he had cried tears of frustration.

There were other churchmen in Poland who had worked longer and more intimately with political dissidents than had Popie-łuszko. But they were either older or less charismatic men who were not as likely to mobilize masses of young workers, students, and intellectuals. In any event none had gained the attention or the following that surrounded the priest from St. Stanisław Kostka. In the Warsaw suburb of Podkowa Leśnia, Father Leon Kantorski had for many years offered his church to human rights activists from KOR, to opposition groups, and to draft resisters. Protest hunger strikes were held there. He invited agnostics like Jacek Kuroń to lecture and organized joint masses with Ukrainian Greco-Catholic priests. He held a mass to mark the heroism of the Hungarians who battled the Soviets in 1956 and he brought workers like Zbigniew Bujak into contact with dissident intellec-tuals. For his efforts, Father Kantorski, the silver-haired son of a prison guard, was carefully watched by the police and frequently admonished by Cardinal Glemp and his associates. But Father Kantorski's church was not often visited by foreign journalists, visitors from abroad, or foreign diplomats, who all regularly came to Kostka. While he was admired and loved by many leaders of the opposition, his name was not generally or widely known.

In contrast, Father Henryk Jankowski, the rector of St. Brygida's church in Gdańsk, had gained a nationwide and even interna-tional reputation as Wałęsa's flamboyant adviser and confessor. He had served mass in the shipyard during the strike that gave birth to Solidarity. He was often at Wałęsa's side and his church frequently provided refuge for the Solidarity faithful. It was a place to meet, to leave messages, and often, as in the case of Kostka in Warsaw, masses would give way to short demonstra-tions as worshippers spilled out of church chanting political slogans. But Gdańsk was less of a media center than Warsaw, and Father Jankowski's ostentatious style alienated some in the opposition. He drove a Mercedes, wore heavy jeweled bracelets and distributed calling cards to foreigners that contained his bank account number. He was also a generation older than Popiełuszko.

Like Polish society, like the party, and like Solidarity, the church, too, had its divisions. The primate's priorities and his formative experiences were very different from that of the young activist priests and their Solidarity friends. Ultimately, he was more interested in negotiating with the government than defying it. He wanted a guarantee of rights for church property and he wanted to extend and entrench church holdings for that day when the pope in Rome would no longer be a Pole—when, presumably, the influence of the Polish church might lessen. To many he seemed more interested in curbing abortion and divorce than extending democracy or contesting Soviet domination. He appeared uneasy that some of the prominent Solidarity figures were former leftists, atheists, or agnostics. In his public statements he related to those prewar Polish political traditions that regarded Polish Catholicism as the sole basis of citizenship. This view contrasted with Piłsudski's vision of a confederation of many nationalities clustered around the Poles. Once, when asked about prominent political prisoners, he replied that he did not understand why the church should show concern for doubtful Christians. Cardinal Glemp was clearly not as enthusiastic about "pluralism" as Solidarity and its supporters were.

For his diffident attitude to political prisoners and for his chastisement of the activist priests, people like Pani Kasia, my devout housekeeper, were calling the primate "Comrade Glemp." Her heroes were the pope, who she perceived as being dissatisfied with Glemp, Father Jankowski, and above all, Father Popiełuszko. The young priest's influence had grown steadily ever since striking steelworkers asked him to serve mass at the Warsaw foundry in 1979. The steelworkers made him their patron. They gave him a white cowboy-style hat of the sort they wore on ceremonial occasions. He was also the chaplain for doctors and nurses. Coal miners made him their religious leader and they gave him their own black-and-purple-plumed ceremonial headgear. A group of actors sought him out and he met regularly with them as well. At Poland's seminaries, his activities were becoming the model of engagement and risk for aspiring priests.

I would often take foreign visitors to the Kostka church to hear Father Popiełuszko. The faces of those who gathered at his sermons formed as broad a cross-section of Poland as I found anywhere. There were the pious, often heavyset black-clad widows mumbling their beads, workers with sport jackets over their coveralls, and young people who wore rock insignia next to religious pins on their denim jackets. There were people who I knew to be rebellious Catholics; people who were divorced and who defended a woman's right to abortion. Within the crowds were city people and country folk, intellectuals, and a few patrician aristocrats. There were black marketeers and private businessmen, former Communists, and even a few who still had their party cards.

Security at the church was provided by by volunteers, mostly steelworkers and people from the Ursus tractor factory. During the fatherland masses they kept an eye out for provocations and plainclothes police. They were organized by a man called "the Mole," a big man who fifteen years earlier had been thrown out of Warsaw University for his anticommunist sentiments. Now he ran a private art gallery and spent his time with workers at the church. There was Maciej, a bearded welder the size of a phone booth, and Ryszard, a sociologist and mountain climber. They had been brought together in the churn of Solidarity, and when the union was crushed, they retreated into the sanctuary at Kostka.

Sometimes when I had nothing much to do, I would go to the church to share coffee with them. The talk tended to be less structured than conversations with people like Michnik and Kuroń, who had refined their arguments in hundreds of lectures and articles and in prison reflection. Once the Mole spoke of the success Afghan tribal warriors were having against the Soviets and he fantasized wishfully about yet another Polish uprising. He was squelched by Ryszard who told him that tactics that work in mountain valleys would not work in modern cities, that Budapest and Prague were probably the last of Europe's uprisings. Another time, Maciej took me to a group of "the boys" who met at the church. He was trying to enlist them in a sobriety campaign. "It's easier to get Poles to throw cobblestones than to stop drinking vodka, but cutting back on alcohol is much more effective if you want to get rid of the Red Ones," he said. Maciej had been reading Gandhi. "Listen, if you can stop drinking, it will make you better. It will make you stronger. Give you more pride. It will make your wives and children happier. And at the same time it will hurt the Red Ones who count on the taxes from the bottles you buy."

Popiełuszko was the catalyst for all such activity at Kostka, but most Poles knew him only through his sermons, which were widely reprinted. The last time I heard him speak was in August of 1984 as he marked the founding of the Solidarity union four years earlier. I had no intimation then that the sermon would be one of his last. What I remember was a low, rumbling voice and the slow cadences that made it easy to take notes. As he often did, the priest linked contemporary acts of valor to heroic deeds of the past, in this case the defeat of the Teutonic knights, Piłsudski's rebuff to the invading Red Army, and the Warsaw uprising. Then he switched from the glorious past to the challenging present.

The solidarity of the nation had its roots in earlier appeals for law and justice in the years 1956, 1968, 1970, and 1976. It had its roots in the tears, injuries, and blood of workers. It had its roots in the humiliation of university youth. That is why it grew so quickly into an imposing tree whose branches spread over the entire land.

. . . Though it developed amid storms, throughout the fifteen months of its legal existence no one was killed or seriously wounded through its fault . . . Two years ago I said that Solidarity had received a wound that continues to bleed, but one which was not mortal, because one cannot murder hopes. Today you can see and feel this even more clearly as we marvel at the faith of our brothers returned from prison. We see and feel more clearly that the hopes of 1980 are alive and are bearing fruit. Today they are even dearer to us because they have entered into human hearts and minds. That which is in the heart, that which is deeply tied to man, cannot be liquidated with this or that regulation or statute. . . . We have to fight our way out of the fear that paralyzes and enslaves reason and the human heart. . . . Our only fear should be the fear that we might ever betray Christ for a few pieces of silver. We have a duty to bear witness to the truth of what happened in August of 1980. We have a duty to demand that the hopes of the nation begin, at last, to be realized. . . . Of course we have to act with care. We have to realize the geopolitical situation in which we find ourselves, but at the same time that situation should never be a convenient excuse to justify the waiver of national rights.

I do not remember being particularly moved by this sermon. I had, by then, grown accustomed to Popiełuszko's outspokenness, and I had come to view the patch around the Kostka church as a tiny enclave where modes of critical expression and moral judgment, unexceptional in the West, were heard regularly. It was only when I reread the notes six months later during the trial of the priest's murderers that I was reminded how remarkable the sermons were for a police state within the Communist bloc. Nowhere else from East Berlin to Vladivostok could anyone stand before five or ten or fifteen thousand people and use a microphone to condemn the errors of state and party. Nowhere, in that vast stretch encompassing some four hundred million people was anyone else openly telling a crowd that defiance of authority was an obligation of the heart, of religion, manhood, and nationhood.

On the morning of October 20, 1984, a Saturday, the priests at
St. Stanisław Kostka Church grew alarmed when Father Popiełuszko did not arrive to conduct the early morning service. Popiełuszko had a small apartment of his own in Warsaw, a room
that had been purchased with money he received from his American relatives. Sometimes he would go there to escape from growing numbers of supplicants. He was not at the apartment. The
priests knew that the night before, Father Popiełuszko had
preached a sermon at a church in Bydgoszcz, a drab industrial
town some 120 miles northwest of the capital. In their anxiety
they called Bydgoszcz and learned that Popiełuszko had left for
home just after dinner the previous night. He and his driver,
Waldemar Chróstowski, had set off in the priest's well-maintained
Volkswagen. Normally, the trip to Warsaw, on a rutted two-lane
highway, should have taken no more than four hours. There were
no accidents reported and no one had called Warsaw to explain
the priest's delayed arrival.

The priests in Warsaw debated whether or not to call the police
or the episcopate. They knew that their colleague had often been
harassed and arrested by the police. His car had been vandalized
and once an explosive device was thrown through his window.
Popiełuszko had told them that police had planted incriminating
evidence in his quarters.

Father Popiełuszko was very responsible and was not likely to
have forgotten his scheduled duties, but the priests wondered
whether he might have veered off on the way home to visit a
colleague or a Solidarity fugitive. They considered the possibility
that they might cause him some difficulties by announcing their
alarm.

Ultimately, they called both the episcopate and the police. By
all accounts, the church bureaucracy absorbed the news slug-
gishly, passing the information up to the primate's office slowly
without discernible fright. However, at the Rakowiecka Street
headquarters of the interior ministry, the report rang bells. Within
hours it was bucked up to Minister Kiszczak.

By afternoon, Kiszczak was informed that his police agents in the city of Toruń had found Chróstowski, Popiełuszko's driver. He had turned up late at night at a church in Torún, shoeless, with scraped elbows and shins. He had roused the sleepy church rector to blurt out an account of how he and Father Popiełuszko were abducted by three men, one of whom had worn the uniform of a traffic policeman. Struggling for coherence, the driver, a former paratrooper, told the rector that Father Popiełuszko had been beaten and bound and then thrown into the trunk of a car. He himself had been gagged and handcuffed and forced into the front seat. Chróstowski told the Toruń priest that he was able to pry open the door latch of the Polish-built Fiat with the pinky of his manacled right hand and that he rolled out of the speeding car. The handcuffs parted when he hit the roadway.

Kiszczak has a reputation of being a careful man who does not jump to conclusions. Still, on that morning, as he heard the sketchy details of the unfolding case, he had to suspect that whatever might have befallen the priest, the circumstances of his kidnapping sounded like, looked like, and smelled like a political provocation. In theory it is of course possible, as a few in the opposition later suggested, that Kiszczak and Jaruzelski were themselves somehow behind the abduction. That they had manipulated policemen to kill the priest in order to frame party rivals, chastise the church, and appease their Soviet critics. Such explanations strain credulity. For one thing, it would have involved too many layers to isolate the leaders from exposure. For another, the events as they unfolded came within a hair of bringing down Jaruzelski and Kiszczak, and it is hard to see how it was in their interest to make themselves so vulnerable. Both army men are extremely cautious strategists who weigh the most minute advantages before they act. High-risk gambles were not their style. Naturally, if Kiszczak had been involved, then the news that morning would not have surprised him. In fact, it seemed to alarm him and he immediately sent his own loyal men to Toruń to watch over the driver. As minister of the interior, he was well aware of other cases where key witnesses had died mysteriously before they could testify. That same day he called Jaruzelski with the details.

The priest was only missing, but to Kiszczak it seemed probable that the primary targets of any plot, if indeed there was a plot, could well be General Jaruzelski and himself.

In the hours before the news of Popiełuszko's disappearance seeped into public awareness, Kiszczak must have weighed several hypothetical explanations. The driver's escape, jumping out of a speeding car, sounded improbable and bizarre. Was it possible that he was an accomplice in the disappearance? Could the whole episode have been faked by some opposition group with the priest's knowledge, to spur mass protests? Could Popiełuszko, at that moment, be hiding out somewhere in the company of his "abductors," awaiting the riots and strikes that news of his kidnapping was likely to inspire? Or, had the abduction been hatched somewhere else, perhaps within party and police ranks by Jaruzelski's rivals? A party congress was scheduled for early October and it was widely assumed that Jaruzelski would use the occasion to demote General Mirosław Milewski as politburo member responsible for police and security. Milewski had been Kiszczak's predecessor as interior minister. He had spent his entire life in the security forces since he first attached himself to a Soviet NKVD unit as a teenage orphan during the war. He had his own networks in the ministry and he often received information that bypassed Kiszczak.

Kiszczak also knew that Milewski had his own lines out to the KGB. Chernenko, who was then the power in the Kremlin, had started his own rise to power in the KGB. Perhaps there was a connection. If a faction of the Polish party was behind the kidnapping, could it have acted without the support of the Soviets, or at least of some Soviets? It was a point that needed very gentle exploration. But there was even more to Milewski.

He was the favored disciple of General Mieczysław Moczar, Gomułka's rival for power in 1968, a master of provocations, and the champion of the hardest of hard-liners. Moczar was ailing and would soon die, but he had scores to settle with Jaruzelski, who had opposed him in the past. In light of the upcoming party congress, the Jaruzelski forces had been anticipating some challenge from their rivals. They had to wonder whether the abduction was related to their fears.

The presumption that political provocation lies behind every unusual event is something of a conditioned reflex in Poland, extending from politicians to high school students. Pani Kasia, my housekeeper, for example, would almost automatically explain dozens of rare occurrences—from the availability of sausage in stores to mine accidents—with the single word *prowokacja*. In the case of the plentiful kiełbasa, she would say that the authorities had been hoarding supplies in order to offer them on the market just before elections, thus assuring a high turnout. As for railway or mining accidents, she would say that they were instigated by murky cabals eager to embarrass local party officials or to cow sectors of society. Many of her examples struck me as fabricated or even paranoid, but in time I came to share her view that provocation was indeed a major—perhaps the major—mechanism for forcing sweeping changes of policy or overthrowing leadership in police states. It lies at the very heart of the system and serves as the dictatorial equivalent of democratic elections or parliamentary votes of no confidence.

For people raised in traditions of Western democracy, the logic of political provocation can be hard to grasp. We are used to straightforward political violence in which the target of the plot is the victim of attackers or assassins. Lincoln, the Kennedy brothers, and Martin Luther King, Jr. were all killed by people who hated them and abhorred their policies. The same was true of Indira Gandhi, who was killed by Sikh nationalists in the same week that Father Popiełuszko was buried. Those acts were essentially vengeful. The rationale for provocation tends to be much more Byzantine. The victim of the attack is never the ultimate target of the plot. Instead, the idea is to set off a tide, in the party or in society, that will force political leaders to either surrender their powers or to reverse their policies and accommodate the plotters. Among the better-known examples in this century was the 1933 Reichstag fire, which Hitler used to force parliamentary elections that increased his Nazi majority. In that same year Stalin exploited the assassination of his politburo rival Kirov—a murder he may have engineered—to launch the great purge in which millions were killed.

In Poland, cases of real or suspect provocations abound. It is generally believed that the 1970 food price demonstrations along the Baltic coast were allowed to develop by members of a party faction who wanted to embarrass and overturn the rule of Władysław Gomułka. There is a growing body of opinion that believes that Solidarity's earliest demonstrations in Gdańsk were also given tacit approval by local bosses who hoped to replace Gierek or force him to reverse his high-spending economic policies. Other lesser known examples of suspected provocation involved mysterious deaths and attacks. Stanisław Pyjaś, a Kraków student and active supporter of KOR, was found dead in a courtyard in 1977, with his head smashed. A friend scheduled to testify at his inquest was found drowned in a pond even though he could not swim and was afraid of water. A priest in Kraków reported he was tortured by masked men who burned his chest with cigarettes and told him to stop associating with Solidarity activists. In the Toruń area there were four kidnappings of Solidarity activists who were beaten by armed men claiming to belong to a murky group that called itself the Anti-Solidarity Organization. The victims said that their abductors had guns and admitted links to the police. Were there actually groups of vigilantes, with police connections, who were brutalizing opposition groups like Latin American death squads? And if so, what were their motives? Were they trying to intimidate the opposition and stifle expressions of dissent? Or were they trying to destabilize Jaruzelski and his fragile policies of fluctuating amnesties and repression?

As Kiszczak gingerly sought to unravel the mystery of Popiełuszko's disappearance, he may have drawn ominous parallels to Moczar's anti-Semitic campaign of 1968. That chapter, which began with a police attack on protesting university students, ended with a full-scale purge of Jews from jobs and schools. By the time it was over more than ten thousand people were forced into emigration. But at the outset those who staged the events that launched the campaign were aiming to overthrow Władysław Gomułka as the party leader. Those who sent out the gangs of police thugs to beat the students and single out Jews were hoping that Gomułka would be compromised in the turmoil and that Moczar would then take over. In this they failed when Gomułka sidestepped their challenge by adding his own voice to the anti-Semitic chorus. But Moczar and his men did succeed in having their own appointees fill many party and government posts left vacant by the departing Jews. The beneficiaries of Moczar's patronage were still a cohesive force in the party, particularly within the police and security apparatus.

In 1968 Jaruzelski himself had watched Moczar's plottings from the vantage point of the cabinet. He had become minister of defense in the same month that Moczar's thugs attacked the students. Two years later Jaruzelski refused Moczar's request to have Polish troops fire at striking workers during the disorders on the Baltic coast. Within the party's inner circles Jaruzelski blocked Moczar's repeated attempts to seek more power. Meanwhile, Moczar kept his own dossier on Jaruzelski. It included a charge that Jaruzelski bought his modest Warsaw home at a ridiculously low price. The men were not friendly comrades. There was enough circumstantial evidence to lead Kiszczak to consider whether Father Popiełuszko's disappearance could have been staged to topple Jaruzelski in the ensuing turmoil just as the anti-Jewish campaign had been ignited to bring down Gomułka.

As word of Popiełuszko's disappearance spread, the situation became more tense and febrile. Masses were being said in every church in the country. At St. Stanisław Kostka, vigils continued through the night as people gathered with candles. Where was the priest? Who had kidnapped him? And why? Rumors on the street said that the priest had been taken to Russia. The underground press quickly reminded the nation that six weeks earlier the Soviet newspaper *Izvestia* had attacked Popiełuszko by name accusing him of turning religious masses into divinely inspired political meetings at which "impudent demands" were made for the return of the cities now known as Lwiw and Vilnius. How long, *Izvestia* demanded, would clergymen like Popiełuszko be allowed to preach "such destructive politics"? Soon after the *Izvestia* article, Urban, the government spokesman, had bitterly attacked Popiełuszko in one of the columns he periodically wrote under the transparent pseudonym of Jan Rem. He labeled Popiełuszko's fatherland masses as "séances of hatred," and insultingly likened them to black masses. In earlier instances when opposition figures accused government agents of a role in suspicious assaults on people who worked in Solidarity, Urban would always defend the police, often with quarrelsome arrogance. "You know," he would say, "even Solidarity activists can get drunk and freeze to death in alleys." When first asked by newsmen about Popiełuszko, he said that it was not the government's job to keep track of every priest. He added that everyone knew of cases in which priests had vanished for short periods in order to escape from their vows of chastity.

In this he continued his chosen role of government lightning rod, attracting and even welcoming the hatred of most Poles and giving some time and room for maneuver to the generals he served. Even as he parried the questions of reporters, Urban was meeting with Jaruzelski and Kiszczak, helping shape a response to the gravest confrontation their rule had faced since the wave of Solidarity strikes five years earlier. They were mindful that when the Przemyk boy had died after a police interrogation, tens of thousands of people had taken to the street, and Przemyk had been a young man who was completely unknown beyond his family and friends. Popiełuszko, on the other hand, was the best-known young priest in a very Catholic country that has always responded to martyrs.

Within a day of Popiełuszko's abduction—by then the chauffeur's story had been confirmed by people who had seen him lunge from the car—Kiszczak knew that the kidnappers had come from inside his police. Suspicion centered on the ministry's Department Four, which was charged with monitoring the work of outspoken priests. Two days after the priest was first reported to be missing, four policemen from that department were secretly arrested. Meanwhile as the search continued for the priest or his body, so did the discussions about how public disclosure was to be made and how, if at all, the culprits were to pay for the crime.

Jaruzelski and his confidants had hoped to move carefully against party enemies, but with the priest's body still missing, and four policemen in custody, they would have to take decisive steps. Kiszczak went on television. On October 27, a week after the disappearance came to light, Poles watched the minister somberly describe the continuing search for the missing priest. Gravely, he revealed some details about the arrest of four officers. He had been coached by Urban and did his job well. He appeared seriously concerned and sorrowful. Some months earlier he had cavalierly dismissed a plan to have Popiełuszko thrown to his death from a moving train when it had been submitted to him by one of the arrested policemen. At that time, his written comment had been, "I'd love to but—" Now in a morbid irony he was desperately trying to convince as many people as he could that the government could and would bring the guilty to judgment.

On the streets, in churches, and in Polish homes, there was an air of uncertainty, but generally Kiszczak was believed. For Poles it all smelled like provocation. Crazy as it seemed, the most logical explanation for why anyone would harm an anticommunist priest was that they wanted to get at the country's Communist leaders.

TEN

THE KILLERS

ON OCTOBER 30, they found the body. Leszek Pekała, the most junior of the four policemen arrested, had broken under questioning. An orphan, raised in state institutions, he feared that he would end up taking the blame for his well-connected confederates. Tearfully he led the investigators to the dam where, along with his partners, he had tied rocks to the priest's body before throwing it into the water. Frogmen searched the deep pool and brought the body to the surface.

"Watch what happens to the murderers," I heard one woman say in a quaking voice to a cluster of tram passengers. "They will disappear from view and years from now we'll learn that they were sent to work in Mongolia as advisers." Rumors were spreading that the families of the four men had already been hurriedly moved from their apartments and that their baggage was on its way to Ethiopia, Mongolia, or Cuba. Many Poles now focused their resentment at Urban for his recent attacks on the priest and his suggestions that the disappearance had been concocted by the opposition.

"This time the poisoned dwarf has gone too far," said a man

I knew who was fully involved in dissent. "He has outraged the nation, and supplied the anti-Semites with many years' worth of ammunition. You know, there are three sources of anti-Semitism in Poland—cultural traditions, religious prejudices, and Jerzy Urban."

With the discovery of Popiełuszko's body a mood of torturously confused sorrow settled over Poland. The vigils at the churches drew more and more people. Memorial candles placed on the sidewalk stretched for blocks around St. Stanisław Kostka Church. People wore black armbands or pieces of black cloth pinned to their lapels. There was widespread grief but there were no stirrings of unrest, no word of strikes.

Just before the priest's murder, Jaruzelski was seeking to have Western creditors ease or remove their sanctions in the wake of his amnesty of most dissidents. At the same time, he was trying to accommodate Soviet demands for greater restraint on the church and more effective cadre formation among youth. In addition he was trying to deflect factional threats within the party. He and Kiszczak realized that their priority now was to head off the assault on their authority posed by the murder. If they succeeded in mollifying the nation, they could then deal directly with the hardheads.

Jaruzelski's position was made a little easier when the opposition, like society as a whole, reacted with uncertainty and ambivalence as it considered the motives behind the crime and who might be responsible for it. *Tygodnik Mazowsze*, the Solidarity underground's most widely read weekly, reacted with a page one editorial signed by Bujak and Kulerski, bearing the title "We Are All Guilty." In it the fugitive leaders reported from hiding that society and the activists of Solidarity had failed to protect Father Popiełuszko. It condemned the workers of Warsaw for not having recognized the threat to his life and for not having protested effectively against earlier police abuses and crimes. The thin, chain-smoking young woman who edited *Tygodnik Mazowsze* spent a difficult week listening to complaints from readers who

felt the editorial was off target. One of my friends, another underground publisher, was outraged. I was with him as he told
her, "The police killed Father Popiełuszko. They worked for the
government. They were paid employees. They were members of
the party. Sure, we should have been more vigilant but no one
should confuse our possibly negligent attitude with seizing a man,
gagging him, beating him to death and then throwing him in the
river. Repentance and remorse are very Christian sentiments, but
everybody knows that some people are very much more guilty
than others." He was incensed that the underground leaders were
letting the government off the hook.

In response to such complaints, the next issue of the weekly
carried this indictment: "In the politics of Communism," it began,
"where everything relates to the struggle for power, the murder
of Father Popiełuszko had to be a part of this struggle, a conscious
provocation. In any case, this crime had to be an attempt to incite
unrest and spread terror on a massive scale." But it declared that
this should not exonerate Jaruzelski and that it was obscene for
him to posture as a victim of the crime.

I had often heard this argument in another context. Michnik,
for example, would repeatedly lecture me not to be taken in by
the "hardhead" versus "liberal" view of the party. "In Western
detective movies you have the good cop and the bad cop, but
they are both serving the same end," said Michnik. "The 'good
cop' warns you that if you don't deal with him, then he won't
be able to hold off the 'bad cop' who is rabid and psychotic. It is
the same thing here. Jaruzelski says if I go, oh boy, it will be
even worse, so you better just submit quietly. The good cop needs
the bad cop and vice versa and the whole thing was figured out
in the Kremlin to confuse innocent and well-meaning reporters
for *The New York Times* who still believe in fairy tales and think
that Communists can be tolerant."

The second editorial in the underground weekly had also declared that it was immaterial which party faction was behind the
killing. Had it not been for the remarkable escape of the single

witness, Chróstowski, the murder would have enabled the authorities to suppress the church and "pacify a persistently defiant society," and here again it did not matter whether the action was "directed in the Kremlin or by homegrown hardheads." The editorial insisted that since the government and party claimed a monopoly of power, they had a monopoly of responsibility. "It is perfidious for Jaruzelski to posture as the victim of the crime that was planned and executed by his police. It is perfidious of him to stand now in the same row as the church and society, posturing as a defender of justice. He wants again to be seen in the eyes of the world as he tried to be seen in December of 1981, as a lesser evil, a real patriot, a liberal, and the only alternative to the hardheads. The West may buy this but we cannot allow ourselves to be cheated, for once he has destroyed his rivals and gained what he could beg from the West, he will deal with us in quite another manner."

The confusion of Poles was not eased when almost a month later, the same weekly printed another editorial under the headline, "It Was Not a Political Provocation." This time *Tygodnik Mazowsze* declared that it was absurd to allege that Moscow or Moscow's agents were responsible for the murder. "No, all indications are that it was not a political attempt to provoke society but a police attempt to frighten the church and part of society," said the newspaper, in its continuing and varying attempts to explain the killing.

The week of Father Popiełuszko's funeral, six of the most prominent recently released detainees, including Kuroń, Wujec, and Onyszkiewicz, the Solidarity spokesman, issued an open letter accusing the Jaruzelski government of creating "the basis and climate" for the slaying. Meanwhile, Solidarity activists announced the formation of civil rights groups around the country which were to collate and publicize information about instances of police harassments and abuses. Edward Lipiński, the then ninety-four-year-old socialist economist and widely respected mainstay of KOR, sent his separate letter to Jaruzelski while issuing copies to foreign news agencies. "You bear responsibility for this cruel assassination. I feel it is my duty to tell you that this murder deprives you of the moral legitimacy to exercise power in the nation. It is high time you resigned." The appeal was heard by many Poles when the letter was broadcast by the Voice of America and the BBC.

Ever since news of the kidnapping became known, the government monitored public sentiment for signs of incendiary anger through its bureau of public opinion research. The bureau's poll takers and analysts were working overtime on their soundings at factories and schools. Having been stunned by the sudden rise of Solidarity, Jaruzelski set up this unit to make and evaluate opinion surveys. Polls taken soon after the body was found showed that almost all people were willing to suspend their responses while they waited for more information.

The funeral was potentially dangerous for the authorities. They were worried about its size. Even before the body was released to the Popiełuszko family by medical examiners, representatives from the office of religious affairs tried to convince Cardinal Glemp to arrange for the burial to take place at the priest's home village, a remote hamlet some distance from Białystok. From the government's point of view, this would be preferable because the crowds of mourners would be limited by the inaccessibility of the place. The world press would cover the funeral wherever it was held, but television shots showing a modest funeral in the countryside would be less damaging to the government than pictures of hundreds of thousands of people, some of whom might carry Solidarity signs in protest. In the rural area, where the crowd was certain to be smaller, it would be easier to confiscate such signs. Furthermore, over the years, a grave in the rural churchyard was less likely to attract large numbers of pilgrims than one in Warsaw.

Cardinal Glemp was sensitive to the government's concerns. Some bishops, however, thought the funeral had to be seen and felt by as many mourners as possible, and Poland's young priests and seminarians all felt that Popiełuszko's death required that he be buried with the greatest honor and attention that church and society could bestow. Their demand was that the burial take place at Warsaw's major cemetery. A requiem mass would be celebrated at St. Stanisław Kostka and then the crowd could follow the coffin in procession. The police were troubled by any procession; it could develop into a political demonstration.

The talks between church and police officials about the funeral were effectively ended by Maria Popiełuszko, the priest's mother. A spare woman, her face etched with years of outdoor work, she knelt before the primate and told him she wished her son to be buried at the Warsaw church where his work brought him to the attention of the nation as well as that of his killers. She said the shepherd should rest near his flock. Her plea provided him with whatever excuse he may have needed to insist that the funeral take place in the capital, at St. Stanisław Kostka.

Some government officials joined in the mourning but the director of the Warsaw steelworks refused to allow workers to keep a flag at half mast and school principals and other directors said that those who missed school or work on the day of the funeral would be penalized. U.S. Senator Edward M. Kennedy had hoped to come for the funeral, but the Polish embassy in Washington denied him a visa. At a diplomatic reception, a Polish journalist and party member who supported Jaruzelski angrily told me that the church would not be allowed to maintain Popiełuszko's grave as a shrine. With his voice rising, the man warned that if the Vatican moved to canonize Popiełuszko as a martyred saint, the government press would intensify its reporting of abuses by priests, portraying them as self-indulgent men living in luxurious circumstances. The authorities were particularly fearful of the cults and passions that sainthood could inspire and even five years after the murder, they had not returned the priest's garments to his family, presumably to prevent them from being treated as relics.

Such disdain on the part of party figures was difficult to fathom in light of the nation's profound grief. In my naïveté I even thought Jaruzelski or Kiszczak would come to the funeral to affirm the unity of all Poles in crisis. It seemed to me that an appearance of the generals, standing with bowed heads at the grave, could have symbolized a desire for reconciliation and shown the chivalrous grace that Poles intuitively appreciate. It would also have underscored the message that the authorities were seeking to project—that Popiełuszko and Jaruzelski were both victims. When I suggested this, Michnik told me—not for the first or last time— that I was an innocent idiot. First of all, he said, I had to understand that because the authorities were weak what they had to communicate most urgently was that they were strong. It is true, he said, that under the rules of literature and morality their appearance at the funeral would have suggested confidence, but because they were Polish Communists, they thought the gesture would show weakness. Secondly, even if the generals had no direct responsibility for the crime—a view he was unwilling to endorse—they still had to contend with those in the party that identified with the killers and those in Moscow who wanted the church to be chastised. Most important, Michnik said, the generals would have had to weigh the prospect of being publicly insulted by other mourners. What if the photographers and television crews from around the world were to show them retreating to their limousines as groups in the crowd chanted "murderers" or raised the slogans of Solidarity?

In any case, among the close to half a million people who gathered around the church on that sunny but cold Saturday, there were none who came as the government's representatives. Less than a mile away, however, thousands of police were deployed with paddy wagons and armored carriers. At the service, eulogies were given by doctors, actors, and workers. Karol Szadurski, one of the mill hands who had worked closely with Father Popiełuszko, touched most of the nation when he addressed the slain priest directly. "My friend, I believe all of Warsaw is here. Do you hear how the bells of freedom are tolling? Do you hear how our hearts are praying? Your ship carrying the hearts of

Solidarity sails on with more and more of us. Let the Lord accept you among Polish martyrs. For the fatherland you have suffered the most. You are already victorious with Christ. It is this that you wanted the most, Jerzy, our priest, farewell."

When Wałęsa took the microphone, he was greeted by a sea of "rabbit ears," the V sign of Solidarity and rhythmic cries of "Sol-i-dar-ność." The burly electrician spoke quickly and directly. "We bid farewell to you solemnly and with dignity and hope for a just social peace in our country. Rest in peace. Solidarity is alive, for you have given your life for it."

Characteristically, it was Cardinal Glemp who struck a note of compromise and conciliation. "Let the strangely latent instinct for self-preservation be awakened and let Poles of different social groups meet not crying over the coffin of a martyred priest, but at the table of dialogue to strive toward peace." The day passed in dignified calm. The ranks of police eventually dispersed to their encampments in the suburbs and at two o'clock in the morning the line of mourners waiting to kneel and pray before the priest's grave was still half a mile long. The memorial candles left by mourners glittered in a sidewalk galaxy.

The government, which had arrested the killers, now signaled that it would not permit its opponents, outside the party or inside the police, to exploit the case politically. The civic watchdog groups formed to monitor police abuses were warned by Urban that they faced penalties for encroaching on government monopolies. When unauthorized groups of demonstrators turned out to mark the November anniversary of Poland's birth in 1918, they were quickly and firmly dispersed by police in Warsaw and Gdańsk. The same thing happened more then a month later when men and women tried to mount marches to lament the imposition of martial law in 1981. Jaruzelski himself took over direct party responsibility for the ministry of the interior, replacing Milewski.

Little by little, Urban released details leading up to the murder. He reported that weeks before Popiełuszko was kidnapped, one of the policemen under arrest for his killing had tried to force the priest's car into a fatal accident by throwing a rock into its windshield as Popiełuszko sped home on a dark night. Another announcement revealed that high officials at the ministry of the interior had been suspended for neglect of duty.

Then, a month after the funeral, Urban reported that two senior investigators working on the case had been killed when their car crashed into a truck. The men had been among a group of army intelligence specialists brought in to investigate links between the suspects and others in the interior ministry. Traffic accidents were indeed a plague in a country of underpowered cars and poorly maintained roads. Throughout Poland, on every highway, tractors and horse-drawn carts stalled columns of impatient drivers. Still, the frequency of such accidents involving politically controversial figures aroused suspicion.

Was it just an accident? Or, was some cabal in the security apparatus striking back? Was this a warning to those in the government who wanted to prosecute the police? Would there be a coup? Perhaps even one that was backed by the Soviets?

As doubts spread, I was summoned to Interpress, the agency that dealt with foreign journalists, and told that I would be permitted to cover the trial of the four men accused of the priest's murder. The trial was to be the government's response.

Again, on a universal or Western scale, the decision to try the accused in the presence of the world press might seem slight. In fact this had never happened in any Communist state. Nowhere had security police charged with any serious crime stood in full view of their countrymen and foreign newsmen. In the past, offenses by policemen were dealt with in secret trials or unpublicized administrative decisions and those found guilty were indeed often sent abroad to serve as advisers or physical training teachers.

The decision to hold a more or less open trial attended by foreign newsmen could not have been made without Soviet approval. In pressing the case for a trial Jaruzelski presumably told the Soviets that it offered the only way to dispel or diminish

Polish suspicions of Moscow's involvement. It is almost certain that in conversations with the Soviets about the trial, the Poles gave assurances that the church would also come under attack in court. And indeed, during the trial it became obvious that such criticism had been prepared in advance. It was noticeable that the reporter for *Izvestia* only came to the courtroom on those days when the prosecution assailed the Catholic Church and its activist priests. And, as it turned out, I was the only American admitted to the trial.

Though unprecedented, the decision to permit full coverage of the trial extended policies that Urban had evolved since Solidarity's heyday. At that time, hundreds of Western reporters were in Poland interviewing opposition figures for newspapers, radio stations, and television. Their dispatches and broadcasts would quickly be translated into Polish for broadcast by the foreign language services on the Voice of America, BBC, and Radio France, among others. This information, heard in Poland, was widely considered much more credible than the censored news of the official media. A closed loop of information had been established which left out the government. Hard-line officials thought the best way to handle the situation would be to expel most Western newsmen, but party liberals pointed out that expulsions would surely bring economic retaliation. Some even claimed that the Western press was needed if only to make the Soviets aware that any invasion they might consider would be well-recorded and documented throughout the world.

Urban, who had twice in his life been blackballed and forbidden to publish for his unorthodox views, devised his own press strategy. He would hold weekly news conferences where he would offer some newsworthy items. The Western press would have to take account of them. He would not only force his way back into the news cycle but would take advantage of the integrity of the Western media to gain a forum for the views of the Polish government.

I was particularly aware of this ploy during the days I spent in the small well-guarded courtroom. Not only were the stories I was writing each day coming back to Poland on foreign shortwave stations but they were being cited by Polish government radio and television in tacit admission that *The New York Times* was a more believable organ than *Trybuna Ludu* or any official Polish source. Moreover, television would often show me taking notes at the trial as if to say that the presence of this American newsman guaranteed the honesty of the proceedings.

One small consequence of this was that my face became well known in Poland and for the next two and a half years I was often stopped by people who wanted to tell me what they thought about many things. The immediate and very major effect of the trial was that it completely dominated life and captivated every sober adult and adolescent and many drunks as well. For six weeks, from December 27 until February 7, when the defendants were sentenced, the attention of virtually every Pole was focused on the court in Toruń. Each night, families gathered to watch excerpts of the proceedings, and at work men and women debated testimony and analyzed the characters of the defendants, the judges, the prosecutors, and witnesses. The initial shock that any trial was taking place quickly gave way to unabashed absorption as the four defendants provided the nation with an unprecedented look at life in the secret police.

All four of the defendants, it turned out, were assigned to Department Four, which specialized in monitoring the activities of religious groups and religious leaders. The disclosures about their duties began when Lieutenant Leszek Pekała, the first witness, told how he and the two others who actually committed the murder had discussed plans to throw the priest from a bridge and at one point tried to stage a traffic accident in which Popiełuszko might burn to death. He described the tying up and beating of Father Popiełuszko and recalled that before the priest was knocked unconscious he had staggered from the trunk of the police car pleading, "Save me, save me! Spare my life, you people." Pekała, who was thirty-two years old, had been raised in a state home for children, and in the dock where he sat with his codefendants, he appeared very much an orphan. His voice was weak. His eyes were perpetually downcast. He cowered and hunched in gestures of submission. He seemed to have been the messenger boy of the group, happy that those he admired as his betters took notice of him and included him in their plans.

He was followed in his testimony by Waldemar Chmielewski, who spoke with a wrenching stammer that had appeared for the first time when the defendant had admitted his role to prosecutors. One of the many small points that were debated by millions of Poles who followed the trial concerned the stammer. Was it like Cain's scar, a proof of guilt, or had Chmielewski simulated it in an appeal for sympathy? Far from being a runt and a stray like Pekała, Chmielewski was born into the police caste. His father and his wife's father were secret policemen. They had engineered his appointment in the ministry of the interior so that his obligatory military service would be cut short and made easier. Once he came out of the army the family found a place for him with the police. Chmielewski's father, by then retired, turned to a former colleague, Colonel Adam Pietruszka, who was a supervisor in Department Four. Pietruszka, who had taken on the young man, was also the highest-ranking defendant in the murder trial. He had not been with the other three when they abducted and killed the priest, but he was with them in the dock, charged with having ordered the crime.

For Poles, however, the most riveting figure in the trial was Grzegorz Piotrowski, the thirty-seven-year-old captain who was Colonel Pietruszka's deputy and the man who directed Pekała and Chmielewski on their final mission. The tallest and best-dressed of the defendants, he mixed moments of contrition with swaggering displays of erudition and confidence. While his co-defendants cried or cringed, he recounted how hard he had worked at his job. Proudly he told of his university studies in mathematical philosophy. He admitted to the court that when he had agreed to harass and intimidate the priest, he was aware that this was an illegal activity, "but I believed a small evil was necessary to end a larger one."

While Piotrowski was testifying, he was studied intently by Andrzej Wajda, who was preparing to direct Dostoyevski's *Crime and Punishment* for the stage. For Wajda the Russian writer had created a figure, Raskolnikov, who prophetically ushered in our era of theoretical crimes. In the afternoons, Wajda read the novel over and over; in the evening he watched televised segments of the trial as Piotrowski rationalized his crime. The articulate, intelligent captain was evoking the rationale of bureaucracy and professionalism. He had, after all, been given a mission. For Wajda the parallels were unavoidable. "Who can kill and who cannot," said the director. "From Raskolnikov's justifications to Hitler's extermination camps to this fresh political murder, behind all is the same argument of authorized, permissible spilling of blood."

But, while Piotrowski certainly resembled Dostoyevski's character in some ways, he was no penurious student. He too was a second-generation member of the police elite. His father had been a secret policeman in Łódź in the days when the Moczar network had its center in that industrial city. His mother worked for the ministry of the interior as a secretary. He had vacationed at the ministry's special holiday camps and bought clothes at special ministry shops. He dressed well and drove an imported car. He had a beautiful wife and several mistresses. He knew that the camera was on him and he appeared to relish the attention. When Adam Pietruszka, his former superior and his codefendant, testified that as a Communist and a law official he could never have authorized a physical attack on a priest, Piotrowski smiled in contempt. Some things, he said in his own testimony, had no logical explanations. One could only understand them through experience.

He told the court that he had been under pressure to stop the priest for almost two years, that Pietruszka had led him to believe that this was a priority assignment, saying, "We have to undertake decisive action. We have to shake the priest so hard that it leads right up to a heart attack. We have to give them a last warning." One of the most compelling moments in his testimony was when, with his voice on the verge of rage, Captain Piotrowski described his frustration with the assignment a half-year before the murder. General Kiszczak had forced him to cancel his plans to raid the Popiełuszko apartment and prosecute the priest for contacts with underground activists. "Grown men cried," said the captain, describing the reaction in his office to the ministerial intervention. He said he learned that a delegation of bishops had complained to Kiszczak about police surveillance of Father Popiełuszko. As a result, months of police work were erased.

As I sat on the first row of benches, there flashed into my mind an image from the days—twenty-three years earlier—when I covered police in New York City. I remembered sitting in bars with policemen who fumed in similar frustration that a drug arrest they had spent weeks to arrange, at great risk, had been thrown out of court on some procedural technicality. "We had the whole operation closed down but now everything is down the toilet," a New York cop once told me. Piotrowski showed the same injured professionalism, except that in his case the criminal activity involved Popiełuszko's persistent involvement with human souls and moral choices.

Police sensibilities and police work were being revealed to the public as they never had before. There was the disclosure that some police had special passes that enabled them to go anywhere unquestioned. That they celebrated a raid with an expense-account lunch in a fancy hotel. There was the testimony that they stole license plates from parked cars to disguise their department vehicle, that for weeks before they kidnapped the priest, they filled the trunk of that car with the rocks eventually used to weigh down Popiełuszko's body. Still, after six weeks the basic question remained unanswered. Had there been an extensive conspiracy? If so, who was behind it?

At one point Piotrowski seemed about to reveal the extent of the plot. Yes, he had said, he had been assured that the orders to go after the priest had originated with senior people above Colonel Pietruszka. Yes, he was sure that the plan had the blessing of those at the top. But after a recess called by the judge the captain's tone was different. Yes, he said, he had thought there was authorization from senior officials. But "since my arrest I have seen that I never had any concrete proof that there was any 'head' who approved. The methods by which things were explained were very suggestive that there was a higher level of authorization and I am not a fool."

Chief Judge Artur Kujawa asked, "And there was no head?"

Piotrowski chose his words carefully. "Perhaps it is better that there was no head?"

Throughout the trial, the judge was in regular telephone contact with someone, presumably discussing points of law or politics, or media. Three television cameras were transmitting the entire trial live, though only chosen segments were shown on the nightly news. One technician told me that key members of the Central Committee were watching every second at party headquarters in Warsaw.

Full disclosure had not been made, but the guilt of the four policemen was affirmed by the judges. Kujawa read the sentences. Pekała was given fifteen years. Chmielewski, fourteen years. Pietruszka, the man who allegedly triggered the plot, received twenty-five years. He had denied everything and had spoken in outmoded slogans of Leninist cant, often thanking the party for his rise from railroad worker. Captain Piotrowski, who, like Pietruszka, could have received a life sentence, was also given twenty-five years.

That night in Łódź, the captain's police friends held a drunken dinner in his honor at which police revolvers were fired at the ceiling. The rambunctious salute to the convicted captain was a clear signal to Kiszczak that nests of discontent still remained as potential dangers. For two years after the trial, some leading members of this old-school police fraternity were quietly dismissed, others were isolated by being shifted to unimportant jobs. At the same time, those rank-and-file cops who had sympathies for Piotrowski and the others were placated with decisions made two years after the trial to cut the convicted men's sentences in half.

For Jaruzelski the trial was a major success. Through it he and Kiszczak strengthened their control of the party and the police. At the same time the trial marked their first successful parody of institutions once disparaged as bourgeois—in this case, an open trial and freer court reporting. Meanwhile, the trial also alerted whatever unindicted conspirators there might have been to disband or lie low. Within a few months all of Jaruzelski's open challengers from the hard-line wing were stripped of power. Milewski was ousted, Stefan Olszowski, once widely believed to be the favorite of the Soviets, was removed as foreign minister and later suspended from the party, allegedly for leaving his wife for a young woman with whom he had a child. Over the next few months, Kiszczak forced several hundred policemen out in a quiet but effective purge.

Concurrently, a bizarre and awkwardly symbiotic relationship was forming between the Solidarity opposition and Jaruzelski. They still clearly hated each other, but for the general the threats from a national resistance movement were proving preferable to the factional phantoms who conspired against him inside the party. The Bujaks, Kurońs, Michniks, and Wałęsas were outlaws, but they were setting the agenda. They were pushing the general in the only direction he could possibly go—toward reform, toward pluralism, toward an increasing sharing of power with non-Communists, even with anti-Communists. This direction was the only one that could end the West's economic isolation of a Polish government sorely in need of help. This was not the Communism with a human face that the revisionists and the Eurocommunists had so often talked about. No, it was more like Michnik's inspired description of Communism with some of its teeth knocked out. The West had linked economic assistance to evidence of expanded human rights. Some Western creditor countries were giving Poland better, perhaps even passing, marks for the amnesty and for the decision to try the police. The United States dropped its opposition to Poland's entry into the International Monetary Fund.

And then, scarcely a month after Popiełuszko's murderers were sentenced, Konstantin U. Chernenko died and was replaced by Mikhail S. Gorbachev. Jaruzelski was to find himself with even more room to maneuver.

ELEVEN

THE GHOSTS
OF JEWS

I FILED A STORY about "democratization" in which I quoted a sociologist named Wojciech Lamentowicz—a prolific critic of the government—as saying that in order to "water down" the impact of a de facto opposition, the government "had come up with a make-believe opposition." He said that the people who were being invited to serve in parliament as allegedly independent and noncommunist legislators were by and large tame and servile collaborators of the regime. The morning after the story appeared in New York, I was asked by Major Górnicki to come to his office at the council of ministers on "a matter of considerable importance." When I arrived, Jaruzelski's aide and confidant, dressed as usual in his officer's uniform, greeted me cordially and asked me if I knew how he had behaved in 1968, during the anti-Semitic campaign launched after the March events. I replied yes, that indeed he had told me about it in each of our previous three meetings.

In 1968 Górnicki had been living in New York as a foreign correspondent accredited to the United Nations. When he learned that fellow Polish newsmen were being dismissed from their jobs

167

because they were Jewish and that lists were being compiled of Jewish state employees or those who were suspected of having Jewish relatives, Górnicki became outraged. He wrote a letter to his editors and to party officials saying that civilized societies do not act in this way. As a result, he was ordered home, lost his privileged job, and was punitively called up as an army reservist.

He reminded me that when he was growing up in Warsaw as the son of a janitor he would often read to his illiterate grandmother from a rabidly anti-Semitic newspaper. That prewar church paper was edited by Father Maksymilian Kolbe, the priest, who in another sad Polish irony, was to join millions of Jews as a Nazi victim at Auschwitz. Father Kolbe changed his views during the war and he has been beatified as a martyr by Pope John Paul II for having volunteered to undergo execution in the place of another inmate. Górnicki, however, told me he has not forgiven the priest for the trash he read as a child. Later, the major said, he saw part of his Warsaw neighborhood sealed in to form the ghetto, where Jews were herded for eventual shipment to death camps. By his own account, he has since his adolescence always been a philo-Semite, working closely with Jews and admiring them as a creative people.

"Now, do you know how this Mr. Lamentowicz behaved in 1968?" he asked me. I said no, but that I was sure he would tell me. In clipped sentences, he said that Lamentowicz had been part of a group of young thugs who terrorized Jews in Łódź. He had gone into an old-age home in that city and driven an eighty-year-old Jewish Communist to suicide by spreading the story that the man lit ceremonial candles on Friday nights, when, in fact, the man had only lit candles during a power failure.

This "revelation," it turned out, was the reason for my being summoned. Górnicki wanted to establish for me, a Jew, that he, an official of the government, was a friend of the Jews, while a man I had quoted as a critic of the government allegedly had an anti-Semitic past.

Though it had no bearing on the story I wrote, out of curiosity

I went to Lamentowicz and asked him about the allegations. He was dumbfounded. He had not been in Łódź in 1968 and had belonged to no clubs or mobs, he said. He was at that time a graduate student at the University of Warsaw, where the campaign had begun.

In the spring of that year of worldwide student protests, a rumor swept through Warsaw University that as a result of criticism from the Soviet ambassador, a Warsaw theater was forced to suspend its production of Mickiewicz's epic *Forefather Eve*. According to the rumor the Soviets had found the characterization of a czarist agent in the play to have offensive contemporary overtones.

At the last performance of the play a group of students marched from the theater to place a wreath on the statue of Mickiewicz. Police and police goons were waiting for the students. Many of the young people were beaten but the only ones arrested were those identified in the newspapers as Jews. In fact there was nothing Jewish about the protest. Among those singled out were Michnik, Jan Lityński, Jan Gross, Barbara Toruńczyk, and Seweryn Blumsztajn, all of whom, incidentally, had until then given little thought to their Jewish origins. All were imprisoned and thrown out of the university in what are now referred to as the March events.

Their arrests were followed up by a press campaign that accused "Zionists" of forming a fifth column in Poland. Day by day the attack mounted. Moczar's journalists fabricated articles claiming that prominent Jewish officials had gleefully celebrated Israel's victory in the Six Day War in open contempt of the Communist line that supported the Arabs. Ministries, universities, and hospitals were asked to compile lists of staff people who were thought to be Jewish or have Jewish relatives, Jewish ancestors, or Jewish spouses. Thousands lost their posts and all but a handful of Poland's remaining Jews emigrated.

In the days after Michnik and the others were arrested, Lamentowicz had signed protest petitions calling for their release, and he took part in campus demonstrations in their behalf that were broken up by club-wielding goons. He admitted that in retrospect, he probably let hopes for his career keep him from speaking out and acting even more forcefully at the time, but he had never hounded or harassed Jews. I checked further with Michnik, Jan Lityński, and later with Seweryn Blumsztajn. All have remained active in opposition politics ever since they were first projected into national prominence during the March events. They all agreed that Lamentowicz had acted decently at the time and they added that since then he has been far more honorable than Górnicki, who according to Michnik was living proof that one "could have a positive attitude to Jews and still be a poor specimen of a human being."

To a foreigner, Major Górnicki's accusation of Lamentowicz and his own declaration of honor must seem very odd. A high official of the government was attempting to win my sympathies, and indeed the sympathetic understanding of the West, by asserting that he and the regime he represented were fond of Jews. And at the same time, he had sought to foist off a fabricated story alleging that a relatively obscure critic of the government had once bullied Jews. And all of this in a country where, in fact, there were virtually no Jews. It was bizarre and yet this some-of-my-best-friends-have-always-been-Jews attitude formed a significant cornerstone of Polish foreign policy, going far beyond a single attempt to influence a Jewish foreign correspondent.

There was, for example, the day when Edgar Bronfman, the president of the World Jewish Congress, arrived in Warsaw on a visit. It was 1986 and Jaruzelski was still being regarded as a pariah by Western leaders. Since martial law was declared they had been refusing invitations to Poland. Only Andreas Papandreou, the Greek political leader, had considered it appropriate to come on an official visit. In light of this ostracism, the presence of Bronfman, the Canadian whiskey magnate, was being treated almost like that of a head of state.

In the lavish, little-known government compound, where the Jewish leader and his associates were housed, I asked Bronfman how he had sized up Jaruzelski. They had talked of plans for the protection and maintenance of old Jewish cemeteries and the possibilities of reestablishing diplomatic links with Israel, which were severed after the Six Day War. "I'll tell you," said Bronfman, "he reminds me of just another Pole who really believes in the Protocols of the Elders of Zion, that we Jews control Western finance and the Western media, and you know, for our purposes, we did not want to entirely disabuse him of that notion."

Then one of Bronfman's aides asked me whether it was true that Solidarity was anti-Semitic. He said government officials had repeatedly charged that Solidarity embraced anti-Semitic views and positions. At its crudest level the political game being played was one in which a government of a country without Jews, which had in fact purged and expelled Jews eighteen years earlier, was asking representatives of Jewish organizations to encourage Western governments to be more sympathetic to the Jaruzelski regime. The Polish officials were also hoping to turn off Western enthusiasm for Solidarity by spreading the charge that the movement was riddled with anti-Semites. In conjunction with this aim, the Polish hosts were offering to trade an agreement for the care of Jewish graves in exchange for an endorsement of Jaruzelski or a castigation of Solidarity by Jewish groups.

There is an old Polish proverb that says, "In hard times, go to the Jew." It refers literally to Jewish pawnbrokers but it connotes the awareness that Jewish moneylenders have come to the rescue of Polish kings and nobles. Now Jaruzelski and Górnicki were also going to the Jews. To win them over they were depicting themselves as friends and admirers of Jews while they smeared their Solidarity opposition as bigots. And, in the meantime, the Jewish visitors ignored the ongoing struggle for democratic rights and seemed solely concerned with whether it was the government or Solidarity which was more sympathetic to Jews. By the time of the Bronfman visit, I had witnessed enough encounters between Poles and foreign Jews to know that they would make my head hurt and my heart ache.

I told the group that had come with Bronfman that probably no single sector in Poland was free of anti-Semitism and that unfortunately there were strains of the sentiment in the government and in the party, as well as in the opposition and the church. Within Solidarity, there had been a faction known as the Real Poles, which was largely defined by its contempt for Jews. Still, when one of the faction's leaders described a rival group in the movement as being led by "Jews and former Communists," he was forthrightly and publicly censured by Wałęsa and the union leadership.

After Wałęsa won the Nobel Peace Prize, he had repeatedly nominated Elie Wiesel for the award. A year after Wiesel won the honor, Wałęsa accompanied him on a highly visible and symbolic visit to the death camp at Auschwitz, where Wiesel had been confined as an inmate. Moreover, among Solidarity's most prominent and persecuted backers were many people who had suffered from government-sponsored anti-Semitism. These included men like Michnik, Lityński, and Blumsztajn, victims of the March events. Czesław Bielecki, the architect and underground publisher who staged his eleven-month hunger strike in jail, always demonstratively identified himself as a Jew in all his court documents. I told the visitors that while I was certain that Górnicki and Jaruzelski were not themselves anti-Semites, they had not, like Wałęsa, disassociated themselves from their own party's anti-Semitic past nor had they ever censured the party faction that continued to openly blame Jews for Poland's troubles. They have never condemned the 1968 campaign, which marked the last time that a European government targeted an entire Jewish population for systematic persecution. Nor has any official ever apologized for the events which were carried out by a government in which Jaruzelski had served as a minister. To this day there is a hard-core lunatic fringe in the party who belong to a club called Grunewald. Despite censorship they are permitted to publish a virulent monthly bulletin that attacks "masons," "internationalists," "cosmopolitans," "old Communists," "Trotskyites," and "Zionists" as well as just plain "Jews" for everything that has gone wrong in Poland and the world. It has a limited readership but it is openly offered for sale at Warsaw's army bookstore.

Grunewald had become quite marginal but even in mainstream Polish society it was people's attitudes toward Jews that more than anything else defined their orientations within every political camp, whether in the government, in the opposition, or in the church. Everywhere the range extended from xenophobic anti-Semitism to sympathy and respect for Jews. What could be called the "liberal" arc of the spectrum included people who felt that the 1968 campaign was shameful. Generally it embraced those who believed that in light of the Holocaust, Poles had a special responsibility to examine and recall Polish-Jewish relations over the centuries. Like Pope John Paul II, these people would cite the lines of Mickiewicz in which the poet, writing for the Polish nation, referred to "Israel, our Elder Brother." Some missed the cultural diversity that Poland had when there were masses of Jews. Such opinions indicated liberal tendencies much more than views on privatization of the economy or Western political values, or freer expression, or contempt for the Soviets, on which virtually everyone agreed, though some loudly and others privately.

And arrayed against these sensibilities was another body of widely held opinion shared by people who generally deplored the Holocaust, but who with the same breath would say that during the war, Poles acquitted themselves better than the other nations of Europe, having no leaders who collaborated at the official level. They would be particularly incensed by charges that Poles bore some special responsibility for the extermination of Jews. In general, many of these people preferred not to delve too deeply into 1968, or they simply categorized the events as Soviet provocations. That was also their response to the last real European pogrom, which took place in the city of Kielce in 1948. In it, an aroused crowd, apparently incited by police agents, killed more than sixty Jews. No Poles would openly applaud what happened at Kielce, but some would deplore the breast-beating of liberals, saying that the nation has nothing for which to apologize or atone. Poles, they declared, had been the first victims of the war. Their country had been invaded by the two most powerful totalitarian powers of the twentieth century. They had fought valorously in such faraway conflicts as the Battle of Britain and at Monte Cassino. Often, these views were coupled with expressions of dismay and anger that public opinion in the West has not been appropriately informed of the scale of Polish losses as it had been of the Nazis' extermination of Jews.

At some point, this generally acceptable and understandable sensibility oozed over into the recognizable slime of bigotry, approaching the views of Grunewald. Here the cogent beliefs were that Poland was better off without Jews, that Jews had introduced cosmopolitan Communism, that Jews were guilty of deicide, or that unlike Poles, who it was claimed fought back against Nazi oppression, Jews went to their deaths docilely.

Whatever the variety of attitudes, it was apparent that an overall preoccupation with Jews and Jewish themes was growing steadily during the years of my stay. The trauma of 1968 was wearing off. Through most of the seventies almost all discussions of the long intertwined history of Jews and Poles was silenced first by fiat, then by shame. In that time there was little writing about the relations of these two tragic peoples who had lived together and died together over many centuries. Historic memories were being obliterated. Historical inquiry had given way to prejudice and officially supported forgetfulness. Then, under the impact of the Solidarity upheavals, all official views and all official acts were challenged, among them the policies of 1968. As the cry for human rights was at last being heard, and suddenly made powerful, the earlier record of anti-Semitism stained the government and made its leaders vulnerable. Jewish issues and concerns began to be raised again. The intellectual Catholic press took a leading role. Even within the government itself there were people who genuinely hoped to redeem the shame of the March events as well as those who, with greater cynicism, felt that gestures to the memory of departed Jews might win the sympathy of people like Bronfman and thus gain economic help from abroad. The new interest was extensive and it often showed itself in surprising ways.

One summer day in 1986 I went to Gdańsk to interview Wałęsa. As we talked in his apartment he invited me to go with him that evening to a performance at the musical theater in nearby Gdynia where he was to be given the seat of honor in the front row. A capacity audience of fifteen hundred people filled the hall to hear a popular song and dance man named Andrzej Rosiewicz. It was not a political evening and the show was built around musical numbers and burlesque bits of sexy patter and double entendres. Scantily dressed chorus girls strutted and kicked to the beat of a heavy-handed drummer. About twenty minutes into the program, the lights dimmed and Rosiewicz put on a tight-fitting cap that resembled a yarmulke. He picked up his guitar and began singing a lament about a long-vanished village, Lumbartow, where the beer was better and the girls were sweeter and the neighbors friendlier than anywhere else. The song was unmistakably Jewish and when the singer came to the first deedle-deedle-deedle refrain, the audience suddenly burst into spontaneous applause, standing and clapping. Rosiewicz stopped singing, peered into the crowd and in the singsong of a Jewish dialect that now exists only in jokes, declared "Aha, so there are many of us here tonight." Again the crowd stood and applauded wildly.

I looked around. I felt I was the only Jew in the theater. Perhaps, I thought, the singer might also be Jewish, but I later learned he was not. Though he was using exaggerated dialect, there was nothing offensive in the act. On the contrary, it was meant as an evocation of something worthy that had disappeared. As for the people in the audience, it was obvious that they were enthusi-

astically and good-naturedly clapping for Jews, for the idea of
Jews, for the memory of Jews. But why? Real anti-Semitism had
fouled Polish history and honor and I knew that many Jews saw
Poland solely as a land of chronic and perpetual anti-Semitism
where their ancestors had forever been scorned and persecuted.
And yet here an ordinary crowd of pleasure seekers, not particularly intellectual or worldly, was spontaneously cheering a few
simulated echoes of vanished Jewish life.

I was startled by the display and I asked people seated near
me what they thought the clapping meant. Perhaps, one man
said, it reflected admiration for the courageous defiance of re-
fuseniks like Anatoly Sharansky in the Soviet Union; just as Jews
had once been perceived stereotypically as Communists and pro-
Soviet, they were now being stereotypically viewed as anti-
Communists and anti-Soviet. Another couple told me that they
considered the outburst as part of a fashion for Jews that stemmed
from a nostalgia for prewar Poland. "You know," the woman
said, "there is an opinion that then the cakes tasted better, the
streets were livelier, and one of the most noticeable differences
was that then, we had Jews." Wałęsa himself said he thought
that Polish society was growing increasingly sympathetic to Jews
as it realized how anti-Semitism was used as an instrument of
rule by the Communists.

All these responses seemed to be partly true. If I had asked
more people I was sure they would have supplied even more
explanations, touching on matters of shame, guilt, honor, and
pride. A few general conclusions, however, seemed obvious. The
attitudes of Poles toward Jews were complicated, deep, and ob-
sessional. It did not matter that there were hardly any actual Jews
left in the country. The ghosts of Jews were everywhere. Much
of the nation was compelled to recall its involvement with a
vanished people who had lived in their midst. Attitudes to Jews
and the Jewish question were moral barometers similar in a way
to American views of race relations. There is, of course, the huge
difference that in the United States there are millions of black

people playing an active role in the dramatic pursuit of justice and honor while in Poland today the Jews are more like Incas or Illyrians, though unlike these lapsed peoples they still stir deep passions among those who survived them.

A photographic exhibit about the scant remnants of Jewish life, put together by a Catholic Pole, drew constant crowds in Warsaw, Gdańsk, and Kraków. Performances of *Fiddler on the Roof* were always sold out. An appearance in Warsaw of the Israeli Philharmonic proved to be a cathartic event. When the musicians played both "Hatikvah" and the Polish national anthem, many in the hall were openly crying. In Kraków, a group of Polish students met in private homes and studied Hebrew. When Claude Lanzmann's remarkable film, *Shoah*, was released, a national debate ensued over whether the movie's portrayal of contemporary Poles making anti-Semitic comments was appropriate or not.

The major Catholic newspaper, *Tygodnik Powszechny*, used the controversy over the film to inspire a national debate over the question of how honorable, in fact, Poles had been in regard to the Jews who lived among them. To prime the discussion the newspaper printed a long piece by Jan Błoński, a literary critic. Błoński cited all the mitigating circumstances—that Christian Poles suffered enormously, that there were no Polish quislings, that there were numbers of gentiles who saved Jews, risking their own lives—but in the end he allied himself with the sentiment of a poem by Miłosz called "A Poor Pole Looks at the Ghetto," in which the poet linked passivity and guilt. Miłosz wrote:

> What am I going to say, me a Jew of the
> New Testament
> Who has been waiting for 2,000 years for
> Jesus to return?
> My broken body will betray me in His
> sight
> And he will include me, uncircumcised,
> among the accomplices of death

The article stimulated a profound reaction and for the next six weeks, the newspaper carried articles that ranged in tone from confessional and apologetic to defensive. Meetings sponsored by the influential Club of Catholic Intellectuals to discuss Polish-Jewish topics began to draw hundreds of people of all ages. University students began writing dissertations on Isaac Bashevis Singer, on the role of the Jew in Polish literature, even on Jewish tavern keepers. Both the official government press and the underground publications devoted more and more attention to Jewish contributions to Polish life. I even heard an intellectual argue drunkenly but eloquently that if Poles claimed Joseph Conrad as their own true native son, despite the fact that he wrote in English, then they should stake equal claim to Singer, the Polish-born novelist who writes in Yiddish.

In addition to Miłosz, other writers were drawing on the Polish-Jewish connection. Ernest Bryl, a popular playwright and poet, taught himself Yiddish. "George Bernard Shaw once said that there were three tragic nations: the Jews, the Irish, and the Poles, and I think he was right," said the writer, who was also learning Gaelic. Konwicki observed that the time was coming when men would be able to choose their culture and that he would then probably choose Jewish culture. As he envisioned it, his preferred circle would be that of people alienated from national life, freed from the rigorous burdens of patriotism, who sat in the prewar cafés of Europe making and extending culture. This half-ironic notion must have germinated, because some months later Konwicki began a novel in which he, the transparent hero of his own fiction, conjures up a Jewish grandfather. He told me that his mother had been born out of wedlock and that he has assumed that the man responsible was a Jew. From another perspective, Hannah Krall, who as a wartime foundling survived Jewish parents she never knew, wrote a moving novel called, *The Subtenant*. It concerns the recollections of a Jewish woman who had been hidden as a child by gentiles in a Warsaw apartment. In her surrealistic passages, her identity merges with that of the daughter of the people shielding her, but then it grows apart; she is only a subtenant. The Solidarity underground chose the book as the best novel of 1986. Another of its annual awards went to the photography exhibit about the remnants of Jewish life.

It was obvious that Jewish ghosts were stirring. There were many of them. Certainly, no one can stand among the barracks of Birkenau, as I often found myself doing, and not sense the passage of Jewish multitudes to the gas chambers. Virtually all Polish pupils visit such places on school trips. In the past their guides may not have always clearly distinguished between the specific sufferings of millions of Jews, of Gypsies, and the agonies of others. There were times when school trips omitted visits to the Jewish pavilion at the adjacent Auschwitz work camp and instead stressed the lives and deaths of those inmates and victims who wore red badges marking them as Communists. Even now, the guides may not always point out—may not be aware—that it was only Jewish and Gypsy children who were doomed for simply being or that it was only Jews and Gypsies who were brought in from other countries of Europe expressly to be destroyed. But, even with the best intentions, exclusive martyrology can give offense. In only remembering some, it is hard not to slight the memory of others. Six million Jews from all over Europe were killed. Three million of those were from Poland. In all, six million Polish citizens died in the war, one out of every six people in the country. Not all the schoolchildren who come on the buses to Birkenau and Majdanek and Treblinka comprehend these statistics the same way as do Jews visiting from the West, but they see the Jewish stars that were carved into the wooden barracks by people awaiting death. They see the display of confiscated prayer shawls and the bales of human hair shorn from victims, most of whom were Jewish. They quite likely may have never known a live Jew, but they are increasingly aware of the millions who died in their land.

There are two reasons for the growing dominion of Jewish ghosts in Poland. The more powerful is the simple but still incomprehensible fact and scale of genocide by the Nazis. More Jews were killed and tormented on Polish soil than anywhere else. But there is another explanation that is also hard to absorb, which is that Jews lived in Poland for a longer time and in greater numbers than anywhere else in their long history. Less than a century ago, 75 percent of all the European, or Ashkenazi, Jews in the world lived in the then trisected historical Polish commonwealth. On the eve of the Second World War, 10 percent of Poland's population was Jewish, a level that until the establishment of Israel was unmatched in any other country. All the Jewish religious national and cultural movements—Hasidism, Zionism, Bundism, Hebraism, and the rise of Yiddish literature—originated or grew largely in Poland, often in an awkward symbiosis with Poles. Only in Poland were there Jewish masses belonging to all levels of society, poor and rich, pious and secular, rural and urban, illiterate and highly educated. Despite anti-Semitism, or perhaps because of it, Polish Jews developed their own thick cultural cohesion.

In the nineteenth century, when new European nation-states were rising, the Poles failed to gain their own state. For 123 years, as their neighbors raised national flags and sang national hymns, they suffered the humiliation of statelessness, of partition and foreign domination, and in that time, among them, the Jews, even weaker, grew in population. Their number increased at a faster rate than that of their Catholic neighbors. Both peoples sustained themselves with romanticism and mirrored dreams of messianic fulfillment. Moreover, Jews, both as groups and as individuals, were more deeply involved in Polish history than they were in that of any other European state. The Polish middle class for long periods of time was significantly, even predominantly, Jewish. Some nationally revered writers were Jews, and Jews took part as Jews in Poland's uprisings. No one could write a history of Poland without significantly including the role of Jews and no one could write a history of the Jews without significantly writing about Poland, and this simply was not the case anywhere else with the exception of Israel, and, to a lesser extent, the contemporary United States.

In my bones I knew that there was much more that united Jews and Poles than separated them, but often it seemed this was my secret knowledge.

There were large numbers of Jews, particularly those now living in the West, who felt that Poles were uniquely and perpetually anti-Semitic. I have heard from some of them how their parents and grandparents experienced persecution and bigotry before the war. The women had been called *parszywe żydówki*, lousy Jewesses. Their fathers, as university students, had been forced by anti-Semitic toughs to sit on separate benches in the rear of lecture halls, or they were denied access to higher education by quotas. At times they were barred from certain occupations. Life was often hard and miserable for many Jews. Every right-wing and centrist prewar political party was in varying degrees anti-Semitic and in churches some priests openly preached against Jews.

From Catholic Poles, I would sometimes hear another set of facts and impressions. They would tell how before the war 40 percent of the houses in Warsaw were owned by Jews and how there used to be a children's street rhyme that said, "Poles live on the street, Jews live in brownstones." Sometimes the Poles would bridle defensively at what they felt was the blanket accusation of national anti-Semitism. With pride as well as injured self-esteem, the Poles would note that while England, France, and Spain threw Jews out, Poles welcomed them, gave them sanctuary and even privileges. If Poland was anti-Semitic, how was it possible that professions such as medicine and law had been virtually dominated by Jews, or that Polish Jews such as Artur Rubinstein could rise to international preeminence in their fields? My Catholic informants would note that for many Poles life was at least as hard and miserable as it was for many Jews. Some would note that Communism was in large measure brought to Poland by Jews and that in the postwar period Jews often served as police and prosecutors interrogating those suspected of

Home Army activity. They mentioned how some Jews, who in 1939 fled eastward from Hitler's invading armies, presented flowers to Soviet commissars who invaded eastern Poland two weeks later.

Often my head would literally ache from trying to sort out the contradictory subjective memories of Poles and Jews who all saw themselves as victimized peoples. Clearly the history of the entire seven-hundred-year relationship between Jews and Poles was viewed very differently by Jews and gentiles, with Poles generally stressing their hospitality to a people banished by others while Jews emphasized their persecution.

As these distinct views of the Jewish past in Poland moved forward to encompass the period of the Second World War, their disparity widened still further and confusion grew. Everyone who was over fifty years old had real memories of horror. At the very least, Poles had seen roundups or street executions of Jews and, in some cases, of Poles. They may have seen mass graves, walled-in ghettos, or trains carrying human, mostly but not exclusively Jewish, cargoes to concentration and death camps. They may have seen Poles taken to work battalions. Many remember hunger. With so many impressions and experiences it was hard to sort it out according to neat categories of guilt, honor, and valor.

For Jews, and for much of the world, the greatest tragedy of the war had been the Holocaust, in which the Jewish people very nearly perished and in which Jewish children, even those too young for any sins, were marked for death by the Nazis. For Poles, the greatest tragedy was that they lost their state, a loss that many of them feel has yet to be redeemed. The stress that each of these peoples placed on their own catastrophic losses often was viewed by the others as insensitivity to their pain. Understandably, Jews see only the awesome murder of their brethren. Often they ignored or belittled the sacrifices of the Poles, and even worse, assigned them leading roles as collaborators in the extermination of the Jews. On several occasions visiting Jews told me that the Germans built the camps in Poland because they could enlist Poles to build them. These assertions were illogical. The death camps were built in Poland because that is where the bulk of Jews lived. The Nazis wanted to limit the costs of transport. As for building the camps, it seemed clear that convict laborers, threatened with death and torture, built what they were told to build, whether they were Poles or Jews. Poles, who rightly view themselves as victims of the war, were often offended by such charges, often noting defensively that they had lost more people than any other group except the Jews.

Among the Poles there were righteous gentiles, people who, at a risk of death, hid and rescued Jews. In Poland, unlike in Western Europe, harboring Jews was punished by summary execution. That is cited sometimes by Poles explaining why there weren't more such people, and this is persuasive. Yet, taking up arms against the Germans was also punishable by death, and this did not prevent more than a hundred thousand Poles from joining the Warsaw uprising, and a whole nation took part in an underground conspiratorial state. Presumably there were many more people willing to run the risk of death for their idea of patriotism than for a sense of brotherhood with a still weaker group of people, who were considered different by many Poles and alien by some. It may be lamentable, but it also seems all too human.

Then there were also numbers of Poles who enriched themselves as *szmalcownicy*, which literally means people who render chicken fat, but which was used to describe blackmailers and extortionists who lived off Jews who were passing as Aryans outside the ghetto walls. They might force a man they suspected of being Jewish into a hallway to check if he was circumcised or not. If he was, they would extort money from him under threat of exposing him to the Nazis. Some took over the houses and properties of Jews. The underground Home Army had declared that the betrayal of Jews was punishable by death, but then that same Home Army had anti-Semitic units who would not accept Jews and who even published in underground papers articles envisioning a victorious Poland free of Jews.

The more I heard of wartime recollections, the harder clear judgments became. What was anyone to think of the man I knew who saved Jews but habitually still used anti-Semitic language, talking of kikes. Or, how is one to judge Zofia Kossak-Szczucka? Before the war she was an austerely pious Catholic whose view of Jews was that as many as possible should convert to Catholicism. She was similar to a good many other people who felt that Jews who did not convert should leave Poland for Palestine or wherever. But when German fascists began herding and killing Jews, she knew it was her duty, precisely as a Polish Catholic, to assist them. This prim, patrician woman, already in middle age, took mortal risks daily as she set up and maintained the Home Army's division to rescue and help Jews.

There was a farmer who told me that he had taken in a Jewish couple one morning and hidden them. That afternoon, when another two Jews came to him, he turned them over to the police. He said he did it to deflect attention from his farm and to save the first two who came to him. That couple survived the war under his care. At the ghetto hospital in Warsaw, a nineteen-year-old Jewish nurse was admired by the staff for the strength she showed in smothering newborn babies to spare their mothers the inevitable pain of watching the children die slow deaths of starvation. Heroes? Villains? I was not there.

As I tried to understand better what seemed so intolerable, I read a good deal of Holocaust literature, particularly the books of Primo Levi, a Jew, and Tadeusz Borowski, a gentile, who bore clear witness to life in Auschwitz. Both wrote what they saw and both killed themselves.

Though, invariably, it was the ghosts of Jews that haunted and fascinated, there were also some living Jews who remained in Poland as remnants. Exactly how many there were was a matter of definition. According to the Polish census there are about three thousand people who identify themselves as religious Jews. There are about the same number who, though not religious, belong to the government-sponsored Jewish cultural society, a group that publishes a Yiddish weekly and maintains a Jewish theater. The theater is a tourist attraction and hardly any of the actors are Jewish. They learn Yiddish as they might learn Greek.

Almost all of the religious and cultural Jews are old, remnants rather than survivors. They are people like the seventy-six-year-old Róża Jakubowicz, who is the guiding spirit and motherly caretaker of the Kraków Jewish community. It is she who maintains contact with Jewish organizations abroad and distributes matzo at Passover. It was she who asked American Jews to send the community a thirteen-year-old boy to celebrate his bar mitzvah with them. "Send us life," she had said, and when Eric Strom, a young man from Connecticut, stood and recited scripture at the synagogue that she had kept from becoming a dance hall, Mrs. Jakubowicz stood with the women in the upstairs balcony crying. She was remembering, she later said, how her own nephew was sent to Auschwitz, an hour away from Kraków, just before he was to have marked his own bar mitzvah. "I wanted Jews overseas to send us a bar mitzvah because we are the last of the Mohicans. We are the oldest people of any Jewish community, and I wanted to bring pleasure to my neighbors that after so much innocent blood was shed, a child could rise here to full Jewish manhood."

In addition to those who, like Mrs. Jakubowicz, designate themselves as religious and observant Jews and those who belong to the cultural organization claiming an essentially ethnic identity, there are others who have blood ties to Jews. Sometimes these people affirm the ties and sometimes they are pointed out by others. Urban, the government spokesman, and Solidarity figures like Michnik, Lityński, Bielecki, Modzelewski, and Geremek, who are known to be Jewish not because of any professed religious belief but because their parents were Jewish and because at some point in their lives they were persecuted as Jews by authorities and labeled as Jews by rivals. Once, at a demonstration, a woman who recognized me from televised news conferences told me that I should inform Urban that the nation was "tired of his Jewish answers." I asked her if she found my Jewish questions more to her liking. She reddened, stammered something about not realizing, and ran off.

There are also people whose fathers, grandfathers, or even great-grandfathers converted from Judaism, who are also still seen as somehow Jewish. One of my friends, Stanisław Krajewski, a mathematician, was in his childhood only vaguely aware of his Jewish ancestry. He is, in fact, the great-grandson of Adolf Warski, a militant socialist and labor union organizer who is claimed as one of the founding fathers of the traditions to which the Polish Communist party lays claim. Krajewski was at the University of Warsaw in 1968, when suddenly his Jewish background became the most important determinant of his life. In the wake of the March events, as many were driven to emigrate and others to denial or self-hatred, he decided to remain in Poland and to become as Jewish as possible, to proudly and publicly affirm that for which he was being attacked. With hardly anyone willing or able to teach him, he taught himself Hebrew from tattered English texts. He observes the Sabbath. His wife, who converted to Judaism, keeps a kosher home and heads a group that identifies and preserves Jewish cemeteries. He wants to live this life in Poland, mindful that there is honor in living as a Jew in a place where so many Jews lived and where so many died.

For those who had been at the center of the March events, the trauma remains profound. They had been singled out as Jews but they had been acting entirely as Poles. Along with other students, they were protesting against Soviet interference in Polish cultural life. Their most dramatic statement had been to defend the work of Mickiewicz, the national poet. Yet, in the furor that was engineered, they were attacked not as dissidents or "revisionists" but as Jews and allegedly aggressive Zionists. It was a paralyzing tactic. Some of these people may have understandably wanted to defend themselves by declaring that they were not acting as Jews, that they were in fact Poles, citizens seeking a better, freer Poland, or that it was only the logic of the Nazis' Nuremburg laws that could lead a government to brand or label others as belonging to this or that group. But twenty-five years after the war, such a disclaimer would have been an act of dishonor to the Jewish dead, to the aunts and uncles who had perished as Jews. One could hardly say, "Look, I don't feel particularly Jewish." And so they went to jail and kept their silence.

But, as the thousands of others who were fired from jobs and hounded at their schools left Poland, most of the students around Michnik who had been targeted to trigger the provocation tenaciously held on, insisting on their right to live in and participate in the life of their country and nation—Poland. They were jailed and then they were thrown out of the university and ordered to work in factories, but they refused to leave. It reversed the situation of the refusenik Russian Jews, who wanted only to emigrate. Friends of Michnik's father, who had settled in America, once offered the young man a full scholarship at any American university if he would live what they called a Jewish life. Michnik realized that within a Polish context to do this would necessarily diminish his Polishness and he turned it down, preferring to get up every morning at five and perform his forced labor on the assembly line of the Rosa Luxemburg light bulb factory.

I sympathized enormously with Michnik. Technically, we were both Jewish in the same way. Our parents were Jews and our aunts and uncles had died in Auschwitz. We were not religiously observant but we were aware and respectful of Jewish history. And yet, I, as an American, knew I could easily determine, affirm, or if I so chose, deny my Jewish heritage without risking much at all. For him, all such options were more painful, much more complicated. In Poland he had been punished for being a Jew and at the same time he was admonished for not being sufficiently Jewish.

And then there is Marek Edelman. Edelman is the most famous Jew in Poland. There are some who think that he is the last Jew in Poland, a gloriously raging, combative, complex, but fundamentally honest man. When Michnik faced trial in 1984, he, like all defendants, was permitted to invite a family member to the court. His own father had died a year earlier and he chose Edelman, who is not related, to come. Edelman's reputation and his authority inside and outside Poland rest on his having been one of the six leaders of the Warsaw ghetto uprising of 1943, a legitimate hero, and one of the few surviving symbols of that resistance. With angry waves of his hand and curses, he scorns the ennobling judgments, saying that heroism is too often a facile, meaningless category. Furiously he attacks those who try to celebrate him for what he did then, when as a young man he led a small group of badly armed men in a doomed and desperate battle against Nazi exterminators. And yet, alone, he still keeps taking bold stands, supporting the Solidarity opposition, attacking the government, attacking the Jews in Israel and the West who he feels want to mythologize the ghetto struggle, and scorning those Jews abroad who he claims have forgotten *rachmones*, the Yiddish word for compassion. Meanwhile he says all that he really wants to do is to go on working as a cardiologist.

"What do you know?" he would ask me whenever I visited him in his apartment in Łódź. "What do any of you know? You are a goy." Then he would smile and pour me a drink and rub his hand over mine and tell me my wife was like a "Modigliani," a woman he considered to be an ideal of Jewish beauty. Often there would be foreign visitors in the two-room apartment. "The sons of SS men from Germany, they want absolution, they want to know what it was like," he once told me, explaining the presence of two young men who were leaving as I arrived. I asked him what he told them. "I gave them absolution. They are good boys, but they cannot understand, you cannot understand." He was right.

When he was twenty-two years old, and the ghetto was being evacuated and the last trainloads of human cargo were being prepared for shipment to the killing camps, he with five others led an uprising of a few score men and women. Their desperate defiance was aimed not at victory but, as he has explained so

188

often, simply to determine the time, the place, and the means of their own deaths. From April 18 to May 7, the poorly armed band held off the Germans, and then most of the leaders who survived killed themselves. Edelman escaped through the sewers to the Aryan side. For his efforts he has been lionized. There is a Polish Catholic playwright, Jerzy Sitó, who is trying to write about the ghetto uprising as the most Polish of all Polish insurrections, because it was the most hopeless and impossible.

Once at my house, Sitó tried to interview Edelman about the uprisings, and Edelman tried to cooperate. Again he tried to tell it, hating the judgments of valor and bravery that he knew his listeners were making. He answered the questions and he kept drinking vodka and he kept trying, as he had for forty years, to keep victims from being turned into heroes, to keep real deaths from being made into legends and to keep others from ascribing false meanings to murder. "The world has decided that it is more noble to die with a gun in your hand than to go silently to your death, but that is not true," he has said.

Before the uprising, Edelman had worked in the ghetto hospital as a helper and a messenger. Each day he would go to the *Umschlagplatz* and watch the trains loaded with Jews going to Treblinka. His job was to look for doctors or nurses who could be useful for the hospital. He had a piece of paper with which he could have people taken off the trains. He watched hundreds of thousands go to their deaths while he had the paper in his pocket. He was disciplined and stern, rescuing only those who could assist the work of the hospital. He ignored the pleas of mothers who wanted him to take their children. After the uprising was crushed, when the other uprising leaders shot themselves, he said no, he would try to live. As he was going through the sewers, he forced back a young woman, a prostitute, who was behind him. He could not look after her and she would endanger his own chances. What does all this have to do with heroism? he asks again and again.

And yet, of course, the antihero is a hero, perhaps not for what he did in 1943, but certainly for what he has done since. The others have gone, to America, to Israel, but he stays. Immediately after the war, when the young who survived gorged themselves and made love in compensation he went to medical school. He said his studies did not keep him from eating and drinking and chasing women. Later, after the anti-Semitic campaign of 1968, his wife, also a doctor, took their children to France when it appeared that their son would be kept from higher studies. But he stayed, bearing witness, working as a doctor. Before the war, he had been a Bundist, a follower of a Socialist political party that sought to maintain some Jewish cultural and social autonomy within a pluralistic Poland. The Bundists opposed the prewar Zionists who saw emigration to Palestine as the only hope for Jews. In a sense, Edelman has remained true to his childhood ideals. He is the last Bundist and sometimes his anger at Israeli policies places him under attack from Jews abroad. Some in the West have explained his decision to remain in Poland as an act of masochism. One American Jewish magazine wrote, indecently I thought, that his decision is the result of his having been orphaned early in life and that he is psychologically incapable of tearing himself away. I asked him once why he stayed. He told me simply, "Somebody has to watch the graves."

Soon after the war, he wrote a booklet about the ghetto battle. Then he withdrew to his medical work, enduring occasional anti-Semitic attacks to head the cardiology unit at the hospital where he worked. He talked to those who came to see him, but he did not seek a wider audience. In 1977, Hannah Krall, then a journalist with the weekly *Polityka*, published a long interview with him entitled "Shielding the Flame." It came out as a book and became a best-seller. In a sense, that interview broke the spell of 1968. Jewish issues and themes started to surface. His stature inside Poland grew and in 1983, when the state sought to commemorate the fortieth anniversary of the uprising, he was to be the guest of honor. In its way, the government may have been seeking to atone for 1968. It may have also been trying honestly to mark a historic moment. And, it may have wanted to gain some goodwill in the West for its gesture. In any case, Marek Edelman, who is a witness to incommunicable truths, wrote to General Jaruzelski that in the wake of martial law, in light of so many people being detained, he would not be able to join in the government festivities.

Instead, he worked with people in the opposition. He offered medical treatment to those coming out of jail and to the families of workers fired because of union activity. He attended Michnik's trial. He would curse his friends and get drunk and say that they, too, did not understand anything. In April of 1988, the government again held anniversary observances for the ghetto uprising, inviting dignitaries from Israel, from the West. Again Edelman would have nothing to do with the ceremonies. The people who came from Israel and from the international Jewish organizations were embarrassed. He was the only surviving uprising leader and he was shunning the celebration. Worse, he was criticizing Israeli policies, reflecting Bundist views that before the war, before the Holocaust, had been utterable—that Jews need not emigrate to Palestine, that they had the right to establish their culture, their autonomy, in those countries where they lived. Genocide had nullified this once tenable proposition.

As the government of Poland prepared to welcome the foreign Jewish visitors with specially produced cookbooks of Polish Jewish cuisine and kosher food in the dollar shops, Edelman organized his own commemoration, unveiling a plaque in memory of two prominent Bundist leaders, Henryk Erlich and Wiktor Alter. They had been members of the Warsaw Municipal Council before the war and in 1941, as they fled eastward from the Nazis, they were murdered in the Soviet Union. They were killed because they were overheard criticizing the Soviet invasion of their country, Poland, at the start of the war. They died as Polish patriots and that is what Edelman wanted to emphasize. Thousands of

Poles, including all the major figures of the opposition movement, came to the unofficial gathering that coincided with the government's ghetto commemoration. As in the government-sponsored festivities, there were elements of exploitation and bad taste. For example, youths from the highly nationalistic opposition group, Konfederacja Polski Niepodlester (Confederation of Independent Poland) or KPN, whose leaders once wrote anti-Semitic articles, turned out in yarmulkes carrying banners in Hebrew. But in general, the tone was dignified and Edelman felt he had made his point that Jews as Jews had their own claims to Poland's history. Wałęsa called the ghetto uprising the most Polish of insurrections. He spoke plainly. "As a son of this land, I ask that the painful excesses of anti-Semitism be forgiven us."

About a year earlier, reporters for an underground publication called *Czas*, or *Time*, came to see Edelman. The interviewers asked him what it meant to be Jewish in Poland. Dr. Marek Edelman, one of the last Jews, and certainly the most audacious Jew, in Poland, replied: "It means to be with the weak, not to be with the authorities because the authorities here always beat Jews, and today it is Solidarity that is being beaten. Today Bujak is beaten by the authorities. I think that no matter who it is that is being beaten, you have to be with them. You have to offer him your apartment and you have to hide him in your basement. You must not be afraid, and you have to be against those who beat. And this is the only thing that makes one Jewish today. Polish Jewry has disappeared. This great Jewish culture vanished and it will not return." At that point the interviewer interjected to say that it had not completely disappeared, that memories remained. Edelman again grew angry with his uncomprehending audience. "No, don't speak nonsense. Nothing has remained. There are memories and literature but nothing remains when it cannot create anything further."

Of course, he is right. Jews are not there to do anything. They are not a social problem in Poland anymore. They are not a force that has to be dealt with politically or economically. But they lived in Poland so long and their deaths were so awesome that they remain a profound historical presence in a country that lives through its history. They remain to prick consciences and validate policies and claims to honor. They torment and they need to be appeased. They are unavoidable. Like ghosts.

TWELVE

MAY DAY, MAY DAY, MAY DAY

IT WAS FOUR o'clock in the morning on the last day of April in 1986 and in one of the high-rise developments around Łódź. The woman I will call Anna Klos had already been up for half an hour. A band of pale sky was forming behind the smokestacks that could be seen through the curtains of the living room where her husband slept noisily. Anna had been introduced to me by mutual friends. I had wanted to see how ordinary workers spent the May Day holiday, which celebrates both the working class and the Communist state. In the years since Solidarity was outlawed the ruling party's claims to the day had been contested by members of the underground union who either infiltrated official parades with their banners or tried to mount their own demonstrations. I wanted to spend the time in Łódź because as a textile center it has had the longest and most developed proletarian tradition in Poland. I chose to spend it with a woman because Łódź is a woman's city, dominated by those who tend the clanking looms. Finally, I suppose, I was drawn to Łódź because my parents both came from there and because my father's first political activities involved participation in what were then illegal May Day celebrations in the 1920s.

Anna invited me into her home, but, unlike almost everyone else who agreed to see me, she asked that I not use her name in anything I might write. "I know I should stand up and not be afraid," she had said, "but some of my friends have already been given 'wolf tickets,' and if I am fired, who will take care of the children?" The children, a boy of twelve and a girl of seventeen, were sleeping in the other room of the small apartment when I arrived. Anna, a heavyset woman, had made them sandwiches to take to school and she was feeding the tropical fish in three tanks. Raising fish, she whispered, was her husband's idea. He planned to sell the young and use the profits to buy his vodka. She said that like most plans in this country it was not working very well. He was spending much more on vodka than the fish were bringing in. "He drinks, you know," she said looking to the bedroom. The per capita consumption of pure spirit in Łódź is eleven liters per person a year, making it the fourth–heaviest drinking region in Poland, and Poland has the highest per capita alcohol consumption in the world. "Most mornings he forgets to feed the fish, so I do it." The elevator was not working. As we walked down from the seventh-floor apartment, there were a number of other women on the stairwell, walking quickly but trying to keep their footfalls as quiet as possible. The apartment walls of the eight-year-old building do not keep out sounds very well.

Like bees leaving their hives, the women streamed out of the apartment house and followed each other to the tram stop. They looked quite similar. Many, like Anna, were plump with the blue veins of their legs as visible as tattoos. They wore cotton dresses buttoned down the front and thin sweaters. When they spoke, you could see that many had missing teeth. The stream thickened, fed by each of the houses. There were just a few men among the hundreds of women. Łódź, a textile city, is maintained by the hard labor of quickly aging women. According to statistics, 51 percent of the work force in Łódź is female, 5 percent above the national average, but the breakdown at the tram stop was far more lopsided. This was probably because of the early hour. Only the textile industry works on three shifts a day and it is primarily the women who have to be at their looms by five o'clock.

Textile production had built Łódź from a nondescript village that in 1809 had only 770 people into the country's second largest city, all in less than a hundred years. Now some of the plants organized by long-vanished merchants still make up the industrial heart of the city, but the tempo of their production is faltering. And, as in the earlier periods, the whole operation depends upon armies of women like Anna Klos who spend their days running back and forth before frames of clattering machinery. They work in noisy rooms at high temperature and high humidity for wages that are about 15 to 20 percent lower than the national average, and every week their shifts change. More than 70 percent of the women who have worked for ten years or more have suffered hearing loss. The rates for respiratory and circulatory diseases are among the highest in the technological world. Ecologically, things are even worse in the areas around Katowice, the industrial belt in the southwest. There, in the town of Bytom, houses and streets are at times swallowed up as the unreinforced shafts of played-out mines give way to suck in the surface. There are areas there where a single cubic meter of ordinary earth will yield enough lead to make a toy soldier. People are warned not to eat vegetables grown in the region. Łódź is better, though the ponds are polluted and the air is gritty.

As Anna waited for the tram to take her to her factory in the center of the city, she met a friend with whom she chatted. Just two days earlier, the official Polish media had confirmed that there had been an increase in radioactivity over parts of Poland as a result of the nuclear accident that had just taken place at Chernobyl. Unlike the Soviets, the Polish authorities were issuing iodine tablets to all schoolchildren as prophylaxis against possible thyroid contamination, but at the same time they were insisting that there was no danger to health as a result of the accident in the Ukrainian facility that lay some three hundred miles east of Łódź.

Anna Klos's friend asked whether anyone was supposed to believe the government's assurances. "Remember when the stores began selling fish with blue bugs in them and the health officials said that the bugs were nutritious?" Anna Klos said that they should watch to see if sparrows fell dead out of the sky over the next few weeks. Her friend said she was particularly worried because her daughter was pregnant. "Maybe she should abort," the friend said. "Heaven forbid," said Anna and she crossed herself.

The women pushed their way onto the tram and continued their conversation. "Are you going to have to march in the parade?" Anna's friend asked. Anna instinctively looked around to see if anyone was paying attention. "I don't know yet, they only asked us once so far. How about you?" The friend sighed and said that at her factory the foremen had told them that they had to gather at eight the next morning to take part in official May Day celebrations and that attendance would be taken. "It looks like I will have to march, but I will not smile." The friend jumped off to change trams.

Anna recalled for me the most memorable May Day of her life. "It was in 1981, when we had Solidarity. No one dared ask us to march. I slept late. It was the only real workers' holiday of my life."

It took forty minutes for Anna to get to the gates of the Marchlewski textile plant at the center of the city. It is a huge complex of red brick buildings behind a well-guarded fence. Originally it had been the Poznański factory, founded around the middle of the nineteenth century by a Hasidic Jewish peddler. From the outside, which is all I was ever able to see of it, the plant was imposing, even beautiful, a monument to an industrial age conceived in steam, risk, and exploitation. In another country it would probably have been turned into studios for artists, restaurants, luxury apartments, malls, and theaters. In Łódź the old factories remain what they were from the beginning, clanking mangles of cloth and cancerous sweatshops that forged despair along with some hope.

Before the turn of the century, the factories had grown rich on the cloth they sent to the Russian market. Along with several German families, some other Jews, and a few Poles, the Poznańskis had grown fabulously and conspicuously wealthy, and even today it is their old palaces that house the city's museums and its music conservatory and art school. Once, when an architect asked the Poznański patriarch whether he should design a particular mansion in Greek, Gothic, Venetian, or Baroque style, he replied, "I am rich enough for you to design it in all styles." The same man once wrote to the czar saying that he planned to pave a ballroom with gold rubles and wanted to know which side of the coins should be facing up, the one with the czar's profile or the one with the imperial eagle. The czar is said to have responded that the coins could be embedded in the floor only if they were placed on their edges.

There was a good deal of excess and lavish vulgarity in this Manchester of the East. But in comparison to the poorly built white elephants of more contemporary Communist style, the remnants of that earlier era stand out like Venetian palaces in a trailer park. Socialist grandeur, modeled on the wedding-cake towers of Moscow, places a high value on open places meant not for walking but for marching, for tanks passing in review. In Łódź, this reached its apogee in the dark gray radio building, the tallest, most massive structure, which like its counterpart in Warsaw, the Palace of Culture, literally frightens people. Often, in both cities, I would notice pedestrians who would cross streets simply to escape from the looming shadows cast by these buildings. By contrast, in Łódź, at least, the most attractive parks, the best-looking streets, the most imposing factories, and the best houses are still those constructed by capitalist exploiters. In many of the factories, the owners built their first imposing homes on the factory grounds, living next to the plants to be around if anything went wrong. The robber barons obviously exploited industrial labor, and there were often violent strikes. Still, there were some paternalistic capitalists who provided worker housing with larger, better rooms than today's standard, and back then, they built churches, chapels, and clinics for the workers.

I pointed this out to Anna, admittedly to provoke her. "Well, you know the old joke," she said. "Under capitalism, man exploits man, but under Communism, it is the other way around."

Anna pointed out the corner where I should meet her when her shift ended, and went in through the gates with thousands of others.

I used the time to wander. Łódź lies seventy miles from Warsaw and with a population of 1.3 million, it is the second largest city in the country after the capital. There are very few foreign tourists; occasionally some Germans and some Western Jews come to look for signs of their ancestors. In general, foreign visitors much prefer the rebuilt Gothic streets of Gdańsk or the baroque squares of Kraków, places that evoke misty half-legendary times. In Kraków, a visitor can easily imagine robed students at a medieval university accosting each other in Latin. In Gdańsk, the canals and gabled houses are picturesque reminders of an early mercantile age. But in Łódź, what is easiest to imagine is open sewers, and rats, and people scratching in Dickensian squalor with Dickensian energy. I like the place as I like Liverpool and Calcutta, other cities of nervous scuffling, though in Łódź the attraction was compounded by the tugs of family. Long before I met Anna, I would drive to Łódź from Warsaw just to walk streets I had heard about from my parents, and I would always end up at the house where my mother was born, which my grandfather had built next to his door and window factory. It is now the social welfare office for trolley workers.

Unlike Warsaw, Łódź was not physically destroyed during the war, when the Nazis annexed it and renamed it Litzmanstadt. It has no quaint rebuilt areas evoking nostalgia for imagined glory of better times. There has not been much investment in Łódź and the old houses, both slums and mansions, remain, though streets and sites once named for the capitalist barons now bear the names of Communists. Anna Klos's factory is now named for Julian Marchlewski, a man who in 1920 was dispatched from Moscow by Lenin to set up a puppet Communist government in Poland. That plan was thwarted by Piłsudski's military genius, which led to the rout of the invading Red Army. There is no street in Łódź named for Piłsudski but at a house where the marshal clandestinely published *Robotnik*, or *The Worker*, in the years before Poland's rebirth, there is a small plaque. Flowers and memorial candles are left there daily. In her apartment, Anna Klos has a picture of Piłsudski along with those of Pope John Paul II and Lech Wałęsa.

After I left Anna, I stopped in at the Hebrew congregation office on the second floor of an old tenement. It was near the house where the pianist Artur Rubinstein was born. Ber Minc, the eighty-year-old head of the congregation, spends his days planning the construction of a new House of the Dead at the cemetery, so that the three or four dozen members of the community will have suitable funerals. There is a wonderful novel by I. J. Singer, Isaac Bashevis Singer's brother, called *The Brothers Ashkenazi*, which documents the growth of Łódź and its Jews. It begins with the patriarch of the family worrying about acquiring a cemetery and a burial house to bury Jews who were beginning to settle in what was then still a village. In the intervening 150 years, Łódź grew to have more Jews than any other city in the world except Warsaw and New York, and in area, the cemetery that the Jews secured was the largest in Europe. Now, at Yom Kippur, those Jews of Łódź who still pray barely fill a normal-sized classroom.

I asked Minc if there were any records that could help me find the site of my grandparents' graves. Minc, who is blind, asked me my mother's maiden name. When I replied "Tyller," he asked whether she was of the same Tyllers who used to live at 11 Tramway Street. I was surprised that he knew the place and felt an irrational surge of vanity. Minc told me that he had once worked as a carpenter for my grandfather, whom I never knew. He gave me the addresses of buildings that my grandfather had built, which included the county courthouse, some schools, parks, and apartment houses. I went off to look at the houses, and though I did not like the sandy-colored courthouse, the others pleased me.

Inside the shabby courtyards of my grandfather's houses, clumps of forsythia bloomed over smelly, overflowing dumpsters. There was much more street life here than in Warsaw, or at least it was more concentrated with people scurrying on the main shopping street that stretched between the old factories. On the broader streets men in cherry pickers were attaching red flags to lampposts for the May Day holiday.

I ran into two street urchins, Tomek and Henryk, whom I knew from my previous visits, when I paid them to wash my car. Normally they spent their days hanging around the Grand Hotel on Piotrkowska, the main street, washing the cars of tourists. Tomek was an undersized thirteen-year-old, while Henryk was a tougher fourteen. They were funny, aggressive kids with the kind of street cunning I often saw in New York but never in Warsaw. They earned twice as much as their mothers, who worked on looms. They spent a good part of their pay in the hotel Pewex shop, buying imported candy, cigarettes, and Western clothes. They also paid off the hotel doorman to chase off older drunks who wanted to compete with them. The doorman made more money from the whores who began gathering at the Grand in early afternoon. They were the best-dressed women in Łódź. Tomek said these women had *klasa*, and he clearly distinguished them from other whores at cheaper hotels, whose clients were mostly visitors from Islamic countries. As in Warsaw these were often disparaged with racist disdain as "arabesques." Tomek said that most of the whores earned fifty times a worker's salary while Henryk said he thought the amount was more like a hundred times as much.

The boys told me that they had spent the early morning shin-
nying up lampposts and stealing red flags. "We took about eighty
of them and threw them down a sewer," said the younger boy.
When I asked them why, they said they didn't like the Russians.
They said they did not think of the flag stealing as a political act
and they said that they really had no allegiance to Solidarity. "It's
fun," said Henryk, who several months later was to be sent to a
reform school on the complaint of a German tourist. As Tomek
later explained it to me, the tourist had stiffed him and he re-
venged himself by washing the man's Mercedes with gritty sand.
As for snatching the flags, "We see who can get the most of them
and sometimes we run from the police," said Henryk.

I bought them a Coca-Cola and as we talked that morning I
was pricked again by a sense of irony. Sixty-seven years earlier,
my father had been suspended from high school for cutting
classes to join an illegal May Day procession where illicit red flags
were unfurled. At least in part he had done it in the belief that
the ideals of socialism would free hopeless young men from lives
of drudgery. Nearly seven decades later, Tomek and Henryk
knew better than that. But, they were still using the flag for rites
and tests of manhood.

When Anna Klos came out of the plant shortly after 1:00 P.M.,
I was waiting for her. I asked her if she wanted to stop for lunch
somewhere, but she said that if she was to get any shopping
done before the holiday she would have to start immediately or
everything would be gone. She said that during her time at work
none of the supervisors had talked to her about showing up for
the May Day parade and she was relieved. Since she did not
have to march, she planned to attend a special church service
celebrating the union movement and the city's proletarian traditions. She said she kept waiting for one of the foremen to say
something but in fact she had not heard a word from anyone
since she entered the gates. "Like always these days, I worked
at the machines until eight, when I had a break of fifteen minutes.
No one talked to me. Not the supervisors and not the other

workers. During the time of Solidarity, we would all talk to each other, or even sing, but now no one talks or asks how you are."

Like almost all Polish women, Anna never leaves her house without a string shopping bag in case she finds something that has been "thrown" on the market, like Cuban oranges. Such occasions arise most frequently just before holidays.

As we waited in the first of what were to be many lines, she answered my questions about her family's budget. Because her husband drinks, it was hard to count on his fifteen-thousand-złoty-a-month salary as a factory janitor. Sometimes he would help with the rent or buy a present for the children but mostly he spent his earnings entirely on his needs. Basically, the family lived on the nineteen thousand złotys she was now making each month. Actually, she had been making twenty-four thousand złotys, but five thousand had come in the form of a bonus for a record of low absenteeism over the previous decade. She lost that when she tore the cartilage in her left knee, slipping on the wet floor as she shuttled between spinning threads of her loom. She had argued with the foreman that since her month-long immobilization was work-related she should not have lost the bonus, but she was overruled.

"If we had a real union, they could never have gotten away with that. But you know what was the worst part? No one, not one of my co-workers, came to me to offer their sympathies. That is how scared everyone has become. Two years ago we visited in each others' homes and sang together and now, once again, we are quiet and frightened like stupid sheep."

A year before, their apartment had cost them six hundred złotys a month, but it had risen to sixteen hundred and was scheduled to go up again. Electricity and gas had also gone up sharply. They had had the apartment for six years after waiting fifteen. Before they moved into it, Anna Klos, who had lived her whole life in Łódź, had never lived anywhere with indoor plumbing. Some foods, such as bread and milk, were low in price, but others were remarkably high. A week earlier, two pounds of tomatoes were selling for three thousand złotys, or twice her rent. As the weather grew warmer tomatoes fell to fifteen hundred złotys. Her family had not eaten tomatoes since they were plentiful and inexpensive ten months earlier. She said she spent a good deal of money on the children's clothes and fees for summer camp. Their biggest expenses had been for a black-and-white television set they bought four years earlier, a washing machine, and a bicycle for their son. Anna Klos had not been to the movies for twenty-five years and she had never gone on a holiday vacation. "I never wanted to go on a bus with people who would be guided about like cattle."

Sometimes during her time off she would spend a few days with an aged aunt who still lived in the farm community from which her parents had migrated after the war. Like many of today's workers, they were peasants who had come to work in the factories. In terms of frayed propaganda these were the people who were being transformed from backward farmers into the vanguard legions of the industrial proletariat.

There was a time when Anna believed that her work was a mission. That was when she first started at the factory twenty-two years ago as a seventeen-year-old. "I thought that, yes, we were building a new Poland and that I would be sharing both the hardships and the rewards." Enthusiasm and hopes withered quickly and when at the age of twenty-four a foreman told her he would nominate her for party membership, she politely declined. From her account I calculated her age as thirty-nine, and it surprised me. From her bearing and appearance I had assumed that she was older than I was, and I realized that in speaking to her, I had adopted a tone I reserved for older people. It turned out she was ten years younger.

The problem with shopping, she explained to me as we inched along, was not only money. For example, here we were on the last day of the month and she had used up all the allotments specified on her family's ration cards. Her children's cards, which she showed me, permit her to buy four pounds of boneless meat or better sausage a month for each child and an additional pound and a half of meat with bones. As manual workers, she and her husband are each allowed to buy a pound more of meat. All the boxes on the card had been punched like a train ticket by the butchers. Some people, she said, were able to stagger their purchases over the month, but she rarely succeeded, and since her rations were used up, she would have to buy some meat *na lewo*, or on the left side. She thought this could be done easier without my tagging along. When she returned forty minutes later with two scrawny chickens, she explained that she had paid more than twice the officially marked price of 240 złotys per kilo. Sometimes, on special occasions, she says, her farm relatives come into town and bring her sausages, veal, and eggs, for which she pays. Before May Day as I accompanied her she bought bread, milk, and butter. The only vegetable she bought was a cabbage. "The cabbage is from last year so it is unlikely to have Chernobyl dust on it."

As we headed away from the market stalls, she spotted some Cuban oranges. We waited for almost an hour so she could buy six of the oranges. Her son, she said, loved oranges. Did he like bananas too? I asked. She said he had never had one.

All together the shopping, which she said was virtually a daily ritual, had taken almost three hours. The ride home was another hour. Once again the trams were filled with women, all of them carrying their string baskets. I thought I recognized some of them from the morning ride, but they did look alike.

During a meeting I had with Solidarity leaders in Łódź, it was suggested to me that the length of the shopping lines was probably determined by the police. Jerzy Dwusz, a man who had been fired from his machinist's job because of his Solidarity union activities, speculated that there was probably a police unit that conducted studies to establish just how long the shopping lines should be in order to sap the women's last reserves of energy and keep them from organizing protests or taking to the streets. He was one of eight former Solidarity officers who had agreed to meet me at a café attached to the Łódź theater.

"I know such a view might seem paranoid elsewhere," said another man, Jerzy Kropiwnicki, a fired university lecturer whose prison diary had recently been published by the underground press. "But this is Łódź, a woman's city, a proletarian city. The symbols are all here and the police know that given the preeminence of the cult of Mary, the cult of the Polish Mother, the image of striking women would be too powerful."

Another union official explained further. "If you think the image of Wałęsa at the Lenin shipyards hurt Communism, can you imagine what it would mean to have textile working mothers march at the same factories where Cossacks shot workers in 1905?" He said that in 1977, the women of Łódź did stage a march against hunger to protest food price increases. Within hours, the government capitulated and rolled back the increase. "The authorities know how incendiary this place could be if the women were to act, so they keep them on the shortest possible leash, with work and with shopping."

"This whole city is a police laboratory," said Andrzej Słowik, a former bus driver and a former national bicycle racing champion who was the head of Solidarity in Łódź, just as Bujak was in Warsaw. "Look around you," he said in a voice meant to carry. "That man reading the paper there is a policeman and so is that one at the next table and the two over there by the door. There must be seven or eight of them who are watching us and there are probably four or five others outside. This is normal."

None of the people he had identified took notice, though they must have heard. After his release from martial-law detention, Słowik had spurned Bujak's invitation to join him in the underground. Słowik's style was to parade himself publicly. He liked to meet his associates with the police watching and he and they were constantly in the courts seeking to regain their jobs and to act as if Solidarity were still a force. He had his differences with

Bujak and Wałęsa, and he openly spoke of his frustrations that Łódź was both too close and too far from Warsaw to be taken as seriously as it should. "We do not visit embassies and very few foreign journalists come here and, anyway, here in Łódź there are just these women," he said sarcastically.

Among the eight who met with me, there was only one woman, and she did not say anything. She was the wife of one of the old union leaders. Even when Solidarity was in full bloom, there were no women in the leadership. Why was that? I asked. "Ah, we talk about this all the time," said Grzegorz Pałka, a fired teacher. "I suppose the women are vulnerable. The men drink or play at politics and the women have to be home to wash and feed the children. The party once had a woman first secretary here but then she disappeared and it was just men. You have to take account of Polish and Catholic traditions, too. We honor women as mothers and we kiss their hands, but they are still encouraged to be timid, to keep to family concerns." This pattern was true all over Poland. Anna Walentynowicz, the welder at the Gdańsk shipyard whose dismissal touched off the strike in which Solidarity was born, was honored for a while as the godmother of the union movement. But after she argued with Wałęsa she was phased out of even a symbolic role. Zosia Kuratowska, a physician, was an influential but informal Solidarity adviser. Other women, such as Barbara Labuda, Joanna Sczesna, and Ewa Kulik, were highly respected for their work within the movement but they were all intellectuals and their names, not generally known, did not figure in any of the national structures.

I thought of the conversation when I ate dinner with the Klos family on the eve of May Day. For one thing, I hoped that none of the neighbors had reported my presence and that Anna would not be threatened or reprimanded for letting me see how she lived. We watched the seven o'clock news, which contained more assurances about Chernobyl. Anna's husband, a bony, short man, was slightly unsteady on his feet as he cleared scum from his fish tanks. He asked me about life in America. How many hours did you have to work for a car? Was it true that there were people who could never find work and were unemployed forever? Like most Poles, he imagined unemployment to be a horror of want and misery. I tried to turn the conversation to the May Day holiday and asked if any of the Klos family felt pride in being workers, or if they had any associations with the traditions of the city.

"My people were peasants and in my heart I am a peasant," said the husband. "When I dream of paradise it is green with fields and not gray with smoke." The daughter said that she had read *The Promised Land*, a classic of Polish literature in which Stanisław Reymont describes the growth of Łódź as a spreading malignancy. The author, who won the Nobel Prize for literature in 1924, deplored the dehumanization of the industrial age. I asked her if she thought that life was much worse in that steam-driven era than now.

"It had to be worse then, didn't it?" she said. "Now people live longer and everybody reads and we have movies and television."

Her father ate his soup silently but her mother said, "You would think different if you worked in the plants, which I hope you will never have to do."

The girl, an attractive young woman, said she had not done well enough at school to get into a university, but she was already working after school at a beauty parlor and she would like to study cosmetology. Anyway, she would be getting married in a few months and she hoped her husband would be transferred to the Gdańsk area. Later, after the girl washed the dishes and left, her mother told me that she was engaged to a young policeman. "I am sad that he is a policeman, but he is a nice boy and I hope he will be good for her. She should leave here, though I will miss her." I asked about her son. He had taken his bicycle downstairs to ride with friends. "He does not work hard at school and I am afraid he will end up in the plants. I do not want him to be a policeman. Maybe he will be lucky and after technical school he will go abroad, to West Germany, to America." By this time, the husband had made his excuses and left to meet some friends. His hand was unsteady as I shook it. Darkness was filtering down outside as Anna Klos and I drank a last glass of tea in the room where she had risen seventeen hours earlier.

As I said good-bye I realized what had been a long day for me was an ordinary one for her.

I was awakened the next morning by the crowds of people assembling on the street below my window to join in the parade. In the previous years the route had been confined to a well-policed area around party headquarters where groups of people were admitted only after their credentials were checked. The idea was to keep out people who might try to subvert or ridicule the representations of the Communists that they reflected the hopes of the working class. That is what happened the year before in Warsaw when a small group that left St. Stanisław Kostka Church in Warsaw quickly swelled into a happy crowd of fifteen thousand. Police units moved in to chase the marchers, who were being cheered on by people at every window. In Gdańsk, Wałęsa had caused a sensation by working his way into the official parade and unfurling a Solidarity banner. Photographers caught the Nobel Prize–winning electrician as he was rushed out of the workers' march by policemen. In Łódź, Słowik and his fellow Solidarity leaders had their own alternate parades that drew thousands, but by 1986, the authorities were confident that hundreds of thousands would march in the official parade and that few would dare to seize the holiday from the state and party.

The calculations seemed correct. At ten o'clock, tens of thousands were marching past the reviewing stands underneath banners of their factories and schools. Foreign students from the university marched under placards of their countries: MONGOLIA, IRAQ, AFGHANISTAN, ANGOLA, YEMEN. When the marchers came to the platform where mostly unidentifiable officials stood, they turned eyes right to look into the posters of Marx and Lenin.

I entered the Church of the Holiest Name of Jesus, just a few streets away from the marchers' route, and sat across the aisle from Anna Klos. She nodded to me and I to her, but mindful that I was probably being watched, we did not speak. The church was not full. In his sermon, Father Stefan Mięcznikowski was praising the sacrifices of working men and women in Łódź over years of foreign occupation and homegrown oppression. The Jesuit priest has run the church as a center of free discussion, providing sanctuary for visiting speakers, theatrical groups, and artists.

At the end of the service the parishioners filed out and some of us walked up two streets toward a plaque that had been put up in 1980 to honor those who had been killed in the Baltic food-price riots. There were several dozen policemen with batons walking in small circles. The parishioners stopped across the street from the plaque, as if waiting for someone to do something. The police kept walking.

I was with a young man who had been in KOR, organized unions, been in prison, and had quarreled with Słowik. His father had been a foreman in the factories, as had his grandfather. Now he was a blacklisted engineer with a six-year-old daughter who lived in a single room without running water inside. He had described his life for me under what he called the *soc*, pronounced sotz, a slang term for the Polish brand of socialism. For him, he had said, the *soc* was simply that one room where his daughter bathed in a tin receptacle with water that he carried in from the pump in the courtyard.

For minutes we waited on the curb in silence with several dozen others. My friend said, "Sometimes I feel that I am an actor in a play I did not write. I am impelled to recite the lines and I wonder where I learned them. When we were arrested after martial law we were all interrogated and we were given a choice, to remain in prison or get one-way visas and emigrate to the West. I said it was dishonorable to leave, but yesterday my daughter asked me why we don't have a bathtub and I know we will never have our own apartment unless the system changes. I ask myself will the day come that my daughter will hate me for the choice I made in jail?"

A few old people walked across the street and placed flowers at the plaque and moved on. The police walked with them. Then five old people knelt at the plaque. Five policemen hurried over and told them to leave. Four of those praying rose, but the fifth, a very thin woman with gray hair tied back in a bun, stayed where she was. Two policemen picked her up forcibly and began carrying her to a paddy wagon. Several people emerged from the crowd, urging the policemen to let her go. "She is overwrought, she is nervous, and she has a history of mental disorders," said a woman, trying to placate the police. The police appeared to hesitate as the crowd called to them. Then the old woman they were carrying said in a clear voice, "I am not ill. You are murderers. You killed workers and I want to pray for them." The police were joined by several others and they rushed the woman to the paddy wagon. My friend shook his head and wandered off in one direction while I went off in another. Across the street, I could see Anna Klos also walking off. Her holiday was almost over.

THIRTEEN

ON THE FARM

Visits from people I did not know were fairly common and sometimes annoying interruptions. The callers usually explained that they had seen me on the televised news conferences that Urban, the government spokesman, held every Tuesday for the foreign press. These sessions were taped and aired late in the evening, drawing more viewers than any other regular program. Urban's confrontational tone in these conferences both attracted and appalled viewers, like a display of terriers chasing rats in a barrel. There, seated in front of the representatives of the world press, the short bald defender of a beleaguered government would pugnaciously take on the great powers. Angered at France, he would announce that Polish high schools might no longer find it necessary to teach the French language. Or, offended by a U.S. State Department comment supporting Polish workers, he would announce a drive to collect sleeping bags from Poles to send to homeless New Yorkers. He once said that if he ever caught his wife wearing a Solidarity badge he would beat her. At every meeting, he would accuse foreign newsmen of alleged misstatements or exaggerations. Quite obviously, he enjoyed the resentment he knew he provoked. Characteristically, his office published transcripts of the news conferences under the title "Duels."

Though it was Urban who usually had the last word in these confrontations, some foreign reporters would reply in kind. The hotter the exchanges, the more we were liked by the public. After all, the bureau of public opinion research once determined that the spokesman was the single most unpopular figure in Poland, "strongly abhorred by 44 percent" of the nation, and his occasional attacks on me served as advertisements that raised my stock with ordinary viewers.

Once after Michnik celebrated his fortieth birthday with a party held in my large home, the spokesman sneered that I had served "charity soup" for a dissident. Another time, television viewers were shown a piglike caricature of Urban and told I had given the insulting statuette to him. In fact, I had bought the figure in a state store in Kraków and when I mentioned its purchase to Urban, he asked me for it, saying he had a shelf of such images. I gave him the pig and he turned that private gesture into a news item that implied that an American newsman had ridiculed him. I was angered but most Poles thought it was wonderful that I gave him a pig. For a while I was cheered wherever I went. One construction worker came down from a ladder to kiss me on both cheeks. Airline stewardesses congratulated me as did shop attendants and school children.

Because of such notoriety, my mail and my visitors increased. Some just wanted to tell me about their lives. Some would describe conditions in the prisons they had recently left, while others would ask for help in finding relatives abroad. Some thought I could help them obtain visas from Western governments or passports from Polish authorities. One man wanted me to introduce him to Jane Fonda. Some were probably police plants, such as the man who wanted to sell me information he said he had gained at a Soviet camp where he said he was being trained as a terrorist along with people from Latin America. Most callers felt themselves aggrieved. They claimed they had been everywhere, to party officials, to the courts, to the watchdog agencies, to the local press, and they were coming to me as the last resort.

That is what drew Stanisław Kułaczkowski to my office from the farm hamlet of Kozlowka. The thirty-eight-year-old heavily muscled farm entrepreneur put on his newest suit and traveled for four hours by bus to enlist my help in his efforts to make and sell cinder blocks. A big, gruff and, as I was to learn, remarkably stubborn man, Kułaczkowski arrived at my house one spring day and told me he had seen me on television quite often and that he was sure I was the man who could help him. Before I could say anything, he pulled sheaves of documents out of his briefcase. "You just ask Urban why I can't make cinder blocks," he demanded, thrusting letter after letter under my nose. Patiently I told him that I was a foreign correspondent trying to explain what was happening in Poland to readers in America. I said I was certain that his case was valid, that he had been victimized just as he said, but that unfortunately our office was not an agency for social work. Perhaps, I said, he might want to contact a lawyer, or some sympathetic clergyman, or people in the opposition.

I was firm but I was no match for Kułaczkowski. There is a stereotype not limited to Poland of the cunning, stubborn peasant: the countryman who is not at all the bumpkin he appears to be. Kułaczkowski is like that. His Tartar eyes narrow as he sizes up a newcomer. He laughs a lot and talks quickly and loud. Before he made his way to my office he had worked his way into offices of deputy ministers, police inspectors, local party secretaries. "If you won't ask Urban about what is preventing me from making cinder blocks, at least come to my farm and see for yourself. Write about it."

I told him I would think about it, but that I was very busy at the moment examining the dim prospects for economic reform. As I saw him out, I formally asked him to call if anything new happened.

Actually, I had for some time been trying to come to grips with conditions in the Polish countryside. Every once in a while I would be seated next to someone at a dinner party who would upbraid me and the entire Western press for our concentration on a few urban centers. Poland, they would say, is not just the Poland of Warsaw, Kraków, and Gdańsk, not just the Poland of the pope, Kuroń, Michnik, Wałęsa, Bujak, and the general. They would tell me that the peasantry fed the nation, that they always fed the nation. Some of my dinner partners claimed that Polish peasants could feed all of Europe if not for misguided government policies. One woman insisted that the basic conservatism of peasants had proven to be a bulwark against Communism, even when those peasants rushed to the cities to work in factories. All of these critics said that Westerners rarely realized just how recently Poland had become urbanized. Before the war more than 70 percent of the population lived on farms or in villages, and the soul and heart of Poland, they would tell me, is still in the countryside.

I suspected this was true. Within the church, for instance, there was a clear and strong rural influence, with Cardinal Glemp reflecting old peasant values of piety that held city life, merchants, and modernity to be suspect. Furthermore, people like Wałęsa, Bujak, and dozens of Solidarity's other worker leaders were the sons of peasants, not long removed from poor farms. The migration to the cities had happened too quickly to be understood or adequately recorded. The process had churned up remarkable people like Henryk Wujec, one of the founders of the Committee to Defend Workers (KOR), who from prison had been offered exile to the Riviera. He had grown up after the war on a very remote and desolate farm with no electricity or plumbing and yet he became a distinguished physicist. Wujec once described for me how he walked two miles to a community school and how he read stories to close relatives who were illiterate. While at Warsaw University he spent his summers helping with the harvest and reading about quantum theory by moonlight. I thought of Wujec as the man who had traveled the longest distance in the shortest time, but there were many who made similar journeys.

Still, whenever I would go to the countryside to seek its qualities, I could not penetrate very far. I was most often met either by intellectual city folk who had purchased old farmhouses as vacation homes, or by old men with lined faces who eyed me suspiciously, confining their talk to the weather.

I thought I had seen the last of Kułaczkowski when I walked him to my door. Three days later he called and said he had been questioned by the police about coming to see me. A week after that he called and said that he chased away two drunken policemen who had come to his farm waving guns and threatening him and his family. After that he used to drop in regularly to tell me of his conflicts and harassments, always with a lot of jokes and a bit of swagger. He would lay the reams of documents on my desk and pick up the case where he had left off. It was often hard to follow, zigging and zagging into a labyrinth of hearings and petitions. Of course, he won. I started visiting him at his farm and through him I learned of rural life and its complaints.

The story of Kułaczkowski's struggle began when he read about a government regulation, part of an early reform package, that exempts private farmers from paying taxes on farm-based businesses designed to aid agriculture. "From the point of view of society around here, that was a smart regulation," he said as we drank tea in the kitchen of his neat three-room house. "The farmers are very good, the land is so-so. The farmers need everything, tractors, fertilizers, pipes, wells, tires. The idea was that if we could produce some of these things ourselves, there would be a ready market and it would lead to more effective use of the land." The regulation struck Kułaczkowski as just the thing that could enable him to start a business.

He was one of those who in terms of the prevailing ideology of the fifties and sixties was being promoted from peasant to the status of industrial proletarian. Life in the cities, forging the technological frontier, was supposed to be the most socially useful life, one that was glorified in the official literature and the official films. Farms, particularly privately held farms, were suspect. He had been born into a peasant family in a house just a few miles from where he now lived. He went to vocational school and when he was eighteen he left for Gdynia to work as a welder at the Paris Commune shipyard next to the Lenin works at Gdańsk. There, Kułaczkowski spent years living in a worker hostel while he labored six and seven days a week on ships for the Soviet fleet. He had been there for two years when the protest and killings of 1970 took place.

Along with his friends and fellow workers he marched to demand a rollback of food price increases. He had been there when the police opened fire on the crowd and he was with the mob when it surged on the Central Committee building, setting it ablaze. He was running with the other workers across the railway bridge leading to the Lenin shipyard when again the police fired and people next to him fell dead. "I remember running into a courtyard. Ten feet behind me a policeman fired. I heard the bullet pass my head." After the protests were crushed, he was detained, questioned, and then kept under house arrest before being summoned back to work in a worse job in a different part of the yard. He worked for nine more years, until his left forearm was crushed by a falling metal bar.

"When I recovered, I realized I had had enough. At the same time, my uncle and aunt, who lived here, were in their nineties. They needed someone to look after them and to tend to the farm." That was in the late seventies just before the Solidarity strikes. By that time the alleged supremacy of the industrial proletariat was, like so many points of ideology, under attack. Officially, peasants had attained coequal status under the law with workers. Government policies were changed and the state buyers began paying higher prices for agricultural yields to give farmers income parity with industrial workers. Then the government claimed that farm incomes were growing faster than those of workers. Actually in some cases farm life had become so harsh that many farmers were abandoning fields. And as this was happening economists inside and outside the government were questioning old decisions that had concentrated investments on heavy industries. Some suggested that Poland would have been better off if it had built its economic development on a base of agriculture and food industries as Hungary had done, rather than on coal, steel, and chemicals.

Kułaczkowski's "farm," as he called it, is just a three-acre field behind the small house, off a major road. It lies two hundred yards from an old castle that is being restored as a museum. Potatoes grow in the field and there is a hothouse, built with the savings that Kułaczkowski sent back from the shipyard. It is used to raise and cure tobacco. "A family cannot live on this," he said gesturing to his holding. He had married while in Gdynia and he and his wife have a son in elementary school. When he first returned home to become what is known as a worker-peasant, he took a job driving a truck for an industrial concern in Lublin. On weekends and evenings he would help tend the farm. His wife became a bookkeeper at a depot where farm machinery was stored and maintained to be leased to farmers at harvest time. Within a year of his arrival, the old uncle and aunt died and Kułaczkowski took over the farm.

It was the time of Solidarity's rise. One of the first strikes had been in Lublin. "It started over a hamburger," Kułaczkowski told me. At the Lublin plant where light trucks were assembled, the canteen had suddenly tripled the price of a subsidized lunch. The workers struck over the issue. "That was before the strikes in Warsaw or Gdańsk, but after that things quieted down in this part of the country. There was not much activity. There is not as much industry here. We are closer to the Russian border and maybe that has something to do with it. There was no chapter of Rural Solidarity," he said referring to the union of private farmers that mushroomed under Solidarity's umbrella. "Most of the farmers here are old, in their seventies. Their sons have gone to the cities. The old ones are cunning and careful. They have seen many changes; the Russians came, the Nazis came. The Ukrainian gangs were here. One of my grandfathers was killed as a Pole by the Ukrainian gangs and the other one was a Ukrainian who died over there." He gestured vaguely toward the Soviet border. "Anyway, these old peasants are not going to rush into anything. They will watch things for a while before they declare themselves."

He, too, had been cautious. But when he read about the tax exemption, he decided to take a chance. Just as he had changed his status from peasant to worker and then to peasant-worker, he would now seek to become a peasant-entrepreneur, the local cinder block baron. The social engineers in Warsaw were favoring just such demographic shifts. Shortly before, he stopped drinking. "I realized that if I was going to achieve anything, I had to gain control over myself. I stopped smoking, too." He began to dress well and he started reading newspapers carefully. "I was excited about cinder blocks. The farmers around here have money. They have saved it and they have nothing to spend it on. I realized if I could mold cinder blocks and concrete forms to make cisterns and wells, I would do quite well. Everybody needs such things around here. I studied cinder block operations. What I would need would be forms to mold the block, a flatbed truck, cement, sand, and concrete. When I made my plans known, the local authorities said it was a fine idea."

When he was ready he dropped in at the farmers' cooperative bank in the next village where Kułaczkowski had been a member since he returned from Gdynia. It is the only place where local people can get credit. The bank is very small, just a one-room office on one of the village's two streets. Jadwiga Chadaj, who is the director of the bank, looks out of place in the bare room. She is a very stylish woman. Her blond hair is fashionably coiffed. She wears heavy gold jewelry on her neck and wrists and she drives to work in an imported car. When Kułaczkowski first reviewed his plans with her, she was, he says, very helpful in offering credit, approving a loan in two parts. "After I received the first installment and bought the truck, she informed me that I was to deliver a truckload of cinder blocks to a house she was building. I did it. I'm not a fool. I knew that here one hand washes the other. I consider that normal. But then two weeks later she stopped me and told me deliver a load of crushed marble to another house she was building for her son. I said, "No, I am sorry, I am proceeding completely within the law. I do not need to give gifts or pay bribes." He remembers that the banker told him he would be sorry, that he had made a very costly decision.

"Three days later two policemen came and asked me to pay what they called a voluntary fine. They were drunk and I told them to get stuffed."

Then it began. He was summoned to the local office of the tax bureau and told that, regardless of the regulation exempting farm businesses from taxation, he would have to pay. His appeals to the ministries in Warsaw were supported, but when he returned from the capital, he was arrested and held for several days in Lublin. The young men he had hired to serve as apprentices were visited by the police and told not to report for work. Reluctantly, they stopped coming. The banker refused to issue the second part of the loan that had earlier been approved. This money was slated to rebuild the dilapidated shed where Kułaczkowski was making his blocks. The roof had literally fallen in. When he went to the finance ministry in Warsaw to obtain a written judgment that the bank had acted unfairly, Mrs. Chadaj had Kułaczkowski charged with slander in a Lublin court. The court found him guilty but before his sentence could be confirmed, it was swept aside in an amnesty. Still, he was periodically detained for two days. He was taken for questioning from his Christmas dinner. Then the local authorities garnisheed his wife's salary. His son's school principal called the parents in and warned them that the boy's grades could be affected by the father's conflict with local officials.

"It was all one cabal. The banker, the police, the tax authorities, and the courts were all tied in together." he said. "At first they were after me, just for the bribes. They wanted to suck my blood. But later, as more and more people saw that I was fighting back, they realized they had to crush me to save face and power." It got worse. His allotment of cement was cut back and he had to buy supplies on the black market. He had been paying back his original loan on schedule, but the bank began proceedings to have Kułaczkowski thrown out of the cooperative bank. If that happened, there was no other bank he could legally use. Through it all, he kept working in the shed without a roof, in the snow, making the cinder blocks and the cistern forms as best he could.

It was at about this juncture that Kułaczkowski came to see me and drew me into his life and struggle. On one of my first visits to his home, he took me on a tour, pointing out several community projects financed by the bank and sponsored by local officials that stood unused and unneeded. These included warehouses, stables, milk storage facilities, and meeting halls. "It is a scandal. None of it was ever used. They got them approved and they all got rich building these things. They know I know about these things and that I am not afraid to criticize them. Mrs. Chadaj was a candidate in local elections but after I started turning up to ask questions, they took her off the ballot."

During that same visit we drove past the local collective farm. In contrast to the private farms, which made do mostly with horses, the state farms had many tractors and farm machines, but they appeared to be rusting in a yard. Three men staggered across a field in obvious drunkenness. It was typical of the state farms. They are very inefficient in comparison to the private farmers, but they and their directors have political clout. They command the greatest share of inputs such as tractors, combines, fuel, and fertilizer, even though their yields are low. Moreover, along with the local police figures and party bosses, the directors make the decisions that favor friends and punish opponents. They determine the placement of a road, a well, a school. Routinely they decide who shall have wood boards, coal, and building supplies. In Kułaczkowski's county, as in so many others, the state farm directors were aligned with the police and the banker.

It was not at all in their interest that private farmers prosper, since they knew that in Warsaw such successes would only further indict their own failures.

As we drove that day we were very conspicuous. My car, a blue Volvo station wagon, often drew stares from people even in large cities. Not only was it twice as large as a Polish Fiat but its license plate marked its occupants as the most suspect outlanders. As in many countries, foreign residents are issued immediately recognizable license plates that identified their origins. They are of a different color than those issued to citizens and they have a numerical prefix that indicate the owner's country of origin. In most countries those prefixes are established alphabetically like pages in a postage stamp album. Afghanistan might be 1, Algeria, 2, Angola, 3, and so on down to Zaire and Zambia. In Poland the prefixes rank the order of suspicion. It is the United States that is 1, Britain is 2, Canada 3, while the Soviet Union is 63. Wherever I drove I would often be able to watch in my rearview mirror as policemen dutifully recorded my passing in their notebooks.

On our initial tour of the neighborhood, I was aware that we were being followed and I asked Kułaczkowski if by using my car we weren't calling a lot of attention to ourselves. "Sure we are, but that's exactly what I want," he said. It bothered me a little, since I did not want to be drawn into his fight as a partisan. I wanted to be the observer, the impartial reporter. But how, I asked myself, do you do that when one side invites you in and the other follows you around?

We dropped in on several farmers. Their sons and daughters had gone off to work at factories. In the summers, the children and the grandchildren would come back to help with the harvests. These farms were larger than Kułaczkowski's and the farmers reflected a sense of well-being if not affluence. The houses all had electricity and most had indoor bathrooms. Several farmers said they had cut back on the planting and turned plots of land over to local authorities because they lacked the resources to exploit them. The authorities kept the land in so-called land banks. Each year, they said, as farmers aged and died, there was less and less land under cultivation. Anyone who wanted to could pick up land for almost nothing from the local authorities but, as one gnarled farmer said, no one was that crazy.

As we sat on an old wooden wagon by his vegetable patch, the farmer's complaints intensified as his confidence in his visitor grew. "You know, through all the troubles in the cities since '56, the peasants have fed Poland. All the bad planning and bad management in Warsaw and we have put food on the table. It is not like over there," he said shrugging in the direction of the Soviet Union. "But the weather has been good for six straight years. One drought and what do they think will happen? I know some people say that we are getting rich and that we have gold under our mattresses but if that is so, why do they think the children are leaving? What happens if they all leave? Maybe they will turn all of our farms into collectives?" He laughed at the thought. "Can you imagine, one great big collective that produces rusting equipment, drunks, and bosses who wear city suits?"

This old farmer had co-signed Kułaczkowski's original loan application along with two of his neighbors. When Kułaczkowski began having his troubles with the authorities, his friends also came under attack. "First thing we noticed was that we were not getting credit for our milk." Like all private farmers in the region, he and his neighbors would regularly deliver the milk from their small herds to a cooperative creamery. The deliveries would be noted and the men would receive payment directly into their accounts. "We thought it was some kind of error but when we noticed that we had not been paid for three months of milk, we went to find out why. They told us that the payments had been held up because of Stanisław's loan. I thought he had fallen behind on payments, but no, he showed me he was paying ahead of schedule. I went back and asked what was happening and at the bank they told me I should be careful who I sign loans for. After some months we finally got our money. But right after that we had the police raid." He explained that a group of the old farmers held a meeting in a church to talk about a variety of problems, including how to make sure the regional officials sent out combines in time for the harvest and how they might try to gain a better price for their tobacco. I never established it outright, but the meeting may also have raised the issue of Kułaczkowski's loan.

"A week later," said the farmer, with some amusement, "four policemen came up right here to this vegetable patch. The old woman was in the house and came to get me from my field. When I got here, they were measuring my vegetable garden with rulers. Two were measuring and the other was writing it all down. They were concerned with the poppies. Last year the authorities told us that you could grow poppies only for your own use. They said that since the young people in the cities were becoming narcotics addicts it would be illegal to grow poppies on a plot greater than two by two meters. Well, most of us have always grown poppies. The wife uses the seeds to bake cakes. But this time instead of having a separate plot, we planted them among the cabbages. The police said that exceeded the limits and said we could go to prison for two years as narcotics traffickers. They pulled out our poppies and took them away. Then all of us, ten farmers, had to go to court. They fined us two thousand złotys each."

When I went to the bank to talk with Mrs. Chadaj, the banker, about the way loans were approved, she at first greeted me politely and offered me tea. But when I asked about Kułaczkowski's complaints, she said brusquely that she had treated him like any other debtor and that anyway, she could not really remember the case. I asked her if there were many members of the cooperative bank who had been brought to court for slander or who were facing expulsion by the bank? No, she said, Kułaczkowski was the only one and, yes, she conceded she was aware of the issue but she did not understand why I was interested. "Why is this your business?" she asked, in apparent outrage that I, a foreigner, was trespassing on private matters. When I asked her about the request Kułaczkowski said she had made for crushed marble to be delivered to her son's homesite, she said she did not wish to speak to me and bid me good day. The only real impression she left me with was how well-dressed and well-coiffed she was. All around were peasant women in kerchiefs and rubber boots. They often walked with a slow, rolling gait and usually they had baskets under their arms. In contrast, in the one-room bank with the foreign car parked outside, a woman whose appearance reminded me of one of the Gabor sisters sat behind a desk.

I wrote about Kułaczkowski's travails for *The New York Times.* I concluded the article in this way: "It would take a battery of lawyers a long time to wade through the amassed court records, letters, and affidavits to apportion degrees of blame and guilt in the arguments between the banker and the farmer. But one thing can be seen with the naked eye: A man wants to make cinder blocks, farmers want to buy cinder blocks, the government wants farmers to obtain cinder blocks and still Mr. Kułaczkowski is not making enough cinder blocks and soon he may not be able to make any."

I thought of sending Kułaczkowski a letter to let him know what I had written, though I still could not understand what he expected to happen as a result of my efforts. But before I was able to do that he called me, obviously happy and excited. "Mr. Michael, I know the story appeared because I heard it last night on the Voice of America. The circus has begun. Already two types from Warsaw have been around here asking my neighbors about me." I said I was sorry if the story would cause him any trouble. "No, no, it is fine. It's what I want. Let them ask, I have nothing to hide."

In the next few days the local police took him to Lublin. There, he said, they told him that I was a Jew and perhaps a spy. They said he should avoid contact with me. He told me he told them to stuff it. Then his uncle, a captain in the Lublin area traffic police, visited him to say that he could be hurt, even killed, if he kept having contact with foreigners. The uncle left, saying that unless Kułaczkowski stopped pressing his case and stopped seeing me, he himself would never again be able to visit his nephew or have any contact with him. Kułaczkowski said he was certain that the uncle had been ordered by his own superiors to pay the call and say what he did.

I had come to like Kułaczkowski and I admired him as the second most stubborn Pole I had met, the first being Czesław Bielecki, the architect who forced his jailers to feed him through a bit for eleven months. I looked forward to Kułaczkowski's visits and calls. But when he told me that his uncle had brought him a veiled death threat, I thought it was best to break off our meetings. Stanisław thought otherwise. "I'll be down to see you next week," he said, his voice booming to compensate for the bad connection from the village post office. I said I didn't think he ought to get killed over a story and that the right to build cinder blocks was, relatively speaking, not such an important human right. "No, no one is going to kill me. You can see they are getting scared. Don't worry, everything is working out just as I planned."

In fact, Urban's office, which monitors the foreign press, had sent its own investigators to the village. Eventually, the spokesman wrote me a letter to say that they could not find any substance in the farmer's allegations. Even in America, Urban wrote, there must be people who had trouble obtaining loans since they were regarded as poor risks. The letter, however, added that the official inquiry would continue. Kułaczkowski received a copy of this letter and was overjoyed. He showed it to whoever came to interview him, implying that he had a channel to Warsaw and that, should he choose, he just might inform the people there where the bodies were hidden, where money had been misspent. He was building his leverage. He had parlayed a visit to a *New York Times* reporter, to a mention on the Voice of America, to a dossier in the office of the government spokesman. Each step enhanced his power. He had figured out how the system works much better than I had and now he was happily pursuing his increasing advantage in his struggles with Mrs. Chadaj and her network. He even started to talk to me about politics. "You realize," he said, "if I can beat them and be seen beating them, then all those farmers will come out to join me. Even now they come over to whisper their support, but if I get my new loan and get this business going, we can chase these gangsters out and take over the bank with our own people."

I realized that the story about one man's thwarted attempts to build cinder blocks drew the attention of the government spokesman because it questioned the government's efforts to paint itself as a promoter of reform and enterprise, but I was still surprised by the amount of time and the number of people devoted to investigating Kułaczkowski's claims as stated in my article. I heard some suggestions that the spokesman, a fan of aggressive journalism, had hoped to encourage some qualified muckraking among Polish newsmen and was looking for models. Or he may have simply wanted to check up on my work. It is possible, however, that what attracted his interest was a paragraph that said: "Mr. Kułaczkowski's situation also illustrates what might be accomplished if the proposed Roman Catholic Church fund for private farmers ever gains final government approval. The concept, which has been a subject of negotiations for three years, calls for the church to administer a hard-currency fund raised in the West and earmarked for agricultural loans and investments. 'If the church fund were functioning,' he said, 'I would have somewhere else to go for credit besides the local cooperative bank. But now there is only the bank and the director and her friends are trying to destroy me.' "

At the time my story appeared, the three-year-long negotiations over the church fund were in fact collapsing, and it is likely that Mr. Kułaczkowski's reference may have been judged too embarrassing to be ignored. The idea for the fund originated with Pope John Paul II's second visit to Poland, which came after martial law, and it was awkward. The pope, who met with Jaruzelski, had seemingly little to offer those who looked to him for rescue. In this situation, the agricultural fund was first suggested by Cardinal Glemp. The money would come from the West in contributions from churches, private groups, and governments. It was to be kept in Western banks, to be used for purchases of farm inputs unavailable in Poland. Polish farmers would pay for these imported goods with złotys. The Polish money would accumulate in another fund that would remain in Poland to be used for rural development projects, such as schools, irrigation schemes, and community storage silos.

In symbolic terms the idea, raised long before Gorbachev's ascendancy, incorporated an acceptance of major taboos of Communism. At its very core it linked the church, Western capitalism, and private farming. For the few remaining ideologues within the party, those who still may have felt that the winds of history were blowing according to Marxist-Leninist design, the idea was repugnant, like setting up a whiskey distillery for a Muslim. For the slightly larger group within the party who rejected historical determinism but accepted Soviet power as the engine of Poland's best hopes, the idea was also viewed as dangerously provocative. But most important for the fate of the church fund was the opposition of people like Mrs. Chadaj and her allies who existed in probably every branch bank and within the *nomenklatura* elites of every town and county. Their power, prestige and prosperity were based upon the monopolies they controlled. To offer alternatives for credit and bypass the sluice gates of patronage and graft would undoubtedly increase production and raise farm exports but the local elites would only lose by that.

The so-called liberals with whom Jaruzelski was increasingly allying himself saw some merit in an idea that might stimulate Polish agriculture and generate a food processing industry. But their enthusiasm waned a bit when the original projection of a billion-dollar fund was reduced to a more realistic twenty-eight million dollars in pledges from the donor countries. By the time my story about Kułaczkowski appeared, the talks on the fund—

which soon were to capsize—were at a critical point. Any reference to a church-administered program as a potential rival to the state-controlled disbursement of credit must have alarmed the hard-liners and ideologues.

Kułaczkowski, meanwhile, sensed that his opponents were weakening in their campaign against him. Mrs. Chadaj was saying hello to him. The police were visiting him less and less. The bank stopped trying to expel him, though the second installment of the loan had not yet been approved. It was time, he thought, for a final campaign.

That took place on a rainy Sunday when a new regional high school was being dedicated in the village. The party dignitaries were coming from Warsaw as well as Lublin. Their cars pulled up by the road and the visitors walked on wood planks set in the mud, leading to the platform. Kułaczkowski again put on his best suit, took an umbrella and a bouquet of flowers and positioned himself next to the platform. When the officials walked by, he shook the hand of each one, offering flowers to the women, and saying "Good morning, comrade." The arrivals obviously assumed he was a local party official. When the newcomers were seated, he mounted the platform and spoke into the microphone. He said it was wonderful to see the new school rising but he thought it was important to point out what had happened to other projects in the neighborhood, the collective creamery, the meeting hall, and so forth. Very quickly somebody disconnected the microphone. Two men, presumably policemen, tried to push him from the platform, but he finished what he had to say.

"It was a real circus," he told me as he showed me the photographs that his wife took of the event. There was no immediate consequence, but some of the local farmers who had been shunning him began dropping by and saying hello to him in public and suddenly he had no trouble buying cement.

I saw him once more just before I left Poland and he said he hoped to get a roof on his shed. Then a year later, I returned and we met again. Everything, he said, was fine. He was in the bank. He had just been issued a ten-million-złoty loan. "You know what else?" he said. "The party committee sent a delegation telling me they wanted me to be a candidate for a seat on the local council. They said it was part of the process of expanding democracy and they said they knew I was a man who had authority in the community." He waited for me to ask him how he had responded. "I asked them what kind of a democracy was it when a committee picked candidates instead of having open nominating meetings. I told them to leave."

FOURTEEN

REFORM, OH YES, REFORM

ENTER MIKHAIL S. GORBACHEV. Predictably, the change that took place in Moscow after Konstantin U. Chernenko died in early March of 1985 did not elicit open shows of joy in Poland. Some Poles welcomed the relative youth of the fifty-four-year-old Soviet first secretary as a notable change, but generally there was little anticipation that anything would or could happen to alter Communism or improve relations between Moscow and Warsaw. There were even some Poles who felt that having a vital and energetic Soviet leader was worse for the fate of Poland than having ailing and weak ones. The overall mood of the country was probably best summed up by a quickly circulating joke: A schoolteacher designates a young boy to carry the flag in the May Day parade. The boy protests: "Why me, teacher, why is it always me? Didn't I carry the flag just before Brezhnev died? And then didn't I carry it the next year when it was Andropov who was the secretary? When he died, and Chernenko was in the Kremlin I again carried the flag. You want me to do it again now that Gorbachev is in power? Teacher, why is it always me?" And the teacher replies, "Because Jacek, you have such golden hands."

No one in Solidarity circles rushed to applaud Gorbachev. "We know from history," said Jacek Kuroń, "that when there is a reformer in Moscow, he holds those on his borders tightly by the snout. It has been that way since Peter the Great." Wałęsa, when asked what he thought about the fate of Soviet reforms, replied: "You know, as an electrician I must have screwed and unscrewed several hundred thousand screws in my lifetime. What I noticed is that whenever I tightened screws I never once ruined them, but sometimes when I unscrewed them, I ended up destroying their heads." The skeptical comments were in some measure a political conditioned reflex. Public sympathy for any Soviet figure has always been risky. One of my friends in the opposition, who had become convinced that Gorbachev did, in fact, represent something new and positive in Soviet politics, agonized about expressing his view in writing. He stalled for months, hoping that one or another of his colleagues would break the ice with some public declaration of even tepid interest. "I am not looking forward to being a kamikaze," he said as his typewriter remained unused.

Jaruzelski's team had no such problem. Almost as soon as Chernenko was buried, the people around the general began to beam and exult. For the first time since the end of the war, they said, a Polish leader had the apparent trust of the leadership in Moscow. Warsaw and Moscow now saw the crisis of Communism the same way, they insisted. Jaruzelski himself told a meeting of party officials that the symmetry of views in Warsaw and Moscow was without precedent in all recorded history. "We support all that Mikhail Gorbachev is doing. His energy, courage and far-sightedness deserve our deep respect and honest Polish sympathy," said the general, echoing the sycophancy of earlier Polish leaders for Stalin, Khrushchev, Kosygin, Brezhnev, and so on. But he went even further. "There is great satisfaction and great opportunity for Poland now that we are moving in the same common current. There is a complete meeting of our class-ideological, state and international interests. We have never had such a convergence in a millennium."

And apparently these Polish feelings were being reciprocated. Late in February of 1986, as Gorbachev sought to entrench and expand his commitment to reform at his first party congress, he quite clearly anointed General Jaruzelski as the first among equals. With the other aging leaders of the Warsaw Pact alliance looking on, a beaming Gorbachev walked arm in arm with Jaruzelski down the center aisle of the hall. East Germany's Erich Honecker was then seventy-four years old, as were Hungary's János Kádár and Czechoslovakia's Gustav Husák. Bulgaria's Todor Zhivkov was seventy-five, while Romania's Nicolae Ceaușescu was seventy. At sixty-four, Jaruzelski was ten years older than the man he was so eager to follow, but that still made him closest in age to Gorbachev.

Throughout the congress, Gorbachev was shown conferring jovially with Jaruzelski, sitting near him and sharing asides with him. The television cameras also followed Jaruzelski when, in a surprising move, with Gorbachev's permission he paid a quick visit to Vilnius, the capital of the Lithuanian Soviet Republic that before the war had been the Polish city of Wilno. He was shown on Polish television chatting with residents on the street. The visit marked the first time a Polish leader had come to Vilnius since 1939, and even opposition critics conceded that Jaruzelski had scored a coup by gaining Gorbachev's consent to make and publicize such a trip. Pani Kasia, my housekeeper, hardly a fan of Jaruzelski, was impressed, though she scorned the general for addressing a young couple on a Vilnius street in Russian even after it was established that they spoke Polish.

Happy as they were with the television coverage, the self-proclaimed liberals around Jaruzelski were happier still with the reform course that Gorbachev had set at his first party conference, seeing it as paralleling the one they had been advocating for almost five years. "Do you know what phrase appears most often in Gorbachev's address?" I was asked by a member of the parliament associated with the party's liberal caucus. "Radical reform," he told me. "I counted." Another member of this group, an economist, said that quite simply, the speech was an endorsement of Poland's schedule of economic reforms. "The way I read the speech, it means that we should have a free hand for the next few years to implement decentralizing policies and to try to rid the economy of unproductive failures," the economist said.

Within the government the enthusiasm was so great that some were claiming that Gorbachev's economic policies were based on Polish experiences with reform. The opposition critics also saw a Polish connection to what was happening in the Soviet Union, contending that it was the Solidarity upheavals that finally convinced Gorbachev that there were more risks in not changing the system than there were in trying to change it. Though such pronouncements occasionally hinted at Polish swagger and self-aggrandizement, they were often persuasive. Nor was the assertion of Polish pathfinding really diminished by the seemingly incongruous fact that just as the Soviet Union was embarking in the footsteps of Polish reform, the Polish economic experiments were quite evidently failing. After all, from whom else could the Soviets learn? Their own experiences with modifying Communism ended in the 1920s. They were hardly likely to openly pattern their innovations after the Chinese, who, after all, were asserting that Peking had become the new vanguard of world Communism.

In the years before his ascension to power, when he supervised Soviet agriculture, Gorbachev studied and became impressed with Hungarian farm management. Far more than any other country in the bloc, Hungary had succeeded in introducing free-market streams into what remained essentially a command economy. It had advanced furthest in the pursuit and development of an as yet amorphous and by no means certain economic hybrid that might someday combine those aspects of capitalism that assure efficiency and competitiveness with some form of state planning and control. Under what became widely known as Goulash Communism, some Hungarian collective farms had branched into industrial production, processing foods, and assembling farm machinery and computers. Small private businesses were being formed rapidly, among them dozens of Budapest restaurants. Joint ventures were established linking state enterprises with foreign capitalists, and a market opened to publicly trade bonds issued by state enterprises. The country had joined the International Monetary Fund.

But it was obvious to most that the evolution of the Hungarian economy was in large measure based on distinctive and specific Hungarian experiences and characteristics that limited its value as a model for a huge superpower like the Soviet Union. For one thing, Hungary is a homogeneous country of only eleven million people, while the Soviet Union has more than 270 million people belonging to dozens of nationalities, speaking scores of languages, and reflecting many religious traditions.

Poland had none of Hungary's economic successes. Its economic record has been among the bleakest in the bloc, and yet, paradoxically, it was the Poles and their experience that served as even more of a beacon for Gorbachev than the Hungarians. Unlike the Hungarians, the thirty-eight million Poles are Slavs, linked at least linguistically to the Russians, Byelorussians, and Ukrainians. In addition, over centuries, Russian culture, political as well as economic, has been influenced by importations from Europe that have come largely through Poland. Most germane, however, was Poland's experience with Solidarity.

Like Communists everywhere, the Soviets had branded the Solidarity upheavals as anarchist outbursts or counterrevolution, but they were too well-versed in their own formative ideology not to have realized that what occurred in Polish mines, factories, and shipyards was a real revolution. In Marxist terms, the Polish ruling elite had lost control of the working class. That had never happened anywhere on such a scale, and, for leaders raised in Communism, this had to be seen as a frightening harbinger, a specter of what might be looming as the force of ideology diminished and economic production atrophied still further in those places where Communism reigned.

Throughout that sphere the notion was spreading that the defects of all command economies were chronic and structural. As the seventies drew to a close, it became quite apparent that not only was Communism incapable of burying the West as Khrushchev once threatened, but they were finding it increasingly difficult either to satisfy or cow those they governed. More than a decade earlier, in the sixties, some top-secret Soviet reports documented slippage in all the significant indexes of modernity, with the possible exception of military might. Scientific innovation, technological implementation, growing agricultural surpluses, and economic growth were all centered in the West. Four decades earlier, Communists were predicting the onset of what they called the general crisis of capitalism, when contradictions in free markets would lead to the political collapse of the Western democracies. To some it now appeared that a general crisis of Communism was occurring first. In a last-gasp effort to show that the Soviet Union was still a pioneering international vanguard at least for the third world, the Soviets intervened in Angola, Mozambique, Ethiopia, Afghanistan, and Nicaragua. The results, from Moscow's point of view, were dismal and generally quite costly. In the process what was left of messianic Communism withered and died.

Then came Gorbachev. He pulled back from the third world, looked to the West and staked his rule on the kind of reform with which the Poles had experimented.

Given the pauperization of the Polish economy, Jaruzelski could not, like Hungary's Kádár, gain grudging support or the good behavior of the population by giving them a chance to own their own homes and drive their own cars, or choose freely at stores where vegetables, cheeses, and salamis were piled high. In Poland, there were no homes and no cars, and meat remained rationed. If that was impossible, the only inducement lay in the area of expanded freedoms. Only through some as yet unnegotiated forms of greater citizen participation could Polish leaders dream of improving economic performance and achieving sustained social tranquility. This also lay at the heart of Gorbachev's premise that *glasnost*, or openness, could lead to *perestroika*, or restructuring.

All of the political innovations that Gorbachev was advocating to prime the pump of radical changes had in fact been adopted in Poland, some of them many years ago. For example, the Soviet leader's desire to transform the rubber-stamp Soviet parliament into a more deliberative and independent body follows the pattern of the Polish Sejm. Though far from a freely elected Western-style parliament, it has had more autonomy than any Communist legislature and it includes some non-party members.

Similarly, Gorbachev's call for establishing new competitive channels of decision-making to force party bureaucrats into greater efficiency has a precedent in Polish experience. Poland has seen a proliferation of such efforts over the last decade. Laws were passed in recent years to establish an ombudsman's office to review complaints of due process violations. A supreme court was given the right to independently review the constitutionality of legislation. Several national fronts were organized to encourage the participation of non-Communists in campaigns of social activism that were never fully spelled out, involving such things as clean streets, anti-alcohol crusades, and tree plantings. A Council on the Economy was impaneled with significant representation of non-party members. A National Consultative Council including a few eminent figures was established and given vague powers of debating and discussing national policies with General Jaruzelski.

Once validated by Gorbachev, such steps were hailed throughout the bloc. It was strange to observe the contortions of Czechoslovakian officials who, having once banned the very word reform, were preposterously insisting that they too favored *glasnost*. But in Poland, where reform had been officially sanctioned for years, government officials saw Gorbachev's views as vindication of their own policies and they redoubled their efforts to exhort the nation to do better now that Moscow had confirmed that their course was right. There was only one problem. Most government leaders knew that reform—the same reform that Moscow was pursuing—was failing in Poland.

The government's economic statistics showed that the crisis that began in 1979 was persisting. Some government and party people clung to the hope that Moscow's endorsement and acceptance of reform would give new life to Poland's flagging economic innovations. But arrayed against them were the critics who contended that whatever the Polish government might offer in the way of democratic inducements would be less than what had been obtained under Solidarity; thus it would have to disappoint rather than inspire. They insisted again that without the participation of Solidarity and the involvement of prominent Solidarity people, all Polish reforms would fail regardless of what the Soviets did or did not achieve.

On the other hand, the initial disdain with which the opposition greeted Gorbachev was giving way to fascination as he took on his party's old guard. Within months, Poles were spinning dozens of intricate, often conflicting, analyses of what was going on in the Soviet Union and what it meant for the world. Predictably, one of the most original views was evolved by Michnik.

It was late in 1987 and Michnik was spending part of his days at the House of the International Press, a neighborhood reading room where people, mostly retired pensioners, read East bloc publications. He went there to read *Ogonek* ("Little Fire"), the Soviet journal that took the lead in publishing articles on previously taboo subjects. One wintry day, on his way there, he met a Russian-born actress who had been the wife of a high-ranking Polish government official. When she said she was also going to the reading room, he asked whether she was also going to read *Ogonek*. "No," she said, "I am looking for a big fire. I am going there to keep warm because the heating in my apartment has failed."

As Michnik told me later that day, the meeting led to his thinking about steam pipes and radiators. In Polish cities, steam is generated at central plants and then transmitted through underground pipes to apartment houses, offices, and other buildings. It seems an inefficient method that allows a great deal of energy to be lost in transmission. The pipes had to be laid deep beneath the surface and when they broke, entire blocks would be without heat for days. Streets were closed to traffic as repair crews excavated. I always thought the steam pipes were an archetypal metaphor for a centralized economy.

However, what surprised Michnik most that morning was that the woman whose home was cold was one of those favored few known as "the prominents," people who lived in privileged apartment blocks. She told him that her home had been without steam for five days, and this, Michnik thought, was unprecedented. "When the house of an ordinary Pole is left without heat, that is not remarkable, but if the former wife of a former high official who lives in the same apartment block with top members of the Central Committee is without heat for five days, it means that the best-maintained, top-priority part of the system has worn out. I realized that the radiators had gone on strike."

Michnik obviously liked his imagery. Like a jazz musician playing with a new phrase, he continued improvising. "In the past, totalitarian regimes have been confronted by strikes and rebellions of people, of workers, even of nations. In those cases the responses were predictable. The czar sent in Cossacks, Jaruzelski or Pinochet sent in his troops. The workers were beaten on the heads with clubs. Some were arrested. Sometimes their leaders were hanged or deported. But what is the response if radiators go on strike? What happens if telephones refuse to work or airplanes fall out of the sky, or computers rebel and trains revolt? Cossacks won't help. You can't intimidate pipes and radiators

239

into working. I suddenly realized that this was what Gorbachev was facing. After all, hadn't he been greeted by the greatest radiator rebellion in the world when the Chernobyl reactor melted? He needed *perestroika*. It was his only chance."

This graphic description embellished Michnik's earlier view that Gorbachev was not so much an original reformer as a man of the Counterreformation. "In the West people are calling him a reformer and that is wrong," he said. "Reform in the bloc began with Solidarity. When our union arose, that was the revolutionary moment. When Wałęsa and the government signed the agreement on free unions and basic freedoms in the shipyard, that was like Martin Luther posting his ninety-five theses to the door at Wittenberg." Just as that act of defiance led to a wave of challenges of church authority, he went on, the demands of the Polish union brought claims on Communism and Communists. Michnik compared Gorbachev and, to a lesser extent, Jaruzelski, to the leaders of the Jesuit-led Counterreformation of the sixteenth century. Like them, they had appropriated some of the criticism raised by rivals and challengers and used it to clean their own house. They advocated versions of reforms that originally arose spontaneously in social turbulence, but they did so to preserve their own ebbing power.

This meant that, as in the sixteenth century, rival groups were all backing reform. Indeed, during my stay in Poland, reform increasingly became a magic, almost incantational word. The original campaign for economic change in Poland began in 1981, five years before Gorbachev arrived on the scene. By the time the Soviet leader introduced *perestroika* into the international vocabulary to offset such earlier contributions as *pogrom* and *gulag*, everyone was ostensibly for it. Certainly no one was openly against it. For years the basic thrust of the Polish reform had been to encourage individual state enterprises to make key economic decisions without much intervention by central authorities. The goal was to have the plants become autonomous, self-governing, and self-financing. At the same time small private enterprises were to be encouraged. The goal was not being met.

I am an economic simpleton, and, at first, when I heard the repeated calls for reform, I could not understand why the problems were so great. It seemed to me that for reform to work all that was necessary was for the political meddling to stop, which would allow organic markets to form. In this, I sided with the many Poles who were raising the cry of *"Nie przeszkadzaj"*—Don't hinder. Their idea was that if the government and party simply turned a blind eye to economic activity, enterprises would proliferate and human energies and talents would find useful and appropriate outlets. Certainly, if people were allowed to acquire land or rent premises, they would open restaurants, beauty parlors, barber shops, garages, workshops, and stores. In theory all such enterprises were possible under reform.

But in fact none of the bureaucrats were willing to dispense with their rights of approval, prerogatives upon which their status was based. As a result the only private restaurants that opened in Warsaw, about six of them, were established by retired policemen who had the right connections. A collective of private cab drivers foundered because officials withheld gasoline rations. It took one man I knew seven years to start a small plant to produce citric acid, even though he had a guarantee of purchases from foreign customers and approval from the key ministries. Another friend, a physician, had spent a fruitless decade trying to set up a clinic that would provide care for subscribers in a private health plan.

Even if privatization were to advance more thoroughly, it would have to be confined to a very small sector. What was to be done with the big state factories, the mines, and the railroads, most of which had been sapped by years of inefficiency and mismanagement? They were overmanned and unproductive, beset with dozens of problems. Every imaginable remedy was costly and painful. There were, for instance, ten coal mines employing more than twenty-three thousand miners, which were obsolete and unproductive. By comparison with competing coal suppliers such as

Canada and Australia, the Polish mines were very inefficient, producing poor grades at higher prices and offering uncertain deliveries. From an ecological point of view the mines were disastrous. In the industrial southwest, forests had withered under acid rain. Kraków's medieval buildings and statues, which survived the war, were blistered by currents of corrosive air. Lead in the air and water was permeating the soil of gardens.

And that wasn't all. One government report claimed that an incredible 40 percent of the coal extracted was then used to extract more coal. Another report pointed out that reserves of coal would not last much beyond the end of the century. Poland had no nuclear plants and after Chernobyl few favored building any. The prospect of a looming energy crisis was all the more haunting because the Soviet Union's easily accessible Caspian oil reserves were being depleted. The Soviets assured the Poles that they would be able to use Siberian oil, but only if they built a pipeline. Only the West has the technology available for such a link, and payment for it would have to be in hard currency. It would cost billions and Poland already owed more than $37 billion to Western creditors.

Some economists argued that because of such problems it made sense to cut back on coal production, storing reserves for the future. A few even urged that the least efficient mines be closed. But they were shouted down by those politicians who noted that inefficient as the Polish mining industry may have been, it was still the major earner of hard currency. Poland was the fourth-largest coal producer in the world. It extracted 193 million metric tons a year, exporting 31 million, of which 17 million went to the West. Earnings from coal provided most of the money used for interest payments on the hard-currency debt. The coal had to be dug and this explained why miners were earning twice the national average and why they were given access to special stores stocked with imports. What did Poland have to sell the world besides coal? Some sulfur, some copper, textiles, ships that no one but the Soviets seemed to want, some ham, and some vodka?

A situation similar to that of the coal fields applied in the shipyards, which as far as anyone could tell were registering even greater losses than shipyards all over the world. They received rubles for the Soviet vessels they built but they spent dollars, marks, and kronor for components and materials acquired in the West. From a purely economic point of view, there were good reasons for shutting down the biggest shipyard or at least cutting back its activities. However, the Soviets, who were receiving inexpensive ships from Gdańsk, naturally opposed such economies. The same was true at plants all over the country where production schedules were integrated into Soviet economic plans.

Just how backward the economy was, was apparent each time I was permitted to visit factories. Occasionally groups of journalists were led to plants presumably selected because they offered the most positive impressions. In each of them, our cluster of newsmen would be led to a conference room, where on tables covered with green felt, we would be offered either black currant juice, beer, or vodka in little juice glasses. The director of the factory and the head of its party organization would then advise us that production was inching up from the low levels of 1979. Often they would say that workers are increasingly aware of the devastating cost of the Solidarity period. If we would ask if any one had been a member of Solidarity, there was usually silence. Then we were led to the shop floor. At one factory which produced electrical switches, the man who led my group was reeling and reeking with drink. He took me aside and told me he drank because it was the only way he could keep from telling us the truth. What was the truth? I asked. "Nothing works and they are all sons of bitches."

At the factory that produced the Polish Fiat, a tiny personal car that was once mistakenly envisioned as a big seller in third world countries, many positions on the assembly line were unoccupied and stools at work tables were empty. I asked the foreman about this. First he said some workers might have the day off. Then, as I pressed him, he said that actually many workers had quit to work in the nearby mines where pay scales were higher. When I said that this explanation would surely not cover women, he answered that women workers were joining so-called Polonia firms, small private companies set up with the capital of foreigners who had some Polish roots. I said I understood that such enterprises accounted for much less than a single percent of Polish jobs and the foreman with some embarrassment conceded that there was a great problem with chronic absenteeism. Later he said that often, people who clock in disappear for extended breaks to smoke and drink *bimber*. Often when I talked to workers, they would cite a well-known rhymed couplet that symbolized the prevailing work ethic—*Czy się stoi, czy się leży, tysiąc złotych się należy* (If you lie down, or if you stand erect / A thousand złotys you expect).

What later became known as the first stage of reform was supposed to have enhanced efficiency by giving directors a freer hand to hire and fire and to change production lines in accordance with market opportunities. To stimulate higher efficiency, the government even approved one of the first bankruptcy provisions within a communist system. It was a very complicated law that mandated an extended period of receivership before failing enterprises could be closed. Three years after the law was passed, despite the existence of hundreds, perhaps thousands, of qualifying enterprises, not one unit was closed. "All such laws are easier to enact than to implement," one government economist explained. "What standard of efficiency are you going to use to determine solvency when every enterprise is somehow dependent on subsidies? If we were to use even moderate Western standards, say those of Austria, I suppose we would have to declare every plant bankrupt."

Along with the bankruptcy provision came other innovations that ended up having little or no positive effect. After five years of discussion, a joint venture law was approved, which so limited the discretion of foreign partners that there were virtually no takers. A regulation that slapped punitive taxes on those state companies that fueled inflation with pay raises and overtime was quickly circumvented by the abuse of another new regulation that permitted directors to contract work out on a piece-goods basis to groups of their own employees who worked after hours. Though they made sense on paper, the reforms often compounded the old confusions of the workplace and further skewed values when they were applied.

In the fall of 1986 Mieczysław Rakowski, the editor and leader of the party's liberal wing who was then serving as an officer of the Sejm, went to the Lenin shipyard to check on how reform was working. Rakowski, who had been hooted in the shipyard when he went there a year after martial law, now was greeted with cool politeness by some workers and ignored by others. But when he met with the director of one division the discussion turned animated.

"Look, you have to get rid of this decentralization, I am getting killed," said the director, according to someone who took notes on the conversation. Under the old system, as the ships neared completion, the management would call a ministerial bureaucrat to requisition furniture. The bureaucrat called the furniture producer in Poznań to place the order. Under the new reform regulations, the shipyard director was supposed to deal directly with the furniture supplier. In theory, this was meant to encourage competition, giving the shipyard some leverage in choosing suppliers, demanding the best deal in terms of price and style and delivery date. In practice, there were not enough competing furniture manufacturers to make a difference. Indeed, there was only the company in Poznań that could manufacture on the scale required. "Now, when I call the director there, he tells me to get fucked, that he has his plant working at full capacity on hard-currency orders for prefabricated furniture for Sweden or West Germany," the shipyard director complained. "What am I supposed to do? If we can't get the furniture, we are liable to pay penalties. So I have to order the cabinets from Finland or Germany and pay real money." Real money, as all Poles understand, is not Polish money.

The director then confided that he routinely kept workers on overtime in violation of anti-inflationary directives. "I have to because on their regular shifts they are borrowing our tools to build their own apartments. Then when they get the apartments, the best workers quit and go to work for private firms." As for the practice of subcontracting work to employees, he said it was leading to two styles of work, each with its own tempo. When the workers put in their regular ten-hour shifts, they worked like snails, but then when they came in on their own time as piece-work contractors, they worked quickly. They had figured out that the slower they worked on their regular jobs the more work they would have on the better paying piece-goods system.

An underlying irritant to all reform was the pervasive suspicion attached to the very concept of competition and hard work. Workers, for instance, were very leery of accepting formulas that would permit more pay for more and better work. Much of this was rooted in the egalitarian ideology in which they had been raised over the last four decades, but there were other contributing causes. As in the defeated American South after the Civil War, generations of Poles viewed working effectively as something close to collaboration with occupying powers, dominating foreigners, or absentee owners. In addition, the penetration downward of values originating in the old gentry class left many with the notion that too much hustle and ambition were graceless, if not absolutely vulgar, traits.

There were some within the government who recognized that what was needed more than anything else was the initiative and even cunning of private-sector pioneers, but on the other hand, they also would label such people as rapacious exploiters, playing to the jealousies and prejudices of large groups of workers. For the party people who were directly responsible for mismanagement, the "privateers" were a convenient scapegoat, just as the Jews had once been.

Obviously, some of those who entered into the new competitive culture were indeed profiteers or black market speculators, just as some of the architects of Western industrial capitalism were robber barons. "The problem is not that private businessmen are vulgar thieves and exploiters," said the friend who finally managed to build the lab that produces citric acid. "The party directors are also vulgar, also exploiters. But they squander and ruin everything they touch. The capitalist barons conserved wealth and used it as productive capital. Our problem is that we do not have a critical mass of such people." Because there were so few of them, the new entrepreneurs could set their own prices and dominate supplies. They could and often did produce sloppy work. They did not want and, indeed, they feared, competitors. Often they included people who would use their party and police connections to thwart any rivals in the "free" marketplace.

A young Warsaw lawyer told me he was shocked to find an almost total lack of capable accountants and bookkeepers. "The tradition has practically disappeared," he said. "Before the war, this field was largely dominated by Jews. The Jews are gone. But beyond that, for the last forty years, the study of commercial subjects was treated with contempt. Working in a bank was less prestigious, less well-paying than working in the police. We simply cannot determine real assets, real worth. I think in China and Hungary, old capitalist skills survived, but not here."

All these tendencies were impeding the stated aims of Polish reform as Gorbachev arrived on the scene in the Kremlin. From a propaganda point of view the Poles were in an uncomfortable bind. In the Polish government and party, people talked about economic reform, yearned for reform, and I suspect some of them prayed for reform. Gorbachev had not only joined their chorus but he was now leading it. But what those Polish party people knew was that in Poland, at least, reform based on *glasnost* was not working. In a rather ingenious, very Polish, resolution, it was decided to simply call the faltering steps a first stage and move on to a "second stage" that, in fact, had not ever been envisioned when reform was first launched.

By mid-1987 a comprehensive list of new measures was compiled, intended to carry the decentralization still further. The provisions tended to be more technical. The number of ministries and the number of bureaucratic decisions was to be pruned. An economic czar was appointed with the theoretical right to name and dismiss managers. In consultation with the International Monetary Fund, which Poland had joined, an austerity plan was designed to balance prices and wages and trim subsidies. The formation of new banks was authorized to break the monopoly on credit. Firms would be allowed to pool or trade their debts, which could mean that well-managed and profitable state enterprises could take over failing factories. There was talk of shutting down unprofitable enterprises, and there was talk also about permitting some limited unemployment even though full employment was guaranteed by the constitution.

One unstated but critical thrust of the new policies was to implant and nurture elements of what might have been called bourgeois, or even petit bourgeois, cultures, had such designations been free of lingering taint. There were people very close to Jaruzelski, people like Rakowski, for example, who believed that the growth of a limited urban class of people tied to property was needed to assure social stability. As Communists they could not surrender even nominal control over the working class but they could, and they did, dream about an embryonic middle class. For one thing, they hoped that this class could draw off the brightest and most troublesome of the Solidarity leaders who might be encouraged to make money instead of revolution. It would be lovely if Wałęsa, Bujak, Frasyniuk, and all the other "boys" suddenly became rich and thus easier to discredit as renegades from the working class.

Beyond this, some of the leaders were also genuinely intrigued by middle-class values, much as an aging bohemian might on his deathbed wonder aloud if the clean and thrifty banker had not had a better life after all. I would sense something like this whenever I heard Polish authorities talk about Margaret Thatcher, probably the quintessential exponent of bourgeois values in the world. In public, it was of course Gorbachev who was portrayed as the world's most interesting and innovative leader, but in private it was often Mrs. Thatcher who seemed most esteemed. Her contemptuous treatment of striking British miners was particularly envied by Communist bureaucrats who yearned to close pits, cut pay and lay off workers but could not do it.

Yet, however strongly they may have fantasized over Thatcherite policies, however much they may have yearned for robber barons on whom to fob off some of society's hatreds, they still could not keep themselves from sabotaging every step, even their own, that led in this direction. There was, for example, the case of the Warsaw Association of Entrepreneurs.

The organization was the brainchild of Aleksander Paczyński, a man who had been an editor and became a builder. Until Solidarity erupted, Paczyński had also worked at *Polityka*, serving as Rakowski's deputy. He had never been a party member and he specialized in writing about economic issues, primarily about the housing problem. Under Rakowski, *Polityka* had become something of a sanctuary of liberal sentiment. When Solidarity emerged, the once tightly knit *Polityka* community split like other Polish environments. Earlier, as the union swelled, Urban and Górnicki followed Rakowski to serve Jaruzelski. But other reporters like Stefan Bratkowski and Dariusz Fikus left to work with the opposition.

Paczyński also quit. After writing about the housing shortage for so long, he and a few partners formed a cooperative that, at first, sold plans and booklets that showed how people could build their own one-family houses. Eventually the cooperative began building houses. "We offer the sort of basic, simple units that are typical all over the world but were unknown here," said Paczyński as he showed me a model house. It looked like an early Levittown ranch house.

By 1986, Paczyński's company had built and sold a few dozen such homes, each one costing about six million złotys. At the official rate of exchange this was about $25,000, but at the black market rate it was about $4,000. The houses were out of the reach of most people but there was still a significant market for them. "We could build and sell thousands of houses if there was no official interference, even tens of thousands," said Paczyński. "Other companies like ours would be encouraged to start up. We could not solve the housing shortage but we could help. The biggest problem is getting title to land. There is plenty of available land in every city, but getting permission to build involves dealings with dozens of officials, most of whom are conditioned to say no and some of whom want bribes."

Paczyński is an apostle for private initiative and as his company grew he felt the time was ripe to extend the inroads of commercial culture. "By the middle of 1987, we felt that the government might be willing to accept innovations that did not directly involve Solidarity." As Western creditors' countries were pressuring the Jaruzelski government to expand the right of association, the regime responded by sanctioning some discussion clubs. Paczyński went ahead and assembled almost a hundred private businessmen, people who ran workshops, garages, restaurants. There were a few architects and contractors. Paczyński's idea was that the businessmen's organization should apply for official status and that once registered, it should function something like a chamber of commerce and a lobby for business interests. The group might eventually sponsor a bank or a credit union, or it might collectively seek loans or credit guarantees abroad. With the backing of the businessmen, he applied for the official registration without which no organization can open a bank account, rent a hall, or buy a rubber stamp.

Quickly Warsaw municipal officials routed him to the Central Committee building. Politburo members told him that what he proposed was impossible. He would not be able to offer membership to businessmen all over the country. The association, they said, should be regional. Paczyński agreed. Then the party officials insisted that membership could not be limited only to businessmen, that this was somehow undemocratic. They said that ministerial and party representatives and academics should also be able to join. Paczyński said that the party people seriously told him, "The trouble with you is that you not only want to discuss economic activity but that you want to become economically active." Paczyński could not accept these terms and the talks were suspended.

Then, suddenly, it was announced that the Warsaw administrative court had approved the formation of an autonomous group calling itself the Entrepreneurs' Association of Warsaw. This was not, however, Paczyński's group. No, this organization was headed by Mieczysław Rakowski, the editor, a man who was then a parliamentary officer and who within a year would be named to the politburo and shortly thereafter was chosen as prime minister. He was telling friends that he was the Pole who was closest in spirit to Gorbachev's reformist desires. He was not, however, nor had he ever been, much of an entrepreneur. Paczyński and his businessmen associates were only mildly stunned by the move. "What we are seeing is the well-known government reflex that forces them to lay their deadening hands on everything," said the builder. "We are used to it but this is even more ludicrous than usual. I guess with its ersatz entrepreneurial committee the party is claiming that its deciding role extends to establishing bourgeois and petit bourgeois institutions."

FIFTEEN

THE LAST CHAPTER

IT WAS SOON after May Day, 1988, that it all started again. A wave of strikes rippled through Poland. First, the two hundred bus drivers of Bydgoszcz, who were represented by a government-sanctioned union, stayed home and paralyzed transport in the middle-sized city. They were demanding raises to compensate for rising food prices. In keeping with the new openness, their action was reported almost immediately by Polish radio and by nightfall television newscasters announced that a settlement had been reached and that the drivers were going back to work, having received a huge sixty percent increase, far exceeding the anti-inflationary guidelines set by reform. But as the bus drivers returned to work, other strikes were mounted in several cities and the cry of "*Solidarność*" was once again being raised.

In Cambridge, Massachusetts, where I had lived since leaving Poland nine months earlier, I watched with fascination as Polish workers once again forced themselves onto the front pages of Western journals and onto the nightly television news. A sitdown strike at an armaments plant at Stalowa Wola was followed by another at the huge steel plant at Nowa Huta near Kraków. There were recurring slowdowns on the assembly line at the Ursus tractor works near Warsaw, and then the Lenin shipyard, the birthplace of Solidarity in Gdańsk, was seized by young men and women who hung up the banners of the outlawed union and demanded it again be made legal.

From my vantage point I wondered how threatening all this was to Poland's rulers. Could the strikes be signaling the final chapter of Polish Communism? Obviously the country had entered another phase in the cycle of worker protests that has been turning since 1956. Even if things were not yet at breaking point, it was clear that masses of Poles who had been dormant were once more advancing their challenge.

I realized I would have to return and I hurriedly obtained a visa and set off for Poland. As I flew eastward it all seemed thrilling and perilous. The wave of strikes was taking place just a month before Gorbachev was to host President Reagan at the Moscow summit. Would that meeting take place? Could it take place if once again Polish workers raised demands for real democracy and liberty? It seemed obvious that the renewed stirrings of Polish workers could easily upset not only Gorbachev's reformist hopes, but also the progress that had been made in East-West relations. Certainly, from a global perspective, there was now more riding on the frustrations of the shipyard crews and mill hands than there was in 1979 and 1980. Then there was no prospect of disarmament or improving Soviet relations with the United States for Polish workers to jeopardize. In 1980 Moscow and Washington were facing each other down with hostile reflexes in Poland as in other parts of the planet. Indeed, things were so bad between the superpowers that it was hard to see how they could get much worse.

Eight years later the situation was very different. The Soviets were pulling their troops out of Afghanistan, and Washington and Moscow were drawing up treaties to mutually reduce nuclear weapons. In the new atmosphere, the potential of renewed Polish disorders was particularly troublesome—this time it was easy to see how relations could deteriorate quite quickly if Poland went up again. Would Gorbachev allow the clamor to continue indefinitely, knowing that it could fan dissent in the Soviet Baltic Republics or even spread to the Ukraine? Or would he send troops as Khrushchev had done to quell the Hungarians in 1956? But if he used force or relied on Jaruzelski to use force, wouldn't that destroy the chances of any understanding on disarmament with the United States, and crush the hopes for a less threatening international political atmosphere?

I landed in Warsaw and took an early train for Gdańsk. There, a few hundred men and women were holding out at the shipyard. In the Baltic city I quickly sensed that the crisis was waning and that my concerns about the international consequences of the strike were for the moment premature. People were going about their business, seemingly indifferent to what was happening on the other side of the shipyard gates. There were no stoppages at any other Gdańsk plants and I was surprised that there was no massive police presence on the streets. Cab drivers talked of the strikers as "they" and not "we" or "our boys" as they had once done.

Only as I approached the shipyard did the emotional climate suddenly change. There, twelve- and thirteen-year-old children were serving as couriers, running food and communications past encircling units of police. The youngsters turned up at St. Brygida's Church on the day the strike began. They organized themselves into teams, some of which led foreign newsmen over the wall. My guide, a twelve-year-old girl, had been interrogated by the police and she was proud that despite their threats to have her suspended from school, she had told them nothing. She said she was helping the strikers because she always wanted to do something heroic like those who fought in the Warsaw uprising.

Inside the gates hope of a general uprising was fading but certain images echoed the days when the union was first established. Once more, grim-faced men and women in coveralls stood under the looming, snatching cranes to face ranks of helmeted

254

riot police. On the gates between the striking workers and poised troopers hung placards drawn in the characteristic sloping red script with which Solidarity signed itself. THERE CAN BE NO LIBERTY WITHOUT SOLIDARITY, the posters proclaimed. Once again, young Polish workers flashed their V-for-victory gestures to the cameras of the world press and played songs of hope on their guitars.

Predictably, Borusewicz was there, helping another generation of workers to frame their anger in protest. He had organized a strike newspaper and was teaching a group of youthful men and women how to run a printing press, instructing them to keep their slogans short and punchy. He knew that the strike was ebbing but he was already preparing for the next one. The man who police had years ago labeled "a born conspirator" was drawing up lists of the brightest young strikers, forging them into new networks that would remain in active contact after they left or were chased from the shipyard.

Borusewicz's most famous and most successful old recruit, Wałęsa, was also back at the shipyard. The two men, who had become estranged by the time martial law descended, had since renewed their close ties and were camping out like old Scoutmasters with a new batch of Scouts. It was obvious, however, that Wałęsa was not enthusiastic about being there. His back hurt and he thought the strike was ill-timed and poorly planned. It had been called without his approval. Furthermore, he did not know the young men and women in their teens and early twenties who were at the heart of the stoppage. Nevertheless, he could not abandon them. He was the head of the union and to keep away from the shipyard would have given weight to government claims that Solidarity was a spent force and a dead issue. So he bedded down among the strikers, offering his presence and his authority. He also shielded them from police assault with his international reputation and his Nobel Peace Prize. When he talked to the press he lavished praise on Gorbachev, saying that Poland would have been better off if Brezhnev had died two years earlier.

Among the few dozen other Solidarity veterans who came to help out at the shipyard was Andrzej Drawicz, a specialist on the Soviet Union, who lectured the strikers about what Gorbachev was doing in Moscow and how his reforms were likely to create new opportunities for political changes in Poland. By late afternoon on the day I arrived, most of the original group of a thousand strikers had peeled off and gone home. The few hundred remaining diehards received word that all the other strikes in the country had ended. They decided that for them, too, further protest was pointless. From St. Brygida's, a phone call was made to the police and the details of withdrawal were quickly worked out. As night fell the strikers marched out, carrying their religious flags but no Solidarity symbols. They were cheered from the windows of apartment houses they passed on their way to St. Brygida's, where a special mass was celebrated. For their part, the police pulled back out of sight. Michnik, who had spent the previous ten days at the church as the strike spokesman, welcomed them, declaring, "We may not have won, but we did not lose, we have emerged with our dignity intact."

Later I joined Michnik, Wałęsa, Drawicz, and Father Henryk Jankowski—as well as some young members of the strike committee—for dinner at the parish house. The mood was genuinely celebratory. It was true, someone said, that the protest had not gained critical mass, but it was equally true that another generation of Polish workers had quite clearly and spontaneously declared their dissatisfaction with the Polish government and the system it still defended. At the other end of the table someone interjected that the authorities would no longer be able to delude themselves that Solidarity has ceased to matter. At one point a young member of the strike committee asked Drawicz whether he thought "Gorbachev was thinking about us even more than we were thinking about him." Drawicz simply said yes, but an older worker blurted out, "You can bet your daughter's virginity on it. When the phone rings in his bedroom at three in the morning what do you think flashes into his mind? At first he may wonder whether it is bad news from Alma-Ata or some other republic, but then he has to be thinking whether the boys in Gdańsk are at it again!"

I returned to Warsaw to talk to government and party people about the strikes. I was certain they would be pleased by the way the strikes had fizzled, but there was no gloating and only a few tried to dismiss the strikes as unimportant. The mood was one of apprehension. While many stressed that the strikes were not the earthquake that some Western newspapers claimed, no one in authority was willing to say that the likelihood of further disruptions had been markedly diminished. Even Urban, the outspoken spokesman, resisted any inclination to crow. Instead he asked me, "Do you know how we differ from the opposition?" When I said no, he explained. "Well, they obviously don't know what they should do next week but they know exactly where they are headed. As for us, we know precisely what we should do next week but we have no idea at all of where we should be going."

Stanisław Ciosek, one of General Jaruzelski's party allies, exhibited similar candor when I called on him a few days later. "We have no illusions—if we are not able to satisfy the needs and desires of the younger workers, they will throw us out," said Ciosek, who at forty-nine was the youngest member of the politburo.

Until my appointment with him I had never before been allowed inside the Central Committee building. In the lobby, a cluster of men in their thirties asked visitors their business. They were policemen but they were very well dressed in checked sport jackets. In their preening, casual postures they clashed with the bronze statues of sinewy miners, welders, and construction workers that stand among the potted palms of the entryway. Upstairs, in Mr. Ciosek's outer office, a secretary painted her nails as she talked on the phone to a friend about plans for a weekend trip to the country. The policeman who escorted me walked over and rubbed her neck. On her desk there is only the telephone. There was no typewriter but there was a shredder.

In Ciosek's inner office, the atmosphere was very different. The desk was piled high with reports and papers. On the wall hung a portrait of Lenin made from bits of wood glued together. Ciosek, an alumnus of the Communist student movement, had negotiated with the Solidarity unions when they won their recognition. He is a comer, a liberal reformer within the party, who believes that the changes Gorbachev is forging in the Soviet Union will enable Poland to evolve a working socialist hybrid that will embrace some market forces and some democracy. I asked him what he thought of the reemergence of Solidarity during the strikes that had just collapsed.

"Look," he declared, "we are condemned to negotiate. There is no other way. We have to talk to some of them." He said that the party was prepared to talk with opposition groups, particularly those that were close to the church. "You will be surprised who we will be talking to in six months." I asked who. No, he said, it would not be Wałęsa, but maybe others who are close to him. He would not name names. In fact, several other high Polish officials quoted General Jaruzelski as saying that given the choice, he would rather shoot himself in the head than meet once more with the head of Solidarity.

Nonetheless, less than four months later, after a new and even more serious round of strikes in September shut down coal mines, steel plants and shipyards, Ciosek, along with Kiszczak, did talk to Wałęsa. They talked about setting up a round of consultations and though no details were announced, the meeting raised the possibility that Solidarity might regain some of its legal status. At the same time Jaruzelski dismissed his government of technocrats, accusing them of economic mismanagement. In the place of the old premier, Zbigniew Messner, a colorless bureaucrat, he appointed Mieczysław Rakowski, the urbane editor who had been energetically portraying himself as a Gorbachev clone.

However, at the time I spoke to Ciosek the government could not yet bring itself to make any direct overture to the opposition, even though it was being informed by its own bureau of public opinion research that every index of instability was rising. After the initial emergence of Solidarity had stunned party leaders, General Jaruzelski established this office and appointed Colonel Stanisław Kwiatkowski, a trusted aide, as its director. The colonel was charged with finding out what Poles truly thought about key issues, and with passing on such information to political decision makers. Before the Solidarity upheavals opinion polling had been carried out by the police or by propaganda specialists, but they normally tainted their findings with wishful thinking. In that earlier period public opinion was largely regarded as a reflection of what Marxists call "false consciousness." It was useful to know what people felt and thought but only to prepare more effective propaganda and bring people to the true consciousness determined by the party. Then as Solidarity flourished it became increasingly clear that the government needed to find out what people were really thinking in order to keep from being overthrown.

I had interviewed Kwiatkowski several times during my years as a *Times* correspondent, and when I again arrived at his office, he greeted me by saying that since I last wrote about him, he had been hospitalized twice with ulcers as a result of resisting political pressures to alter his findings. He added that he had succeeded and he was proud that the Soviets were about to set up a similar bureau imitating his methods.

When I asked about the strikes, he handed me a study entitled "The Upward Spiral of Frustrations." "Here is what we wrote two weeks before the strikes began," he said, pointing to the conclusion: "The situation is explosive. Pressures and hardships in social and economic life are very high."

What was particularly significant, he noted, was that tolerance for violence was growing throughout the country. For years Kwiatkowski's opinion surveys had shown that the maintenance of law and order was the second most frequently cited yearning after reform of the economy. "That has started to change radically," he said. "In the last six months fewer and fewer people have been concerned about social tranquility and now this point has fallen sharply to seventh or eighth place in our polls. It even ranks behind such concerns as building more apartments and more nursery schools."

The colonel then explained where he considered the potential for violence and disruption to be greatest. He showed me a poll in which people were asked to assess their standards of living. The most recent version, compiled just before the May strikes, showed that 38 percent of all Poles saw themselves as impoverished and needy. "These are people who cannot make ends meet, people who we would expect to be angry and rebellious," said the colonel. The group, he explained, included retired people on low pensions, single mothers with children, poorly paid teachers, doctors, workers in smaller state enterprises, shop clerks, and office workers. "We knew such people would be hurt by price increases but we also realized they are not in any position to incite instability. After all, can doctors or teachers or single mothers strike?"

There was, however, one subgroup among the list of disaffected that Kwiatkowski isolated as troublesome. "These are the younger workers in the larger plants, the people between nineteen and their early thirties." There are, in fact, 3.6 million Poles between the ages of 18 and 24 and most of these are manual workers. There are another 6.5 million more between the ages of 25 and 34. Together these two age groups account for 26 percent of the Polish population. Many of the older workers who originally formed Solidarity—people over thirty—have in material terms been mollified by government policies. Some have been allowed or even encouraged to emigrate and others have become private entrepreneurs. Those who stayed on at the big plants and mines are among the highest-paid income earners and most of them have by now received some kind of living quarters.

It is the younger ones who do not have the apartments. "Many of them are still apprentices and messengers who go get tea for the others," said Kwiatkowski. "We did not think they would have the authority or the confidence to lead a strike. Some of us thought they would be inhibited by the older workers. In that perhaps we were wrong."

I wanted to learn more about such frustrations so I asked Bujak to set me up with some of these younger workers. I followed his instructions and on a rainy day I turned up at the train station at Ursus, the Warsaw suburb that is dominated by a huge tractor factory. I was met by two men who took me to talk with a dozen other tractor workers waiting in a nearby apartment. Their ages ranged from twenty-one to fifty-five, but it was the youngest who were most articulate, most forthcoming, and most excited.

"The government has had almost eight years to do something since Jaruzelski sent tanks into the street, and do you know what has happened in that time?" asked Henryk Tacharczyk, a twenty-six-year-old mechanic. "Before, according to their own statistics, we young workers had to wait twenty years for our own apartments and now in some places they say we will have to wait fifty years, or our whole lives."

Mariusz Ambroziak, a twenty-one-year-old, who along with Tacharczyk had been a member of a quickly assembled strike committee at the Ursus plant, focused his anger on the party bosses in the country and at the factory. "They are pretending that all this was just a juvenalia, a spring frolic of young people. But they are fooling themselves. They really know that our concerns are fundamental. We want the hope of a normal life and they cannot guarantee that. They keep saying that things will not change until we change, until we work harder. But most of us are working overtime as it is and we know that things will not change until they change, until they accept real pluralism and real democracy."

Ambroziak was thirteen years old and living on his family's small farm when Solidarity was suppressed. He remembers how

his mother cried when martial law was declared. Since then he
has graduated from vocational school and has worked at Ursus
for two years. More than a year ago he joined Freedom and Peace,
an organization founded by university graduates which uses a
strategy of draft resistance, pacifism, and ecological crusading in
its struggle against Communist rule. Ambroziak does not yet need
to shave regularly and he could pass for a Boy Scout or a choirboy.
Yet in that room, he and Tacharczyk, and a third young man,
Marek Jarószewski, who is twenty-seven years old, clearly commanded the respect of their more timid elders.

During the conversation, which lasted all afternoon, none of
the older workers volunteered his or her name. One, a forty-six-
year-old mechanic, explained why he insisted on anonymity.
"You know I have a temporary apartment. After twenty years
my wife and I and our two children were finally able to move
out of the rented quarters we shared with two other families."
At Ursus as well as other large plants all housing is secured
through the factory. "They tell me that maybe in five more years
we will get our own place. You should know that in my whole
life I have never lived anywhere without having to share bathrooms and kitchens. So for this reason I would prefer not to give
you my name, but I support everything these young people are
saying. They are right."

Tacharczyk continued to list grievances. "The authorities have
tried to make it appear as if we were selfishly seeking even more
money. They say we should work harder. We work six days a
week now. We can't save very much and there is nothing to buy.
We get letters from friends who emigrated and they tell us about
their houses and cars and holidays, and it hurts that we are like
orphans in our own homes. Poland is the poorest country in
Europe after Romania and Albania, and remember, we won the
war."

Later Tacharczyk led me to the hostel where he has lived for
eight years. Five people share his suite of two small rooms. "It
is like barracks life in the army, but you finish the army in two

years and this goes on and on," he said. "How can I get married? How can I have any serious relationship? We are doomed not just to bachelorhood but to celibacy. You can't invite any woman here. Where do you go? The system forces you into whorehouses, into a degenerate life. Priests take vows of poverty and chastity but why should industrial workers? Last year, for a few months, one of our assigned roommates was a fifty-five-year-old alcoholic, a wreck of a man who had been in hostels all his life. All of us, I think, looked at him and wondered if he once had hopes like ours. For forty years, the Red Ones have been making promises and asking us to sacrifice. We believe in the idea of reforms but unless there is some major compromise, unless the government makes some real dramatic gesture like Gorbachev has done in Afghanistan, why should we trust them, why should we or the West trust them?"

During the last days of my visit and during the months that followed, I often returned to thoughts of the young men from Ursus wondering what real chances they had for a normal life in their own land. Who or what could save them from a system that guaranteed only tedium and drab impoverishment? One thing seemed certain—if Poland was to be rescued at all, it would have to be from outside. The country simply lacked the internal resources to stabilize itself and prosper. Even if, somehow, social divisions were to be bridged, mortal economic problems would remain unresolved. Wałęsa used to say that Poland was not a poor country, that it was merely mismanaged. To me it seemed poor as well as mismanaged. It might in the future be managed better, but it would stay poor and weak for a long time.

The idea of international rescue was, in fact, circulating within both party and opposition circles. Some people in the Solidarity camp were even fantasizing about a new Marshall Plan under which the West would unleash flows of investments and offer technology to Poland once the government came to terms and accepted the opposition. The idea was not entirely fanciful. As its advocates pointed out, the ascension of Gorbachev had for the first time in the century created a situation in which the stability and prosperity of Poland was arguably in the interest of all major European and world powers. The Soviets obviously did not want turmoil in Poland that could spread elsewhere and sap their reserves. The United States, which may have once viewed an unstable Poland as an open wound that burdened Moscow, now had to wonder whether further burdening Moscow with Polish troubles would profit anyone. And in Western Europe, some industrialists and politicians were raising the prospect of eventually bringing Poland and Hungary into an expanded continental market that would be more competitive with Japan and the United States. At their most cynical, those Poles who dreamed of deliverance through a new Marshall Plan would simply argue that the stability of Poland was too important for the peace and security of the continent and the world to be left to Poles, who, in any case, could not bring it about.

Such assertions of Poland's pivotal importance for the continent appeared all the more relevant as the fiftieth anniversary of the Hitler-Stalin Pact neared. In 1939, the two major totalitarian regimes of our time implemented the pact by dismembering Poland and starting the war. There were some people in Poland, admittedly romantics, who saw it as fitting that a Germany shorn of fascism and a Soviet Union retreating from its darkest deeds should at least consent to the reconstruction of the Polish state that lay between them and thus secure and ennoble all of Europe.

The entire notion was very Polish and very elegant. It was rooted in earlier Polish dreams of deliverance in which the sufferings of the "Christ of Nations" would eventually bring about the redemption of all Europe. From those who hoped for a Marshall Plan, I heard echoes of earlier Polish generations who believed that they would be freed by Napoleonic legions or that the Allies would pull Poland into the Western democratic camp at the end of the Second World War. Napoleon never came and the Allies consented to Yalta.

264

As with those earlier dreams, contemporary Polish hopes for dramatic rescue from the West were politically unrealistic. Some limited growth in capital from abroad was probable, particularly if state and society established a truce, but full-scale rescue by a consortium of benefactors seemed a chimera. The United States no longer had dollars available for reconstruction and development of foreign countries. The Soviets were hardly likely to agree to more Polish independence from Moscow while their own republics clamored for greater autonomy. And, while the West Germans have both money and moral reasons to make the investment, they would not strengthen Poland over East German objections, and the East Germans are not eager to have a strong Poland as a neighbor.

But if salvation from abroad was improbable, what then? I did not see any way in which the young men at the Ursus plant could obtain their own apartments, and I knew that if they and thousands like them were to remain without hope of the most routine domesticity, new and more violent upheavals were certain. After all, how long could young men wait for a room into which they could bring a decent girl?

So far, the leadership of the Solidarity opposition has channeled resentments and rebellious instincts to nonviolent action. Solidarity could indeed placate the disaffected by pointing to concessions it had wrested from the custodians of a withering system without violence. It had significantly changed Polish Communism and introduced a new political culture, unique in the Soviet sphere. As a result of its legal and clandestine activities Poland was the only Communist country where cohesive social groupings had formed outside of government and party control. It was not at all difficult to imagine how this de facto opposition might some day form a spectrum of legal parties if it was allowed to do so. Under Solidarity's umbrella there were embryos of right-wing, centrist, and social democratic parties that were straining to mature. Perhaps, just perhaps, the zigzag course set by Jaruzelski can be kept from capsizing. Perhaps a government aware that it cannot fulfill the needs of Poles will continue to divest itself of power, slowly offering political concessions in compensation for the diminishing standards of quality of life. And perhaps, as the process unfolds, Poles will continue to endure with discipline.

But even my Solidarity friends, who have devoted their lives to changing the system through evolutionary means, often wonder if things will remain peaceful as the real last chapter draws near. They are aware that because the government and party have been so weak, the possibilities of establishing new political institutions have increased. But they also know that paradoxically, because prospects of profound change are close, the situation is the most dangerous it has ever been.

Certainly, my short return to Poland made me aware that despite the relative tolerance of the regime—there were no political prisoners, and strikers suffered rare reprisals—the crisis was mounting. Everywhere I sensed so many frustrations, so many deferred hopes and delayed solutions. I asked myself and others if even Wałęsa, Michnik, and Kuroń or even the pope would be able to hold off a people's mounting rage as the seams of the Soviet empire were seen to be fraying and as Communism's repressive power eroded.

As I headed back to the United States I kept wondering whether any extensive economic and political system had ever been transformed without violence. Maybe that is what happened in the New Deal, or when Britain freed its colonies and nationalized key industries after the war. But the United States and Britain are countries with long democratic traditions. Can Poland work its way out of the dead end in which it is trapped without murderous consequences?

With the intelligence of the opposition and the continuing weakening of the government and party, Poland may yet attain Michnik's view of a civil society not modeled on utopian dreams but based on due process, legal rights, openly contestable views, and participatory citizenship. But I am just Polish enough to look to Konwicki's contention that what Poland has always depended on was a fine miracle every fifty years or so. The last one had come in 1918, when unexpectedly three European empires simultaneously collapsed and the long-lapsed Polish state was reborn. The next one is overdue.

ACKNOWLEDGMENTS

In the preceding pages I have included the names of many people for whose trust and friendship I am grateful. Mostly, these are men and women who accompanied me on journeys of discovery above and below the surface. The identities of my foremost guides are apparent in what I have written. But there were many others who provided me with insight, information, friendship and, when necessary, chastisement. They included Czesław Bielecki, Konrad Bieliński, Seweryn Blumsztajn, Grzegorz Boguta, Ernest Bryl, Andrzej Celiński, Jacek Czaputowicz, Marek Edelman, Jacek Federowicz, Father Leon Kantorski, Stefan Kisielewski, Tadeusz Konwicki, Witold Kulerski, Ewa Kulik, Dr. Zofia Kuratowska, Barbara Labuda, Jan Lityński, Jan Józef Lipski, Ewa Milewicz, Leszek Moczulski, Zbigniew Najder, Janusz and Joanna Onyszkiewicz, Krzys Pusz, Joanna Szczesna, Barbara Toruńczyk, Andrzej Wajda and Henryk Wujec.

I am grateful to Alexander Wiechowski, the translator for the Warsaw bureau of *The New York Times*; Anna Białoskurska, my secretary in Warsaw; and Witek Szulecki, the bureau's photographer. They were always around when I needed them.

With less warmth but with some appreciation, I would also like to thank the Polish officials for the usually correct treatment they accorded me. They provided me with visas when I needed them and offered me as much access as I suppose they dared. Some offered confidences that I imagine involved risks. A few were redeemed by humor. In almost every case they were better at their jobs than their counterparts in neighboring countries. There is no need to cite their names since they know who they are and they may not really want anyone else to know.

On this side of the Atlantic, I had the good luck to work with

Bob Loomis of Random House. He handled me and my words with grace, knowing exactly when to let matters lie and when to intervene.

Joseph Lelyveld, the *Times*'s foreign editor and a very old friend, and Max Frankel, the paper's executive editor, offered me the encouragement and the time to write. Earlier, A. M. Rosenthal of the *Times* sent me on my assignment to Poland. The Guggenheim Foundation supported my work with a fellowship. At Harvard, Professors Marshall Goldman and Adam Ulam provided me sanctuary at the Russian Research Center. And Eric Fay, a graduate student, helped me to transcribe tapes.

Finally, and most important, I want to thank my father and my wife. My father for having given me the Polish language and for infecting me with romantic prejudices. And my wife, Rebecca, for having known better than I that I needed to go to Poland, and for accompanying me on the quest.

MICHAEL T. KAUFMAN was born in Paris and came to the United States on an emergency visa in 1941. From 1975 to 1987, he was a foreign correspondent for *The New York Times*, and served as bureau chief in Nairobi, New Delhi, Ottawa, and finally Warsaw. In the years before he went abroad, he covered major events in the United States from Martin Luther King's march on Washington, to Woodstock, to the Attica prison riots.

He has won the George Polk Award for international reporting, was given a Guggenheim Fellowship, and spent a year as a fellow at the Russian Research Center at Harvard. He is married, has three children, and lives in New York City.